Southern Campaigns of the American Revolution

Southern Campaigns of the American Revolution

by

Dan L. Morrill

The Nautical & Aviation Publishing Company of America
Mount Pleasant, South Carolina

Library of Congress Catalog Card Number: 93-41018

ISBN: 1-877853-21-6

Printed in the United States of America

First Printing, 1993
Second Printing, 1999

The portraits in this book are courtesy of Independence National Historical Park.

The cover painting is reprinted with the permission of the State of South Carolina.

Cover design by Robert Bischoff.

Library of Congress Cataloging-in-Publication Data
Morrill, Dan L.
     Southern Campaigns of the American Revolution / by Dan L. Morrill.
     p.   cm.
     Includes bibliographical references and index.
     ISBN 1-877853-21-6
     1. Southern States—History—Revolution, 1775-1783—Campaigns.
2. United States—History—Revolution, 1775-1783—Campaigns. I. Title.
E230.5.S67   1993
973.3'3 dc20   93-41018
                                                  CIP

for my wife

ACKNOWLEDGMENTS

The history of the war in the South during the Revolution has always been my favorite subject as a student, writer, teacher, parent and general promoter of local history in any forum. Apparently I have not been alone. One day the idea for such a book intended for the general reader was suggested to me by another resident of Charlotte, Wilton Connor, who came to visit me along with the publisher of this volume. I want to thank Wilton for starting me on a task that I have enjoyed immensely. I am sure he will join me on this journey through old by-ways and battles as closely as I could trace them.

CONTENTS

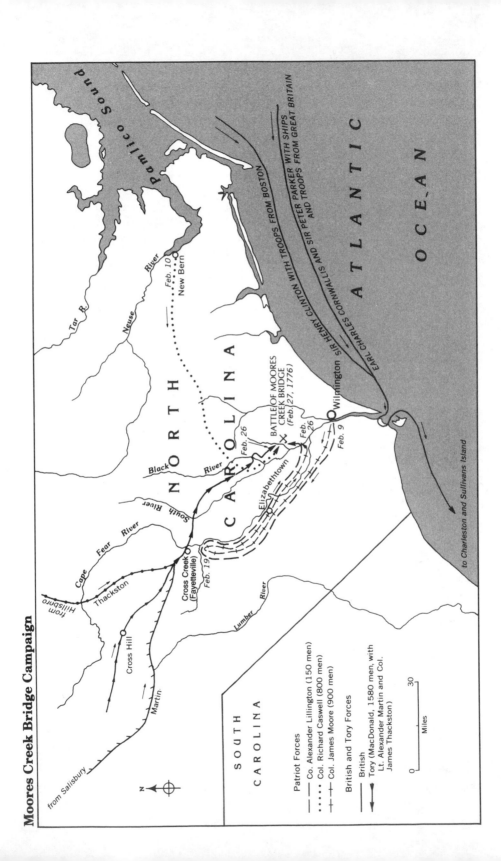

Moores Creek Bridge Campaign

Pamlico Sound

ATLANTIC OCEAN

NORTH CAROLINA

SOUTH CAROLINA

Tar R.

Neuse River

Black River

South River

Cape Fear River

Lumber River

Martin

New Bern
Feb. 10

Wilmington
Feb. 9

BATTLE OF MOORES CREEK BRIDGE
(Feb. 27, 1776)

Feb. 26

Feb. 26

Elizabethtown

Cross Creek
(Fayetteville)
Feb. 19

Cross Hill

Thackston

from Hillsboro

from Salisbury

SIR HENRY CLINTON WITH TROOPS FROM BOSTON

SIR PETER PARKER WITH SHIPS
AND TROOPS FROM GREAT BRITAIN

EARL CHARLES CORNWALLIS

to Charleston and Sullivans Island

N

Patriot Forces
——— Co. Alexander Lillington (150 men)
········· Col. Richard Caswell (800 men)
+ + + Col. James Moore (900 men)

British and Tory Forces
British
——— Tory (MacDonald, 1580 men, with
Lt. Alexander Martin and Col.
James Thackston)

0   30
Miles

Chapter One

Moore's Creek Bridge

The story of the American Revolutionary War in the South is a tale told mainly in half-tones and subtle images. Contrary to popular belief, it was not the large engagements, such as the battles at Camden, Charleston, Guilford Court House, or Yorktown, that determined the eventual military outcome of the contest. As dramatic as these clashes of sizeable armies and fleets might have been, the crucial battles were primarily small engagements, like those of Moore's Creek Bridge, Kettle Creek, and Hanging Rock. Because the conflict in the South was fundamentally a struggle for the allegiance of the rank-and-file of the colonies' white population, these battles were often fought between neighbors. It was a civil war, with all the pain and agony that such a political catastrophe brings upon a people.

At the time, there were many new settlers in the colonies, especially in the South. The population was diverse in terms of national origin and religious affiliation. Slavery and the Indian frontier were volatile issues. In this environment, commitments to be for or against the king were often spasmodic and mutable. Consequently, it was vital that when the British first summoned Loyalists to take up arms against their neighbors that the Royal military not act prematurely. The British needed to protect their colonial allies. An early Tory defeat would prove devastating to the British cause, dampening the enthusiasm of countless potential Loyalists. Instead of taking up arms for the king, they would stay home and keep still instead. It is against this background that the three-minute engagement that occurred in North Carolina at Moore's Creek Bridge on February 27, 1776 takes on a significance far greater than that suggested by the size of the forces that fought there.

The perpetrator of the foolhardy campaign that culminated in the merciless slaughter at Moore's Creek Bridge was Josiah Martin, the Royal governor of the colony. Ensconced in his magnificent palace in New Bern, the governor watched the tide of the Revolution surge around him. An ambitious, young, energetic bureaucrat, Martin was determined to restore the king's prerogatives and to destroy the "monster of sedition" who had "dared to raise his impious head in America."[1] Believing that legions of Tories were eager to gather under the king's banner, the governor, like other British officials, discounted the fighting resolve of the patriots. Thus he devised a grandiose scheme to quell the colonial foe.

Martin, aware that bands of patriot militia were swaggering through the town and nearby countryside, dispatched his wife, who was "big with child," and his children to New York City. He then ordered the cannon in his palace spiked, buried the ammunition in the cellar and beneath the cabbage patch in the palace garden, and fled south to Fort Johnston on the Cape Fear River, arriving there on June 2, 1775.[2] A little more than a month later, on July 18, the governor had to retreat again, this time aboard the *Cruizer,* a British war sloop anchored in the river. However, these events in no way dampened Martin's enthusiasm to recapture political supremacy in North Carolina. Indeed, his imagination soared to fanciful heights.

Governor Martin sent word to Lord Dartmouth, Secretary of State for the American Department and the minister responsible for the conduct of the war, requesting that General Thomas Gage, His Majesty's commander in chief in North America, dispatch 10,000 stands of arms, six brass six-pounders, and field supplies to North Carolina. Martin's plan was to distribute these items mainly among the Highland Scots who had settled in the upper reaches of the Cape Fear River. The Highland Scots were firm Loyalists, Martin argued, and would protect the throngs of Tories who inhabited the Carolina backcountry. This would assure that a force of some 20,000 troops would rally to the Royal banner and, at least in the governor's fecund imagination, clear the Carolinas and Georgia of all patriot opposition.

A perfunctory perusal of Martin's scheme suggested that it might be feasible. North Carolina Whigs were known to be less powerful than their counterparts in most other colonies, especially in the North. Indeed, the North Carolina patriots had succeeded in establishing only six committees of safety by 1775. Sanctioned by the First Continental Congress, this network of committees was the principal instrument by which local patriots organized militia units and obtained pledges of support for the revolutionary cause. Further complicating the political landscape of North Carolina and putting the intensity of patriot resolve in doubt was the legacy of the Regulator Movement of 1770–1771. Centered in the piedmont hinterland, this uprising had been caused by the resentment of many settlers in the backcountry against the colonial assembly, which was controlled by the political elite of coastal North Carolina. No doubt many former Regulators realized that the prominent Whigs of 1775–1776 had been the leaders of the legislature against which they had revolted just a few years before.

To strengthen his case with British officials, Martin sent a personal emissary, Alexander Schaw, to London to argue the wisdom of dispatching arms and men to North Carolina. This ploy brought success. In November 1775, British authorities agreed to begin preparations for a fleet commanded by Sir Peter Parker to transport seven regiments under Lord Charles Cornwallis across the Atlantic to the Cape Fear River, although the ultimate target of the campaign was to be elsewhere. General William Howe, who had replaced General Gage as head of British troops in America, was instructed to select an overall commander for this venturesome foray into the South. This commander, who turned out to be the enigmatic Sir Henry Clinton, was to send a body of troops from New York City to rendezvous with Parker's fleet off the North Carolina coast and, if possible, to put troops ashore.

On January 3, 1776, Governor Martin received dispatches from Lord Dartmouth telling him that Cornwallis's troops were ready for embarkation and would be escorted across the Atlantic by nine warships of the Royal Navy. Imagine how excited Governor Martin must have become when he read Dartmouth's communiques. Chased like a common criminal from his sumptuous palace in New Bern and compelled to take refuge aboard ship as he watched "patriot ruffians" occupy and wreck Fort Johnston, the beleaguered chief executive could finally lash out at the despicable rebels.

Martin was not surely alone in his desire to strike back. One can only guess how many Tories were hunkered down in the towns, pine forests, and coastal swamps of the Carolinas, frightened by the savage political turmoil that swirled around them and hoping that somehow British authority and order could be restored.

Janet Schaw, a Loyalist who lived in Wilmington, North Carolina, was in just such a predicament. In June 1775, looking down from the balcony of a friend's home on a humid, sultry summer afternoon, she observed a large body of patriot militia parading through a nearby field and described what to her was a most disturbing event:

> Before the review was over, I heard a cry of tar and feather. I was ready to faint at the idea of this dreadful operation. I would have gladly quitted the balcony, but was so much afraid the victim was one of my friends that I was not able to move; and he indeed proved to be one, tho' in a humble station. For it was Mr. Neilson's poor English groom. You can hardly conceive what I felt

when I saw him dragged forward, poor devil, frightened out of his wits. . . .

Oh Britannia, what are you doing, while your true obedient sons are thus insulted by their unlawful brethen; are they also forgot by their natural parents?[3]

A prudent politician would have proceeded cautiously in such an explosive atmosphere, but Governor Martin was never one to practice forbearance. Martin cast aside any concerns about the success of the complicated plan, which depended upon the timely and coordinated arrival of two fleets of British warships and their ability to cross the shallow waters at the mouth of the Cape Fear River. In January 1776 he implemented his plans to summon the Highland Scots and other Tories to assemble and make ready to march to the coast. The governor assumed that the Loyalist militia, once it arrived on the lower Cape Fear, would join with coastal Tories, and together the two groups would assume a defensive posture until the British regulars arrived by ship to reinforce them.

On January 10, 1776, Martin empowered the Tory leaders in the counties of Anson, Cumberland, Chatham, Guilford, Mecklenburg, Rowan, Surry, and Bute to recruit militia, select officers, take control of weapons held by the local rebels, and choose a place where the various Tory forces could merge to begin their trek to the Cape Fear port of Brunswick. They were to arrive at the coast no later than February 15. Accordingly, a meeting of Loyalist militia officers was held on February 5 at Cross Creek, the main residence of Highland Scots in Cumberland County. Primarily due to the insistence of the ex-Regulators who attended this Tory powwow, the assembled leaders decided to proceed immediately with Governor Martin's scheme to gather troops for the march to the lower Cape Fear.

The commander of the Loyalist throng that gathered in mid-February 1776 in the Cumberland County town of Cross Hill was Donald MacDonald, an elderly Scotsman sent to North Carolina in 1775 by General Gage to recruit men for the Royal Highland Emigrant Regiment. Marching his 1,580 troops southeastward to Cross Creek, MacDonald, already behind schedule, made preparations on February 17 to begin his thrust toward the sea. The next day, the Highland Scots and their ex-Regulator compatriots ventured forth from the town. Many of the Scots were decked out in colorful tartans. As the mournful sounds of their bagpipes reverberated through the forests and their broadswords glistened in the wintry sun, Whig eyes were watching.

Unlike the participants in most revolutionary movements, the American patriots and their Loyalist foes were thoroughly familiar with firearms. Only during the Seven Years' War (1756–1763) had redcoats appeared in appreciable numbers on the American side of the Atlantic. Until that time, American settlers had had to defend their homes and villages from the Indians, the Dutch, the French, and the Spanish without meaningful help from the British military. Thus the male population of the colonies had acquired significant experience as militiamen. Expected to spend no longer than six months in continuous active service, members of the militia would assemble at regular intervals, frequently after church, to practice the rudiments of 18th century battlefield tactics. Often illiterate, frequently unwashed, sometimes intoxicated, the rum-filled rank-and-file of the colonial militia were often almost comical in appearance, especially to someone familiar with the professional standards and deportment of the British army. Janet Schaw wrote thus of these militiamen:

> We came down in the morning in time for the review, which the heat made as terrible to the spectators as to the soldiers, or what you please to call them. They had certainly fainted under it, had not the constant draughts of grog supported them. Their exercise was that of bush-fighting, but it appeared so confused and so perfectly different from any thing I ever saw, I cannot say whether they performed it well or not; but this I know, that they were heated with rum till capable of committing the most shocking outrages. . . . I must really laugh while I recollect their figures: 2000 men in their shirts and trousers, preceded by a very ill beat-drum and a fiddler, who was also in his shirt with a long sword and a cue in his hair, who played with all his might.[4]

In early February 1776, word reached the coast that Tories were gathering in substantial numbers on the upper Cape Fear. Patriot militia units began to make ready to oppose them. The New Bern Committee of Safety selected Colonel Richard Caswell to lead its fighting men, while the Whigs in Wilmington entrusted military command to Colonel Alexander Lillington. Even more menacing to Donald MacDonald and his legions was a force headed by Colonel James Moore. The nucleus of what was to become a regiment of the Continental Line, these troops eventually numbered about 1,100. They marched northwestward from Wilmington along the southern bank of the Cape Fear River, and on February 15 assumed a defensive stance beside Rockfish Creek just a few miles southeast of the Tory stronghold of Cross Creek.

Moore exercised the overall strategic command of the Whig troops, including those serving under Caswell and Lillington. Moore assumed that MacDonald would stay on the south side of the river, endeavor to move directly across Rockfish Creek and smash the patriot defenses, and, if successful, take the most direct route to Brunswick. On the night of February 18, the Tory force stopped within four miles of Moore's encampment; the patriots made ready to defend their position against an anticipated frontal assault.

In this instance, however, MacDonald outwitted Moore. Refusing to heed the pleas of some of his younger officers who wanted to rush pell-mell against the patriots' formidable defenses, the wily Scotsman ordered his militiamen to retreat a short distance to Campbell Town. There they crossed over to the northern side of the Cape Fear River, where no patriot troops stood in their way. Moore was unaware that the Tories were no longer along his front until February 21, when he learned that MacDonald and his men had slipped away and had moved across the Cape Fear the day before.

With a formidable body of armed Tories now heading unopposed toward the sea, Colonel Moore acted quickly and decisively to rescue the situation. Knowing that two tributaries of the Cape Fear, the South River and the Black River, stood in MacDonald's path, the patriot commander ordered Caswell's militia to place themselves at Corbett's Ferry on the Black River. (Caswell's militia had the decided advantage of possessing two light artillery pieces, nicknamed Old Mother Covington and Her Daughter.) Moore then directed Alexander Lillington and his soldiers to move quickly from the patriot camp at Rockfish Creek to reinforce Caswell; if a juncture could not be made, they were to dig in and defend the bridge across Moore's Creek, a murky, languid stream situated a few miles south of Corbett's Ferry and about seventeen miles north of Wilmington.

Meanwhile, the Tory troops lurched forward, completely unaware of the efforts to block their advance. MacDonald, by instinct a chary commander, proceeded cautiously. He ordered Donald McLeod to establish a cavalry force of 100 Highland Scots and travel ahead of the main body of Loyalist militia. McLeod's force was to reconnoiter the countryside and to locate and take control of key bridges. On February 23, McLeod sent word back to MacDonald that Caswell was encamped at Corbett's Ferry, only four miles in front of the Tory vanguard.

At this point, the boats the Tories had used to cross the Cape Fear had been burned by the Loyalists themselves to prevent easy pursuit. With Cross Creek now occupied by a contingent of Moore's patriot army, MacDonald had no choice but to prepare his men for attack. A volunteer force of 100 men commanded by Captain John Campbell and armed with broadswords (also called claymores), the principal ground attack weapon of the Highland Scots, was placed at the center of the Tory army to lead the attack. Brandishing their cumbersome, 35-inch, singled-blade swords with basket hilt and fishtail grip, these gallant lads were to swarm forward to the beat of drums and the clamorous din of bagpipes to act as shock troops, spreading panic and dismay among Caswell's untested Carolina militia.

But shortly before MacDonald was to give the signal to mount the charge, a body of Tory cavalry learned from a black man who lived in the immediate neighborhood that the Black River, unbeknown to the patriot militia, could be crossed a few miles north of Corbett's Ferry by using a flat-bottomed boat that was submerged just below the surface and that could easily be raised. Realizing that his fundamental objective was to deliver his men safely to the coast, not to engage the enemy in combat, MacDonald decided to avoid a direct assault. The inventive Scotsman sent a small force to demonstrate on Caswell's front, directing them to play bagpipes, beat drums, fire muskets, and generally make a fuss, while he and the main army moved to the alternate crossing site.

It was a brilliant maneuver. After dispatching McLeod's cavalry across the Black to continue its scouting operations, MacDonald oversaw the construction of a bridge to carry the weight of his troops and their supply wagons. Shortly after daybreak on February 26, the rear echelons of the Tory army reached the far bank of the Black, and MacDonald and his ebullient men were once more marching unopposed toward the sea.

When Colonel Moore, encamped at Elizabethtown on the Cape Fear River, learned that MacDonald had bypassed Corbett's Ferry, he ordered Caswell to make every effort to reinforce Lillington at Moore's Creek Bridge, which stood athwart the route the Loyalist would have to take to the coast. In the interim, Moore's troops would sail down the Cape Fear and march overland in a desperate attempt to reach Lillington before MacDonald's force arrived.

Moore did not get there in time, but Caswell and his 800 men beat the Tories to Moore's Creek Bridge. The patriot troops arrived with their two artillery pieces and joined Lillington's much smaller force of 150 militiamen on the afternoon of February 26, while MacDonald and the Loyalist army approached from the northwest.

The ground that Lillington and Caswell occupied was superbly suited for defensive operations. Moore's Creek, a tributary of the Black River, meanders through a dense, forbidding swamp in a series of severe, twisting loops. Five feet deep and approximately fifty feet wide at the location of the log and plank bridge, the slow-moving, ink-black stream was an imposing barrier. The patriot militiamen knew that the Highland Scots and their Regulator allies could not mount a successful flanking maneuver, but would have to come straight at them. Accordingly, during the afternoon and evening of February 26, they prepared formidable defenses on the already tortuous terrain.

Caswell originally ordered his men to begin constructing entrenchments on the west bank of Moore's Creek, but then wisely decided to place all his troops on the east side instead. About half of the flooring on the bridge was removed, and the logs that supported the superstructure were covered with soft soap and tallow. Caswell's force of about 950 men, crouching behind embankments, their muskets and two artillery pieces aimed at Moore's Creek Bridge, were now ready to resist the frontal attack they knew was coming.

MacDonald, ever hesitant to order a frontal assault, dispatched James Hepburn, his secretary, under a flag of truce, to the patriot camp before nightfall on February 26. Although he carried an ultimatum demanding Caswell's surrender, Hepburn was not sent to secure the capitulation of the patriots but to see where they had placed their defenses. Hepburn, as expected, was rebuffed by Caswell, but he returned to MacDonald's headquarters and told the Tory leader that the patriots were taking position on the west bank of the creek. If true, that would have meant that a substantial number of Caswell's men would have had to fight with Moore's Creek at their back.

MacDonald followed his usual custom of calling a council of his officers to discuss the situation. Believing that most of the rebels would be unable to retreat across Moore's Creek before the Highland Scots were upon them with their claymores and muskets, the Tory leaders decided by a slight majority to attack at daybreak on February 27. The plan was to set out on the six-mile march to Moore's Creek Bridge in the middle of the night, divide the invading force into three columns, and achieve complete surprise by sneaking silently into the patriot camp at dawn.

Matters began to go awry for the Tories from the outset. Donald Mac-Donald, ill and exhausted from the rigors of the march, had to stay behind, thereby depriving the rank-and-file of the presence of the commander who had brilliantly outwitted the patriots at Rockfish Creek and Corbett's Ferry. Moreover, the Loyalist troops, completely unfamiliar with the immediate countryside, became lost in the swamps and waded for hours in the muck and mire of the Carolina coastal lowlands before reaching the woodlands bordering Moore's Creek just before dawn. But the worst setback of all was discovered once the Tories moved into the camp itself: all of Caswell's men were on the east side of the creek, across Moore's Creek Bridge.

Donald McLeod was a young, impulsive officer, and did not recognize the utter folly of mounting a direct assault against an unseen enemy arrayed somewhere across a forbidding stream within the confines of an unfamiliar swamp. He should have pulled back and consulted MacDonald, who almost certainly would have called off the attack. But the impetuous young Scot's blood was running hot that fateful morning. For McLeod and his men, the moment of truth had arrived.

McLeod ordered the Loyalist force to form a battle line. The Tory troops were 1,600 strong, but only about 500 of them had firearms. With the rallying cry, "King George and Broad Swords," McLeod and Campbell's men, resplendent in their long socks and kilts, moved forward, searching for the bridge. The dingy waters of Moore's Creek lapped around the pilings of the mutilated structure. When McLeod and Campbell came upon it in the half light of dawn, they saw that most of the planks had been removed from the floor. Undaunted, the two Scotsmen began to climb gingerly out onto the sleepers, thrusting their claymores into the slippery logs to steady their advance. A billowing chorus of drums and bagpipes drowned out the drone emanating from the frogs, crickets, and countless other critters that resided in the obscure eddies of the surrounding swamp.

Caswell and Lillington steadied their untested militiamen, waiting for the most opportune moment to fire a killing, crushing volley. This apprehensive assortment of citizen soldiers, none of whom had yet to participate in combat with the Tories, had no doubt sat up all night, now and again catching a brief moment of sleep between swigs of rum, constantly searching the horizon for any sign of ominous movement. One can imagine how they must have felt: tingling flesh, quivering hands, queasy stomachs.

Suddenly the faint images of McLeod and Campbell appeared, teetering atop the sleepers of the bridge. Smoke surged across the battlefield from the patriots' muskets. Old Mother Covington and Her Daughter belched with deadly force. A horrible scene of agony, dismay, and confusion began to unfold at Moore's Creek Bridge. "On reaching a point within thirty paces of the breastworks," a Whig newspaper account reported, "they were received with a very heavy fire, which did great execution."[5]

McLeod and Campbell fell mortally wounded, their bodies riddled with bullets and shrapnel. Other Highland Scots, flailing their claymores in a vain search for the enemy, lost their balance and fell from the bridge into the creek, where many of them drowned as the weight of their water-soaked tartans dragged them into the murky depths.

At least thirty Tories died in the battle, while the Whigs lost only one man. The Highland Scots and their Regulator allies, after directing ineffectual fire from the opposite bank, broke and ran into the swamp. Colonel Moore, arriving with his men at Moore's Creek Bridge several hours after the engagement, launched an organized pursuit of the Loyalists. Donald MacDonald was captured in his own tent. The majority of the rank-and-file Tories were allowed to return home on their oath that they would never again take up arms against the patriot cause. Governor Martin's dream of raising a mighty Loyalist force in the North Carolina hinterland had met an ignominious fate.

The defeat at Moore's Creek Bridge was unquestionably a calamitous setback for the southern supporters of the king, although it was not the first military encounter between Whigs and Tories in the South. On November 11 and 12, 1775, ships loyal to the king had attacked patriot vessels in the harbor at Charleston, South Carolina. A larger battle had occurred later in November at the inland South Carolina stronghold of Ninety Six, where Major Joseph Robinson and Captain Patrick Cunningham had led a force of about 1,800 Tories in laying siege to a fort held by the Whigs. In December 1775, patriots had routed a sizeable Loyalist force at the Battle of Great Bridge near Norfolk, Virginia. Still, the Tory defeat at Moore's Creek Bridge was especially significant because it forcefully diminished the likelihood that colonists would come out for the king in the North Carolina backcountry, where Tory sentiments were particularly robust.

An overall assessment of the Moore's Creek Bridge campaign reveals that North Carolina Governor Josiah Martin was a haughty, arrogant man. Indeed, his record of misdeeds and miscalculations, especially his premature summoning of Tories to take up arms when they had no reasonable chance for victory, suggests that Martin was a fool. Clearly, the enormous military advantages that the patriots possessed doomed Donald MacDonald and his men from the very outset of the campaign. The Tories had no artillery, and they demonstrated by their use of broadswords that they had no understanding of the tactics appropriate for the swamps and pine barrens of eastern North Carolina. Colonel Moore, on the other hand, was familiar with the terrain. Knowing that MacDonald was seeking to reach Brunswick on the lower Cape Fear, he was able to place his troops astride the only routes the Tories could take to the coast. In other words, Moore and his subordinant commanders were able to choose when and where to fight, able to occupy the battlefield first, and had ample time in which to erect formidable fortifications. The only hope the Tories had depended on the timely arrival of Henry Clinton and his sizeable body of regular British troops. Clinton's first ship, however, was delayed by bad weather, and did not reach the lower Cape Fear until April 18. The entire armada did not assemble until May 3, more than two months after the Loyalist troops had been overwhelmed.

The crucial defeat at Moore's Creek Bridge was political, not military. It is important to remember that the majority of patriots and Loyalists were not firm or resolute in their political commitments. In many instances, the decision to be for or against the king depended upon which course of action seemed to hold the greater prospects for personal benefit. If Governor Martin had waited for the arrival of British forces on the lower Cape Fear before ordering the Tories to form militia units, he could have at least provided some legitimate prospect that the Loyalists would have emerged as victors and heroes, not prisoners and fugitives. It takes no great imagination to realize the dampening impact this sorry episode had upon the Tories and their sympathizers in the Carolina backcountry. *The New York Packet,* a patriot newspaper, predicted that "this, we think, will effectively put a stop to Toryism in North Carolina."[6]

Battle for Sullivan's Island

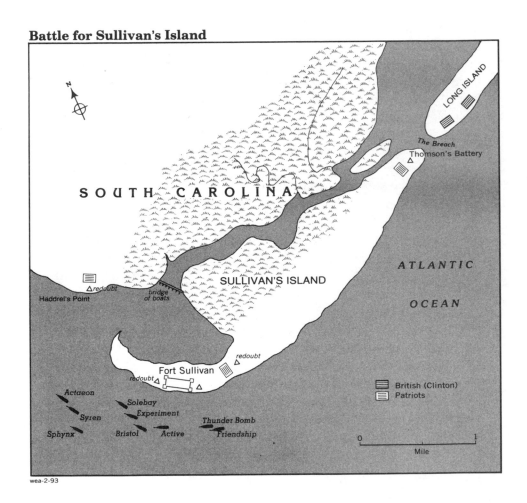

LONG ISLAND

The Breach
Thomson's Battery

SOUTH CAROLINA

ATLANTIC

OCEAN

SULLIVAN'S ISLAND

△redoubt
Haddrel's Point
bridge
of boats

redoubt

Fort Sullivan
redoubt △

Actaeon

Solebay
Syren
Experiment

Sphynx
Bristol
Active

Thunder Bomb
Friendship

British (Clinton)
Patriots

0   1
Mile

wea-2-93

Chapter Two

Charleston: The First Time

The British generals were arrogant and contemptuous at the outbreak of the American Revolution. Experts in the mechanics of eighteenth century European combat, they thought their disciplined troops would easily transform the American rebels into a sorry lot of penitent supplicants. One British general told Benjamin Franklin that with 1,000 grenadiers, "He would undertake to go from one end of America to the other and geld all the males, partly by force and partly by a little coaxing."[1] Francis Lord Rowden, who would command the British garrison at Camden, South Carolina, minced no words in his estimation of how the Whig forces would fare against him. "We shall soon have done with these scoundrels, for one only dirties one's fingers by meddling with them."[2] No less haughty were these remarks made by the Earl of Sandwich in the House of Commons on February 10, 1775:

> Suppose the Colonies do abound with men, what does that signify? They are raw, undisciplined, cowardly men. . . . Believe me, my Lords, the very sound of a cannon would carry them off . . . as fast as their feet could carry them.[3]

Great Britain did enjoy noteworthy military advantages over its rebellious colonies in the American Revolution. The population of Britain was approximately 8 million, whereas the number of people in the colonies totaled about 2.5 million, of whom roughly 500,000 were black slaves, 500,000 Loyalists, and 200,000 neutralists. Unlike Great Britain, where the Industrial Revolution was beginning, the colonies possessed an economy that was almost exclusively agricultural and had virtually no manufacturing facilities other than those that produced light or household goods. The American rebels, who had no professional military organization at the outset of the war, were facing the greatest military power in the world. Great Britain had an army 50,000 strong and the greatest navy afloat.

The British placed their ultimate trust in the invincibility of European military strategy. Created to avoid the kind of devastation brought on by the wars of attrition, especially the Thirty Years' War (1618–1648), the standard rules of engagement were supposed to limit the scope of armed conflict and to make war more rational. Each maneuver on the battlefield had its intricate list of commands, and the British troops were expected to learn and execute them by rote. In doing battle with the American patriots, the redcoats and their Tory allies would surely be an unconquerable killing machine, or so the British thought.

The tactics of the eighteenth century battlefield were largely dictated by the assets and liabilities of the infantry's principal attack weapon, the Brown Bess muzzle-loading, smooth-bore, single-shot, flintlock musket with socket bayonet. There was no problem with the musket's ability to mutilate, maim, and annihilate the enemy. The bullet, a leaden ball nearly three-quarters of an inch in diameter, left the muzzle with sufficient force to penetrate a pine board six inches thick at a range of 1,000 feet. To increase its lethal impact, troops would sometimes add several buckshot to the solid slug to guarantee that a hit would produce a gaping, horrible wound. An English surgeon was sickened by the ingenuity that the American rebels displayed in loading their guns:

> Their muskets were charged with old nails and angular pieces of iron, and from most of the men being wounded in the legs, I am inclined to believe it was their design, not wishing to kill the men, to leave them as burdens on us, to exhaust the provisions, as well as to intimidate the soldiery.[4]

The major deficiencies of the Brown Bess musket and its American counterpart were accuracy, rate of fire, and reliability. Even in the hands of a skilled marksman, the standard musket, because it had no rifling or spiraling grooves in the barrel, was hopelessly inaccurate at more than 150 yards. One soldier wrote:

> Brown Bess will strike a figure of a man at 80 yards. It may even be 100 yards, but a soldier must be very unfortunate indeed who shall be wounded by a common musket at 150 yards provided his antagonist aims at him; and as to firing at a man at 200 yards with a common musket you may as well fire at the moon and have the same hope of hitting your object.[5]

It was not uncommon, at least at long range, for whole battalions or entire lines of troops to fire at one another without anyone being hit. In addition, the cumbersome process of loading and discharging the eighteenth century musket meant that even seasoned troops could deliver only about three to five volleys per minute.

Twelve commands orchestrated the laborious procedure by which the infantryman prepared his musket for action. He began by reaching into his cartridge pouch and lifting out a little paper cylinder which contained a charge of powder and a leaden musket ball. After biting off the end encasing the bullet, he shook a bit of powder into a trough called the priming pan at the breech end of the musket, from where a touch hole led into the interior of the barrel. With the musket cocked, the infantryman then placed the butt of the musket on the ground, tapped the rest of the powder into the muzzle end, spit the slug down the barrel, and poked in the empty paper cartridge. The final movement involved withdrawing a long ramrod from its housing under the barrel, reversing the stick in the air, inserting it into the muzzle end of the musket, pushing the paper firmly down on top of the bullet, and returning the ramrod to its housing. Only then was the eighteenth century soldier ready to fire his Brown Bess musket.

No end of difficulties and disappointments awaited the beleaguered infantryman even after he finished loading his musket and pulled the trigger. Any moisture, including an early morning dew, that somehow seeped into the cartridge pouch or the firing mechanism would render black powder useless and make the musket misfire or not shoot at all. Colonel Henry Knox, serving in the Continental army in September 1777 wrote:

> After some days' manoeuvring, we came in sight of the enemy, and drew up in order of battle, which the enemy declined; but a most violent rain coming on obliged us to change our position, in the course of which nearly all the musket cartidges of the army that had been delivered to the men were damaged, consisting of about 400,000. This was a terrible stroke to us, and owing entirely to the badness of the cartouch-boxes which had been provided for the army.[6]

The flint, because it was stone, would become dull after several rounds, fail to ignite the charge in the priming pan, and have to be replaced. If the touch hole became clogged or stopped up, the black powder would flash in the priming pan without setting off the main charge in the barrel (hence the phrase "flash in the pan"). Even worse, soldiers caught up in the excitement of battle, with waves of musket fire rolling like claps of thunder across the landscape, would sometimes not realize that their weapons had malfunctioned. Consequently, trained to respond like robots to a sequence of commands, the troops would keep pouring powder and spitting bullets into the muzzle end. Imagine the horrifying calamity that would occur if the initial charge ignited after several rounds had misfired. The barrel of the Brown Bess musket or its American counterpart would explode, blowing off or disfiguring the hands and arms of the soldier holding it and propelling red hot metal and fire into the torsos and faces of that soldier and others near him.

With a weapon so inaccurate, so unreliable, and so arduous to load and discharge, military strategists and tacticians of the eighteenth century, in order to obtain a sufficient rate and efficiency of fire, devised a system of concentrated engagement which dictated that the infantry march to the battlefield in columns and deploy in long lines two to four rows deep to fight the enemy. "The strength of well-disciplined armies lay not in the motivation or prowess of individuals, but in the capacity for collective action," observed one analyst.[7]

Picture what it was like. Weighted down with a formidable jumble of paraphernalia, including bayonet, musket, cartridge pouch, water bottle, knapsack, and a haversack containing bread, flour, or rock-hard biscuits, the infantryman stood shoulder to shoulder with his compatriots, sweltering beneath a felt hat, a shirt of coarse linen, a waistcoat, a coat, breeches fastened below the knee, spats, and high-heeled shoes. Arrayed across the battlefield like a row of deadly dominoes, he and the other troops, resplendent in their colorful uniforms so they could be seen through the thick haze created by smokeless gunpowder, strode stoically toward the enemy, each army hoping that the other would fire the first volley.

The initial rounds, delivered at a distance of about 150 yards, brought few men down, so the two armies would gradually converge until they were little more than 40 yards apart. The men in the front row would load, crouch, and shoot, synchronizing their movements with the troops standing behind. At this range the carnage was ghastly. Whenever the troops sensed that the opposing force was faltering, they would fix their bayonets onto the muzzle end of their muskets, point the tips forward, and close with the enemy in ferocious, hand-to-hand combat and claim the field.

The patriot militia, organized by state and expected to serve only for a few months or to meet an immediate emergency, lacked the cohesion and discipline needed to excel on the eighteenth century battlefield. George Washington, who insisted that the rebellious colonies must create a professional army, was frequently harsh in his assessment of the capabilities of the part-time soldier. "I solemnly declare I never was witness to a single instance, that can countenance an opinion of Militia or raw Troops being fit for the real business of fighting," he pronounced.[8] Writing in the fall of

1776, Washington insisted that relying upon militia "is, assuredly, resting upon a broken staff." The American commander further lamented:

> Men just dragged from the tender Scenes of domestick life; un-accustomed to the din of Arms; totally unacquainted with every kind of Military skill, when opposed by Troops regularly train'd, disciplined and appointed, makes them timid and ready to fly at their own shadows.[9]

The most accomplished militia companies were along the frontier, where the Indian menace mandated that they remain ready to fight, but even they were largely unsuited for traditional eighteenth century combat. Many frontiersmen used rifles, which in the hands of an expert could hit a target as small as a man's head at a distance of 200 yards. While effective in the hit-and-run, guerrilla tactics that the white man had learned from the Indians, rifles could fire only about one round for every three volleys delivered by muskets; more importantly, they could not be fitted with a standard bayonet. As for the militia units along the coast, they had only recently bestirred themselves from years of virtual inactivity, in which they had become little more than social clubs where men came together to drink and cavort.

Not surprisingly, General Henry Clinton, an aloof British aristocrat reared in New York, and Commodore Sir Peter Parker, leaders of the British land and naval forces, respectively, assumed that they could wreak havoc with impunity upon patriot strongholds anywhere along the Southern coast. The soldiers and sailors under their command bore little resemblance to the pitiful band of Tory blunderheads who had marched to Moore's Creek Bridge four months before. Consequently, Clinton and Parker reasoned that these 2,500 troops, many of whom were seasoned and battle-tested, would be able to defeat any military unit the patriots dared to send against them. After all, their force included such crack British units as the Fifteenth, Twenty-eighth, Thirty-third, Thirty-seventh, Fifty-fourth, and Fifty-seventh Regiments and seven companies of the Forty-sixth. The redcoat fleet was even more impressive; the Whigs had no chance whatsoever of matching the might of the British navy on the high seas. Commodore Parker commanded the fifty-gun flagship *Bristol*, the twenty-eight-gun frigates *Active, Actaeon,* and *Solebay,* the twenty-two-gun *Friendship,* the twenty-gun *Sphynx,* plus assorted smaller craft. The fifty-gun *Experiment* arrived from Boston to join Parker's fleet in late June.

The crucial question was, where would the British strike? Clinton and Parker knew that they must act quickly, because they were under orders to join Sir William Howe's army for a summer campaign in the North. Clinton wanted to land on the shores of the Chesapeake, but Parker dispatched a reconnaissance party instead to Charleston, South Carolina. Discovering that the patriots were building a fort on Sullivan's Island at the entrance to Charleston Harbor, the two British commanders agreed that they had identified a military objective with sufficiently limited scope to satisfy their restricted timetable. Consequently, on May 30, 1776, Clinton and Parker ordered the powerful British fleet to hoist anchor and sail south from the mouth of the Cape Fear River. The redoubtable Royal armada, its menacing masts silhouetted against the Carolina horizon, arrived off Charleston Harbor on June 4, 1776.

The town of Charleston occupies the tip of a peninsula formed by the Ashley River to the west and the Cooper River to the east. Low barrier islands and impassable salt water marshes dominate the coastal landscape. To the north of the harbor entrance is Sullivan's Island, a snake-like, sandy spit of terrain about three miles in length and just a few hundred yards wide at its broadest point. Since late February, the patriots had been erecting a palmetto log fort, which was to be capable of accommodating up to 1,000 defenders, near the southern tip of Sullivan's Island. Designed as a conventional square citadel with bastions at the four corners, it had sixteen feet of sand and marsh packed between its interior and exterior walls. The commander of this curious but durable edifice was Charleston-born Colonel William Moultrie, who had moved to the island in early March on orders from President John Rutledge, head of the rebel South Carolina government.

Fort Sullivan occupied an especially strategic position. Any large vessel seeking to reach Charleston had to proceed northward via a U-shaped course. From Five Fathom Hole, an anchorage off shore, large ships had to sail westward through the narrow main channel that ran between Sullivan's Island and a treacherous shoal called the Middle Ground before turning northwestward across the harbor toward Charleston itself. This route dictated that ships would sail bow first toward Fort Sullivan, be able to bring their powerful broadsides to bear upon the Whig citadel only briefly, and then expose their vulnerable sterns to the deadly, patriot batteries.

Commodore Parker knew the types of artillery shells Moultrie's gunners would shoot toward the British fleet. Smoothbore, flat trajectory cannon would fire solid, iron balls to penetrate the wooden ships at the waterline. Chain shot, consisting of two cannonballs connected by a chain and fired from a single gun, would be launched to cut the sails and rigging. Hot shot, simply cannonballs heated cherry red in an oven and placed in the barrel with wet wadding, would be let loose in hopes of setting the fleet afire. But the most awesome weapon in the artillerymen's arsenal would be grape shot, composed of several small balls clustered around a wooden core. Upon impact, the balls would break loose and become shrapnel, spreading destruction in all directions.

William Moultrie described the apprehensive atmosphere which enshrouded the patriot troops at Charleston in late May and early June 1776, when the British armada began to come into view:

> The sight of these vessels alarmed us very much—all was hurry and confusion, the President with his council busy in sending expresses to every part of the country to hasten down the militia; men running about the town looking for horses, carriages and boats to send their families into the country. . . .[10]

Major General Charles Lee, a lean, intelligent military strategist and scholar who was married to the daughter of a Seneca Indian chief, arrived in Charleston on June 8 to assume overall command of the patriot defenses. Regarded by George Washington as the leading military expert in the American army, Lee was troubled by what he saw. The patriot militia suffered mightily from the unrelenting summer heat, swatted incessantly at swarms of pesky mosquitoes, and frequently developed diarrhea from contaminated drinking water. Only the judicious use of courts-martial allowed the Whig commanders to maintain even the bare rudiments of discipline among the troops.

Lee was particularly apprehensive about the strength of Moultrie's position on Sullivan's Island. He observed that the western and rear walls of the island fortress were barely seven feet high and therefore that they offered little or no protection against fire directed from any British ship that succeeded in sailing into the cove behind the island or from an attack by hostile troops approaching overland. Lee therefore urged Moultrie to withdraw his troops to the mainland. "When he came to Sullivan's Island," Moultrie wrote of Lee, "he did not like the post at all. . . . nay, he called it a 'slaughter pen.'"[11]

The logic of Lee's tactical thinking seemed irrefutable. It is true that the platforms and bastions fronting the entrance to Charleston harbor contained an impressive array of weaponry capable of inflicting grievous damage on any ship that dared to approach the palmetto fort. The west side had six 24-pounders and three 18-pounders, while the south side bristled with six 9- and 12-pounders. In each bastion there were five guns, ranging from nine to twenty-six pounds. In all, the unfinished fort on Sullivan's Island could bring twenty-one guns to bear upon the harbor entrance. But Parker's fleet, if properly positioned, would be able to aim more than 100 guns at the patriot citadel, and Lee was correct in his contention that the troops in Fort Sullivan would find it virtually impossible to repulse an attack from the rear. The soundness of Lee's calculations notwithstanding, knowing that the British fleet would have to pass directly in front of the citadel's artillery platforms if it sought to move toward Charleston, the South Carolinians refused to vacate Moultrie's precarious post at the southern tip of Sullivan's Island. The patriot garrison would stand and fight.

Whatever advantages the British brought to the auspicious engagement at Charleston in June 1776 were more than offset by faulty intelligence, inadequate planning, and plain bad luck. At first intending to land his troops on Sullivan's Island, Clinton persuaded Parker to put the redcoats ashore on Long Island, which was separated from Sullivan's Island to the south by a narrow estuary known as the Breach. The British general, a vain, headstrong commander, reasoned that his men would find Long Island, now the Isle of Palms, a more suitable spot from which to launch their attack upon Fort Sullivan. He was wrong.

The redcoats began to land on Long Island on June 8 or 9, 1776. On June 17, Clinton, having accepted the veracity of several local residents who had claimed that the Breach could be easily traversed by foot at low tide, waded from the shore only to find himself quickly engulfed by water up to his shoulders. This was a most unsettling discovery. Captain James Murray, an officer in the Fifty-seventh Regiment, described the situation:

> So much was the General prepossessed with the idea of this infernal ford, that several days and nights were spent in search of it. . . . It appears to me, but I speak it with the diffidence natural to one that has been an witness of the affair, that we might have abandoned the idea of attacking that part of the Island upon the first discovery of our mistake.[12]

Clinton and his formidable force of about 2,500 well-trained troops found themselves essentially cut off from Sullivan's Island unless they could launch an amphibious assault across the Breach and overwhelm a contingent of about 400 patriot soldiers who were dug in amid the sand dunes on the far shore. The British had suffered a severe setback. There was now little prospect that the Royal infantry would be able to participate in a coordinated land and sea attack upon Fort Sullivan as planned. The British fleet would most likely have to act alone in attacking the palmetto citadel.

On the morning of June 28, 1776, Commodore Parker ordered his fleet to lift anchor and commence its assault upon Fort Sullivan. His tactical scheme was to sail the *Bristol, Solebay, Active,* and *Experiment* close in to the citadel so that British troops stationed in the masts could bring the fort's gun platforms within range of small arms fire. "It was evident, from the manoeuvering of the British ships, that we were to have hot work," wrote Edward Hall, a patriot defender of Fort Sullivan.[13]

This bold British plan of attack began to unravel when the black South Carolinian pilots of the *Bristol* and the *Experiment* refused to come within 400 yards from shore. Parker's intention to dispatch the *Sphinx, Actaeon,* and *Syren* through the harbor entrance to attack the vulnerable rear of the palmetto log citadel from the cove also miscarried. Again the fault lay with the native blacks who piloted the British ships. The three frigates, led by the *Sphinx,* sailed too far to the west and ran aground on the Middle Ground, one of the many treacherous shoals that bordered the main channel. Moreover, the *Thunder,* a British ketch that was ordered to rain bombs from mortars upon Fort Sullivan, was anchored some 2,600 yards off shore and so was out of range. Almost laughably, the only fatalities from Royal mortar fire that day were three ducks, two geese, and one turkey.

As for Henry Clinton, until the *Sphinx, Actaeon,* and *Syren* failed to enter the cove, he had planned to transport his troops to the mainland and put them ashore at Haddrell Point just across from Sullivan's Island. After the frigates ran aground, Clinton had no choice but to attempt a direct assault across the Breach. After the patriots successfully resisted this strike, Clinton could do nothing more than observe through a spyglass the dramatic battle that was unfolding at the southern tip of Sullivan's Island.

The engagement at Charleston ultimately evolved into a gruesome, nine-hour artillery duel between the gunners aboard the *Active, Bristol, Experiment,* and *Solebay* and the Whig troops manning the ramparts along the southern and western faces of Fort Sullivan. Clearly, the advantage lay with the British in terms of the overall rate and volume of fire. The *Experiment* alone, for example, consumed nearly 160 barrels of gunpowder, and the British delivered approximately twenty shells for every round the patriot batteries succeeded in pouring down upon the Royal fleet. An eyewitness in Clinton's army described Parker's ships as "an eternal sheet of fire and smoke," while another redcoat stated, "I think it was by far the grandest sight I ever beheld."[14] A patriot soldier observed that "for hours it seemed that all the devils from the pit were let loose."[15]

Although the barrage of fire from Parker's ships was impressive, it did surprisingly little damage to Fort Sullivan and its defenders. Expecting patriot resistance to last thirty minutes at the most, Captain James Murray of the Fifty-seventh Regiment looked on with amazement as Colonel Moultrie and his troops fought on hour after hour: "After the first hour we began to be impatient and a good deal surprised at the resistance of the battery. But when for 4 hours the fire grew every moment hotter and hotter we were lost in wonder and astonishment."[16]

The performance of the 1,430 officers and men who operated and defended the patriot batteries at Fort Sullivan on June 28, 1776 was truly extraordinary, especially when one takes into account their relative inexperience. Particularly noteworthy was the ability of these unseasoned troops to maintain discipline under attack. "All along the fort, on the sea face, from our side and angle our brave men were returning this fire," wrote South Carolinian Edward Hall.[17] Militiamen always tended to perform best when they occupied defensive fortifications, were led by officers whom they trusted, and fought to protect their own homes. Major Banard Elliott described in a letter to his wife how one Whig soldier, "after a cannon ball had taken off his shoulder and scouped out his stomach," had exhorted his compatriots to fight on.[18]

An unexpected benefit resulted from the fort's walls being constructed of palmetto logs. Unlike rigid masonry, the porous timbers splintered but did not break under attack, and the patriot gunners took maximum advantage of the protection provided by the palmetto citadel. The Whigs concentrated their fire upon the two 50-gun ships, the *Bristol* and the *Experiment*. By using chain shot to destroy the masts, rigging, and sails and hot shot and grape shot to set the ships afire and to mutilate the crews, the Whigs succeeded in severely damaging Commodore Parker's fleet. "During the action no slaughter-house could present so bad a sight with blood and entrails lying about," observed an officer aboard the *Bristol*.[19] Another sailor was almost overcome by the ghastly scene that played itself out on the British flagship and described it thus: "I was on board the *Bristol* during the action and suffered much from the sight of so much slaughter. I am perfectly satisfied with what I have seen of civil war and devoutly wish that omnipotence would arrest the progress of the destroying angel and say it is enough."[20]

Six miles away sat the citizens of Charleston on their picturesque porticos, along their wharves, and high in their church steeples, apprehensively watching great clouds of smoke billow atop the water on the far side of the harbor. They were astonished when nightfall did not bring an end to the bloody engagement. Balls of fire continued to illuminate the dark horizon, revealing that the tide of battle was turning more and more against the British. The Royal gunners, who had tended to overshoot Fort Sullivan even in daylight, now could barely discern the patriot citadel through the sultry darkness. The *Bristol,* its anchor chain severed, drifted stern first toward the patriot batteries, its decks ravaged by incoming hot shot and grape shot. The *Actaeon,* hopelessly grounded in only seven feet of water at low tide, came under merciless artillery bombardment and was set afire by its own crew the next morning.

Finally, shortly after 9:00 A.M., Parker ordered the British ships to cut their cables and drift seaward on the ebb tide. Forty were killed and seventy-one wounded on the *Bristol* and twenty-three were killed and fifty-six wounded on the *Experiment.* There were fifteen casualties on the *Active* and *Solebay* each. Of the patriots, twelve were killed and twenty-five wounded. The verdict was clear. Britain's attempt to subdue Fort Sullivan and to invigorate Tory resolve in South Carolina had failed. Charleston would remain firmly in patriot hands, and no major British initiative would be taken in the South for another three years.

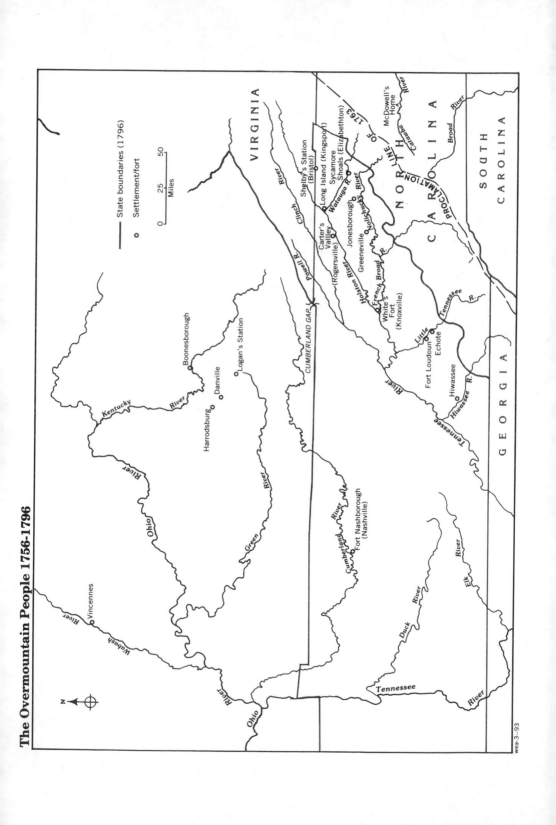

The Overmountain People 1756-1796

— State boundaries (1796)
○ Settlement/fort

Miles
0 25 50

VIRGINIA

Clinch River

Powell R.

CUMBERLAND GAP

Holston River

Nolichucky River

Watauga R.

French Broad R.

Shelby's Station (Bristol)
Carter's Valley (Rogersville)
Long Island (Kingsport)
Sycamore Shoals (Elizabethton)
Jonesborough
Greeneville
White's Fort (Knoxville)

NORTH CAROLINA

PROCLAMATION LINE OF 1763

McDowell's Home

Catawba River

Broad River

SOUTH CAROLINA

Little Tennessee R.
Fort Loudoun
Echote
Hiwassee

Tennessee River

Hiwassee R.

GEORGIA

Elk River

Duck River

Tennessee River

Cumberland River

Fort Nashborough (Nashville)

Green River

Ohio River

Kentucky River

Boonesborough
Logan's Station
Danville
Harrodsburg

Ohio River

Vincennes

Wabash River

N

wea-3-93

Chapter Three

Indians and Slaves

The final phase of the opening round of the American Revolution in the South occurred on the frontier. Barely had the people of Charleston begun to celebrate their victory over General Clinton and Commodore Parker when news arrived that the Cherokees, native Americans who lived in the mountain valleys of western North Carolina, northwestern South Carolina, northeastern Georgia and present day Tennessee, were on the warpath. Contrary to rumors circulating among rank-and-file patriots, this violent Indian uprising in July 1776 had no connection with the British assault upon Sullivan's Island the month before. It was instead a tragic milestone in the sordid tale of interactions between the native Americans and their white neighbors.

Since the end of the French and Indian War in 1763, when Great Britain had wrested control of the entire eastern basin of the Mississippi from France, His Majesty's government had stipulated that no white settlements were to exist beyond the crest of the Appalachian Mountains. Despite this prohibition, small bands of pioneers, carrying their belongings in wagons, on pack horses, or even on their backs, migrated over the mountains throughout the 1760s, especially into the valleys of the Holston, Watauga, and Nolichucky Rivers in what is now extreme northeastern Tennessee and southwestern Virginia. Legally nothing more than squatters, these "over-mountain" settlers, known as Wataugans, cleared plots in the forest, erected log cabins, and began raising crops on land that Great Britain insisted still belonged to the Iroquoian Cherokees.

About 22,000 Cherokees, whose tribal name roughly translates as "mountaineers" in English, resided in the lush meadows and along the sparkling, fast-running streams of the southern highlands. They were a fascinating folk. Their rich mythology taught them that the Milky Way was created by bits of grain falling from the mouth of a dog that had scampered across the heavens, that revengeful animals had created human diseases, including rheumatism by the deer, and that their forebears had emerged from the mother earth in the midst of the mountains where they lived.

The Cherokees were a hardy, resilient people, loyal to their friends but unrelenting in opposing their adversaries. "They are a very gentle and amicable disposition to those they think their friends," commented a British lieutenant who traveled among them in the early 1760s, "but as implacable in their enmity, their revenge only completed in the entire destruction of their enemies."[1]

Of olive complexion and medium height, the Cherokees were skillful hunters. Before white traders brought guns and powder into the Appalachian Mountains, the Indians had used bows and arrows, spears, hooks, and blowguns to kill animals, principally deer. They also practiced extensive agriculture. Their main crop was corn. A visitor to a Cherokee town in 1776 wrote, "All before me and on every side, appeared little plantations of young Corn, Beans, &c. divided from each other by narrow strips or borders of grass, which marked the bounds of each one's property, their habitation standing in the midst."[2]

Obviously, the coming of white farmers to the southern frontier had a profound impact upon the Indians' welfare. Among the destructive consequences of this encounter was the arrival of smallpox, against which the native Americans had no immunity. Alcoholism also ran rampant, as the Cherokees eagerly traded deerskins for the alluring pleasures provided by white man's rum. But the greatest threat resulted from the new settlers' insatiable appetite for land.

John Stuart, British superintendent for the Southern Indian Department, whose headquarters were in Charleston, and his special deputy to the Cherokees, Alexander Cameron, labored vigorously to protect the rights of the Cherokees. But the Indians were not united in how they should respond to the influx of white people, or "Long Knives" as the Cherokees called them. The younger warriors, especially the fiery chieftain Dragging Canoe, believed that the only solution was armed resistance. Older chiefs, like Attacullaculla and Oconnostota, sought accommodation with the white man. Meanwhile, the Cherokees' economy had become dependent upon the trade of deerskins for manufactured goods, mainly guns, ammunition, and rum, from the British colonies. Thus in 1772 the Cherokees agreed to lease land to the Wataugans for ten years.

In March 1775, without consulting Royal authorities, the Cherokees signed a treaty at Sycamore Shoals on the Watauga by which they consented to sell huge tracts of land in what is now Kentucky to the Translyvania Company, which was headed by North Carolinian Richard Henderson, who had hired Daniel Boone as his principal agent. That same month Attacullacula and Oconnostota also approved the sale of land in the valleys of the Holston, Watauga, and Nolichucky Rivers to the overmountain families who resided there.

The outbreak of hostilities between Great Britain and its North American Colonies in 1775 created a grim dilemma for the Cherokees. Not only would trade with the white man be interrupted, but the Indians would also be forced to choose sides in the conflict. Moreover, war would increase tensions with the frontiersmen, who were always eager to take advantage of any justification for seizing land from the Cherokees.

Initially John Stuart, who was forced to flee Charleston and settle in St. Augustine in British Florida, advised the Indians to remain neutral. In October 1775, however, he received orders from General Gage to secure military assistance from the Cherokees. Accordingly, in April 1776, Stuart dispatched his brother, Henry Stuart, to Chota, a major Overhill Cherokee town near the mouth of the Little Tennessee River, to plead with the Indians to gather under the Royal banner. Also present in the Overhill communities of the tribe was Alexander Cameron, whose wife was a Cherokee. The patriots were active as well in pursuing an alliance with the Cherokees, but logic dictated that the Indians would ultimately side with the British. It was Royal authority that offered the greater protection for their beloved tribal territory.

John Stuart and his associates regarded the Cherokees' sale of land in March 1775 to the Transylvania Company and the Wataugans as invalid because the Indians had acted independently. On May 2, 1776, at a Great Council of Cherokees meeting in Chota, Henry Stuart endeavored to negotiate a peaceful settlement to this dispute. He sided against the vitriolic Dragging Canoe, who continued to insist that the Cherokees should attack the Wataugan settlements and take back the territory illegally sold to the whites. Stuart won approval instead for a petition that instructed the frontiersmen to leave their farms within twenty days and move elsewhere, perhaps to British Florida, where land was plentiful.

The Wataugans simply ignored the petition and began making preparations for war. To win support for their illegitimate seizure of Indian territory, the conniving frontiersmen went so far as to produce a clever forgery of Cameron's handwriting and distribute a letter in which the British agent purportedly warned that an Indian attack was imminent and that Loyalists should immediately identify themselves so they would be spared. This malicious, wicked act prompted the majority of Cherokees to abandon the older chiefs and support Dragging Canoe instead. Adorning battle dress and decorating their bodies with war paint, the Cherokees took strength from the words of their ancient battle songs:

> Where'er the earth's enlightened by the sun,
> Moon shines by night, grass grows, or waters run
> Be't known that we are going, like men, afar,
> In hostile fields to wage destructive war.[3]

In July 1776, the southern frontier exploded into violence as hundreds of Cherokees rushed from their mountain havens, pillaging and plundering the countryside. From the lower towns the warriors advanced into upper South Carolina, while those in the middle and valley communities marched into North Carolina and bands from the Overhill towns moved against the Wataugans. On July 14, General Griffith Rutherford, who would lead the North Carolina militia in retaliation against the Cherokees, described in flawed grammar and spelling what he was hearing about events along the frontier:

> I am Under the Nessety of sending you by Express, the Allerming Condition, this Country is in, the Indins is making Grate Prograce, in Distroying and Murdering, in the frunteers of the County, 37 I am informed was killed Last Wednesday & Thursday, on the Cuttaba River, I am also Informed that Colo McDowel 10 men more & 120 women & children is Beshaged, in some kind of a fort, & the Indins Round them, no help to them before yesterday, & they were surrounded on Wednesday ... pray Gentlemen Consider oure Distress ... three off oure Captans is kild & one Wounded. This day I set out with what men I can Raise for the Relefe of the Distrest. ...[4]

Punishment of the Cherokees was swift, massive, and devastating. Like Donald MacDonald and the Highland Scots who had marched to Moore's Creek Bridge the previous February, Dragging Canoe and his compatriots were to pay a heavy price for siding against the Whigs. "In the perception of the patriots," argues one scholar, "the Indians had no reason for existence on the earth, save as the other wild beasts."[5]

On September 1, 1776, Rutherford led 2,500 North Carolinians through the Swannanoa Gap in the Blue Ridge Mountains and then westward to the Cherokee middle towns some eighty miles away. Joined by about 1,800 South Carolinians under Andrew Williamson, the invading force burned villages and ruined corn fields, thereby depriving the Indians of their essential food reserves. In October, a second patriot army, commanded by Colonel William Christian of Virginia, invaded across the Holston River on its way to the Overhill towns of the Cherokees. The proud Cherokee Indian nation never fully recovered from the defeat it suffered in the Cherokee War. Hereafter, any hope of securing help for the Tories from the Cherokees was a dead issue. Also, the perception persisted that the British had prompted the Indians to attack and murder innocent frontiersmen and their families—hardly an inducement to persuade white settlers to support the Loyalist movement.

John Murray, Earl of Dunmore, the Royal governor of Virginia, was also detrimental to the Tory cause in the South. The Earl of Dunmore was rashly insensitive to the political and social entanglements of the region. In April 1775, when a patriot throng was threatening to seize a store of ammunition in Williamsburg, Lord Dunmore suggested that slaves who rose up against their patriot masters and bore arms for the king might gain their freedom. "By the living God, if an insult is offered to me or to those who have obeyed my orders," the governor warned, "I will declare freedom to the slaves and lay the town in ashes."[6]

The institution of human bondage hung like a menacing shroud over British America. It gnawed away at the foundations of colonial society like a ruinous, corrosive acid and had a profound impact upon the course of the American Revolutionary War. The War for Independence, writes one expert, "had complexities overlooked by historians but all too real for eighteenth-century Americans. In short, two wars of liberation were taking place concurrently in which black and white objectives sometimes converged but just as often diverged."[7]

Supposedly fighting for freedom, the patriots nonetheless continued to administer onerous slave codes to control the behavior of their bondsmen. Any slave giving false testimony in court, for example, would "have one Ear nailed to the Pillory, and there stand for the Space of One Hour, and the said Ear to be cut off, and thereafter the other Ear nailed in a like manner, and cut off, at the Expiration of one other Hour."[8]

The first blacks had arrived in the British provinces in North America in 1619 at Jamestown, Virginia as indentured servants. By 1700, the importation and enslavement of blacks had become the chief means by which large landowners acquired and sustained an adequate labor supply. This was especially true in the plantation colonies of the South, such as Virginia and South Carolina, and the number of blacks held in bondage was substantial. For example, in 1775, South Carolina had 110,000 slaves and just 90,000 whites; in Georgia, there were 18,000 slaves and 10,000 whites; Virginia, the most populous colony, had about 200,000 slaves. Of the southern colonies, only North Carolina had relatively few people held in bondage in terms of a percentage of total population—20,000 slaves and 70,000 whites—primarily because it lacked a sufficient number of deep water ports to support a far-flung plantation economy.

A recurring fear among the wealthy landowners of the South was that a ferocious slave rebellion would explode across the region. Nightmarish images of bestial, sweat-soaked blacks rising up against their masters, destroying or grabbing everyone and everything that stood in their path, haunted the imaginations of the slave masters, many of whom were prominent Whigs. Janet Schaw commented in the summer of 1775 that the Whigs were insisting that the British had promised "every Negro that would murder his Master and family that he should have his Master's plantation."[9] In June of that year the Wilmington Committee of Safety sent out "Patroles to search for & take from Negroes all kinds of Arms whatsoever."[10] Obviously, anyone who dared to encourage the servile population of the South to defy established authority and to seek their freedom would evoke great anger, even fury, on the part of the region's economic and political elite.

The Earl of Dunmore did just that. On November 7, 1775, safely aboard ship in Norfolk Harbor, the governor issued a proclamation announcing that all able-bodied, male slaves in Virginia who abandoned their Whig masters and took up arms for the king would be free: ". . . and I do hereby further declare all indented servants, Negroes or others, (appertaining to Rebels) free, that are able and willing to bear arms, they joining his Majesty's Troops as soon as may be, for the more speedily reducing this Colony to a proper sense of their duty to His Majesty's crown and dignity. . . ."[11] "Hell itself could not have vomitted anything more black than this design of emancipating our slaves," wrote a patriot newspaper correspondent.[12]

Unquestionably, Lord Dunmore's proclamation greatly diminished Britain's ability to persuade the rank-and-file white population of the South to take up arms for the king. "Whatever loyalty there was in Virginia pretty much flickered out with Dunmore's call," states one scholar.[13] The offer of freedom for the slaves also had a dramatic impact in neighboring North Carolina. "Twelve Negroes, termed 'Dunmore's banditti,' invaded one plantation, robbed the owner of all his valuables, and carried off two Negro women," writes Jeffrey J. Crow in *The Black Experience in Revolutionary North Carolina*.[14]

Patriot leaders had not hesitated from the outset of hostilities to circulate rumors that the redcoats would embolden hordes of slaves to rebel against their masters and gather under the Royal standard. To say the least, it made for potent propaganda. In May 1775, radical Whigs in South Carolina had reported that word had arrived from friendly sources in London that the British were concocting a slave uprising and an Indian assault against the colonists. "Words, I am told, cannot express the flame that this occasioned amongst all ranks and degrees; the cruelty and savage barbarity of the scheme was the conversation of all companies," proclaimed William Bull, Royal governor of South Carolina.[15]

It is true that runaway or captured slaves gave meaningful support to the Royal military during the American Revolution. Historians have lionized such famous black patriots as Crispus Attucks, who was killed in the Boston Massacre, but the "evidence suggests that those blacks who took action in the Revolution were more likely to join the British."[16] Relatively few saw service in combat, but slaves were especially helpful as laborers, teamsters, carpenters, blacksmiths, foragers, naval pilots, spies, informers, guides, and the like. However, whatever assistance the slaves did provide to the redcoats was more than offset by the political damage wrought by Lord Dunmore's emancipation decree of November 7, 1775. Moderates such as Robert Carter Nicholas in Virginia, who had been most reluctant to sever his ties with Great Britain, became convinced of the need for separation because of Lord Dunmore's disregard for the right of property, even property in human beings. At a more visceral level, Lord Dunmore became a convenient hate symbol for the radical Whigs and racists of the South. Even the yeomen farmers of Virginia, the two Carolinas, and Georgia, most of whom had no expectation of owning slaves, were now more likely to accept characterizations of the Virginia governor as a sneering, leering tyrant who epitomized the insolent, uncaring British bureaucrat.

It was outside places like Bruton Parish Church in Williamsburg, Virginia that country gentlemen gathered to hear who had or who had not signed the oath of allegiance. The calamitous division of the South into Whigs and Tories had begun.

Chapter Four

Whigs and Tories

In late 1776 and throughout 1777, the South saw no large military engagements. It was in the North, primarily in New York, New Jersey, and Pennsylvania, that the major clashes were occurring. The absence of big battles below the Potomac did not mean that the South was devoid of tension, however, for unrest festered beneath a thin veneer of civility. Tragically, distrust and hatred persisted among neighbors and within families. This lamentable circumstance was especially widespread in the southern hinterland, where Tory sentiments remained surprisingly strong even after the defeat of the Loyalist troops at Moore's Creek Bridge.

The factors that prompted individuals to become or remain Tories defy simple classification. One scholar writes, "On present knowledge their cultural, economic, occupational, racial, ethnic, class, religious, and age backgrounds were virtually indistinguishable from those of other Americans who took the revolutionary course."[1] "Neither wealth nor occupation explains the division on the frontier," affirms historian Rachel N. Klein.[2]

Naturally, those persons whose economic welfare was intimately bound up with Great Britain overwhelmingly sided with the king. They included British merchants or merchants who did substantial business with Great Britain, officials who held office under Royal authority, and Anglican clergymen outside the South. They also included most of the participants in the Regulator movement (especially in North Carolina) and recent immigrants, such as the Highland Scots, who had settled in North Carolina's Cape Fear River valley.

A widespread phenomenon was for neighborhoods "to coalesce around key individuals."[3] The area between the Broad and Saluda Rivers in upper South Carolina became a notorious Tory stronghold largely because Thomas Fletchall, a militia colonel, supported the Royal banner. "Col. Fletchall has all those people at his beck, and reigns amongst them like a little King," deplored one Whig observer.[4]

Another prominent Loyalist in this district was Robert Cunningham.

According to Andrew Pickens, who would gain fame as a militia general during the American Revolution, Cunningham abandoned the patriots because he had been the loser in a contest to be elected colonel of his local militia regiment.

The most common characteristic of the Loyalists was that they "tended to be members of minority groups ... within their immediate environment."[5] "The proportion of loyalists seems to have been highest among the cultural and religious minorities," asserts Don Higginbotham in *The War Of American Independence.*[6] Many of the Germans who lived in eastern Rowan County, North Carolina, for example, sided with the king because they believed that the end of British rule would enable their more numerous Presbyterian neighbors to dominate local politics. In other words, they would rather obey George III than submit to being governed by the Scotch Irish Presbyterians who lived just up the road.

In 1777, Loyalists, who comprised about one-third of the colonial population, came under severe pressure to join the local patriot militia and sign oaths of allegiance to the permanent state governments that the Whigs had established. Any adult male not meeting these requirements was regarded as a traitor. The North Carolina oath read in part, "I will bear faithful and true allegiance to the State of North Carolina, and will to the utmost of my Power, support and maintain, and defend the independent Government thereof, against George the Third, King of Great Britain, and his Successors. . . ."[7]

Poignant stories of the mistreatment of those Tories who refused to comply with the patriots' stipulations were commonplace in the South. A merciless mob of about 100 backcountry Georgians assaulted Thomas Brown near Augusta, tied him to a tree, beat and kicked him until he lost consciousness, and scorched his feet with hot irons so badly that he lost two toes. "They burnt his feet, tarred, feathered and cut off his hair," reported one eyewitness of this dreadful but all too typical encounter.[8] Not surprisingly, Brown was to become a venomous opponent of the American rebels.

A series of incidents that occurred in Rowan County, North Carolina also demonstrates how frightening matters had become for the supporters of the king. Put yourself in the shoes of this harassed minority and consider what it must have been like for Tories in the North Carolina backcountry, where Whig sentiments reigned supreme in 1776–1777. The backers of the king were isolated and especially vulnerable because the British army was occupied elsewhere and was unable to protect Loyalists in the South during these years.

John Dunn was a wealthy Rowan lawyer, a respected leader in his community, and the Crown's attorney for the Court in Salisbury, the county seat. In 1774, when the final break with Great Britain was still two years away, he had signed a private declaration of support for Royal prerogatives. Dunn's adversary was William Kennon, a fiery patriot who served as chairman of the Committee of Safety in Rowan County. According to Kennon, Dunn, whom Kennon keenly disliked, had endorsed a document that was "in the highest degree false and contemptible and even bordering upon Blasphemy."[9] Never officially charged with a crime and never permitted to argue his case before a jury of his peers, Dunn was kidnapped in his own home by a patriot posse. "A number of Armed persons Entered into my house," the beleaguered Tory reported.[10] This sorry band of patriot ruffians then forced Dunn, who didn't have "a shift of any kind of apparel nor a shilling" in his pocket, to march under guard to Charleston, South Carolina, where he languished in a damp, dingy prison until late 1776.[11]

Is it any wonder that in 1776–1777 many Loyalists decided to flee or hide in the dense forests and coastal swamps of the South? Archibald Hamilton, a merchant in Halifax, North Carolina, bought a ship in New Bern and transported many of his Tory friends to New York City. Neil Snodgrass sailed from North Carolina "in a very small crazy Boat which happily brought him to New York."[12] Some Loyalists escaped to British Florida; others journeyed into the mountains to live among the Cherokee. Predictably, many Tories signed the oath of allegiance simply because they had no real choice. These duplicitous backers of the king waited for the day when Royal authority would return to the South, so they could reveal their true sentiments and retaliate against their oppressors. James Glen of Surry County, North Carolina, proclaimed that "a time would soon come" when the Whigs "would be obligated to take as many Black Oaths contrary to their conscience."[13] He would soon be proved right.

In 1778, a complex combination of considerations induced the British government to cast its eyes once more toward the South. His Majesty's Prime Minister, Lord Frederick North, and Lord George Germain, Secretary of State for the American Department and the person answerable for Britain's performance in the American Revolutionary War, came under intense political pressure to achieve a military breakthrough and subdue the rebellious colonies.

The previous year had not been kind to the king's fortunes. Weakened by a series of jolting setbacks culminating with the Battle of Bemis Heights on October 7, 1777, Major General John Burgoyne and his command had been overwhelmed and compelled to capitulate to Horatio Gates's American army at Saratoga, New York. After transporting his troops from New York City to Head of Elk at the northern end of the Chesapeake Bay in August, pushing Washington's army aside at the Battle of Brandywine on September 11, occupying Philadelphia on September 26, and repulsing an American charge at the Battle of Germantown on October 4, Sir William Howe and the main British army had found themselves essentially under siege in the Pennsylvania metropolis.

Another serious setback for the British was the entry of France into the American Revolutionary War in February 1778. Motivated primarily by a desire to avenge the reverses it had suffered in the Seven Years' War, France brought inestimable assets to the struggle to secure independence for the American colonies. Most conspicuous in this regard was its navy. Heretofore, Lord North and George Germain could at least be certain that Great Britain enjoyed absolute mastery of the sea, but now the French fleet, operating from its bases in the West Indies, could mount a serious challenge to Britain's naval supremacy in North America. Indeed, in August 1778, a French fleet commanded by Vice Admiral Comte d'Estaing cooperated with a Whig army and 4,000 French soldiers in an abortive attempt to seize Newport, Rhode Island from the British.

With Burgoyne's once powerful army destroyed, with General Howe's command under virtual siege in Philadelphia, and with the British fleet no longer invincible, Germain faced an increasingly hostile opposition in Parliament. William Pitt, a highly respected former prime minister and an outspoken advocate for ending the war, proclaimed in a speech on November 20, 1777:

> I know that the conquest of English America is an impossibility. You cannot, I venture to say it, cannot conquer America. If I were an American as I am an Englishman, while a foreign troop was landed in my country, I never would lay down my arms—never— never—never.[14]

Even more damaging to Germain and his ministerial colleagues were statements made by Major General Charles Grey, who had just returned from a tour of duty with the British army in North America: "I do not think that from the beginning of June, when I landed in New York, in 1777, to the 20th of November, 1777, there was in that time a number of troops in America altogether adequate to the subduing of that country by force of arms."[15]

Sir William Howe, who resigned as commander in chief in North America and was replaced in March 1778 by Henry Clinton, shared Grey's contention that defeating the rebels would require sending a much larger Royal Army across the Atlantic. Howe also publicly disputed the assumption that undergirded Germain's overall military strategy—that the Loyalists were capable of assuming a leading role in overwhelming the patriots.

In March 1778, George III, eager to extricate his government from what had become a political quagmire, established the Carlisle Commission, which was named for its chairman, the Earl of Carlisle. The Carlisle Commission was dispatched to New York City with conciliatory proposals. As expected, the American government refused to meet with Carlisle and his two associates. American emissaries insisted that peace negotiations between Great Britain and the rebellious colonies could occur only if His Majesty's government agreed at the outset to set its North American colonies free, a concession George III adamantly refused to make. Faced with this irreconcilable impasse, Lord North and his colleagues understood that the war must continue.

Germain recognized that the anti-war faction in Parliament might make "it almost impossible to the present Ministry to remain in office."[16] Consequently, he searched fervently for a strategy that would demonstrate that the war was winnable. How could he show that the Loyalists, if protected by a British army, would rise up in great numbers to support the king? To secure what he thought would be a sufficient number of troops to safeguard the Tories, Germain used such traditional recruiting techniques as offering bounties to volunteers, obtaining criminals convicted by the courts, and hiring German mercenaries, especially from Hesse-Cassel, which sent 17,000 soldiers to serve in North America with the British. But would the number of troops ever be enough to induce the Tories to come forth in sufficient numbers to win the war and silence Germain's critics in Parliament?

Not a few interested parties argued that the South continued to offer the best hope for a successful Tory uprising. Among them were such notable figures as Governor William Campbell of South Carolina and Governor James Wright of Georgia. "From our particular knowledge of those Provinces," the two banished Royal officials proclaimed, "it appears very clear to us, that if a proper number of troops were in possession of Charleston . . . or if they were to possess themselves of the back country thro' Georgia, and to leave a garrison in the town of Savannah, the whole inhabitants of both Provinces would soon come in and submit."[17] Major General James Robertson, a veteran of the American war, insisted that the Tories below the Potomac were merely waiting for the help that would "enable the loyal subjects of America to get free from the tyranny of the rebels."[18] Finally, James Simpson, the crown's attorney general for South Carolina, who was sent to the South to gauge the strength of Loyalist sentiment, suggested that "whenever the King's troops move to Carolina they will be assisted by a very considerable number of the inhabitants."[19]

On March 8, 1778, Germain sent a dispatch to Henry Clinton in New York City informing His Majesty's commander in chief in North America that the conquest of the South was "considered by the King as an object of great importance in the scale of the war."[20] According to the Secretary of State for the American Department, the capture of Virginia, the two Carolinas, and Georgia would deprive the rebel government of its ability to export tobacco, rice, and indigo, which were the principal crops the Whigs sold to acquire the money to purchase crucial supplies from Europe. Germain's instructions gave Clinton broad latitude in deciding where and when the invasion of the South should occur. He wrote:

> But your own knowledge of those provinces, and the information you can collect from the naval and military officers that have been upon service there, will enable you to give the officer to whom you may entrust the command better instructions than I can pretend to point out to you at this distance.[21]

For Germain to provide so much discretion to Clinton in devising a strategy for an armed intrusion into the South was characteristic of British military practice during the American Revolution. The officer class was not composed of trained professionals. Indeed, commissions through the rank of colonel could be bought, and most of the redcoat generals, including aristocrats like Howe, Burgoyne, Cornwallis, and Clinton, were members of the Parliament. Therefore, political considerations were always uppermost in the minds of the officer corps. By giving a high level of discretion to Clinton, Germain could absolve himself of direct responsibility if the campaign should fail. Such actions, while politically shrewd, tended to sow discord and distrust among the upper echelons of the British military, as well as cause them to eschew bold, decisive action. Cagey subordinates like Henry Clinton would likewise protect their own reputations by giving broad latitude to their own field commanders, including Lieutenant Colonel Archibald Campbell, a 39-year-old Scot who was to lead the first foray into the South.

Chapter Five

Savannah: The First Time

"Certain false assumptions and miscalculations underlay the Southern campaign from the very beginning," asserts Don Higginbotham.[1] The greatest of these was the belief that His Majesty's government could expand the war into the Carolinas and Georgia at minimal cost because Loyalists were so numerous there. In November 1778, Clinton, whose army was only about two-thirds as large as that which William Howe had possessed the previous year, took the dangerous step of splitting his forces by sending 3,500 men south by sea with Archibald Campbell from New York City to join General Augustine Prevost, who commanded about 2,000 soldiers in St. Augustine, Florida. Clearly, this bold adventure, which had as its initial objective the conquest of Georgia, could succeed only if Britain retained absolute mastery of the sea. Remember, however, that since March 1778, when Germain had first proposed that Clinton commit substantial numbers of troops to offensive operations in the South, France had brought its powerful fleet into the war. The dire consequences of Great Britain losing, even temporarily, naval superiority to France was to become all too obvious at Savannah, Georgia in the late summer and early fall of 1779.

Matters went well for the British in the beginning of the invasion. Taking full liberties with his imprecise instructions, Archibald Campbell, instead of making a juncture with Prevost's army before engaging the enemy in combat, sailed directly for Tybee Island at the mouth of the Savannah River. On December 29, 1778, the intrepid redcoat began putting troops ashore on the right bank of the river at Girardeau's Landing, a spit of firm ground bounded by rice plantations about two miles south of the Georgia capital.

Campbell knew that Georgia was especially vulnerable to invasion. Small bands of Tories and redcoats had periodically moved northward from their haven in British Florida to plunder the Georgia countryside, and the Creek Indians had not hesitated to send raiding parties into the backcountry. The population, almost half of whom were black slaves, numbered only about 40,000, and most of Georgia's residents lived within a narrow strip of land forty to fifty miles wide to the west and the south of the Savannah River. In addition to the capital, the major strategic settlements were Sunbury, about forty miles down the coast from Savannah, and Augusta, the gateway to the hinterland, some 120 miles upriver from the Georgia capital.

The Whigs had endeavored on three occasions between 1776 and 1778 to make Georgia more secure by launching invasions against British Florida. During the summer of 1776, Charles Lee had seen his small patriot army succumb to yellow fever and malaria in the steamy swamps and marshes of the Ogeechee River. In 1777 the Georgia Provincial Congress had attempted to mount a second attack against St. Augustine, but this assault was aborted when two patriot officers bickered over who was to command the expedition. Finally, in 1778, Brigadier General Robert Howe, a North Carolinian who had been appointed by Congress early in that year to head the Department of the South, had ordered his Continentals to cooperate with elements of the Georgia and South Carolina militia in invading Florida.

"The situation of this country is a circumstance of exceeding anxiety to me," Howe wrote. "It is a melancholy truth that our regulars do not exceed 550 effectives."[2] Again partly because of disagreements over who should command the expedition, the patriot army failed to achieve its objective. In September 1778, the Continental Congress, hearing considerable criticism of Howe's performance in this ill-fated campaign, selected Major General Benjamin Lincoln of Massachusetts to replace Howe as head of the southern district. "Think, Sir, the underserved mortification I must feel upon an occasion like this," Howe had lamented in a letter to Henry Laurens, president of Congress.[3]

His removal notwithstanding, Howe was still responsible for the defense of the Carolinas and Georgia until Lincoln arrived from the North. Consequently, when rumors began to circulate in late 1778 that Henry Clinton was about to order a fleet to set sail from New York City and invade Georgia, the embattled North Carolinian started making preparations for fortifying the state. To his dismay and consternation, Howe learned that Governor John Houstoun and the patriot militia of Georgia refused to admit that they should obey a Continental commander's orders or requests, which they regarded as Howe's "attempts to dictate to them."[4] "It is impossible for me to give an account of the confused, perplexed way in which I found matters in this state upon my arrival," Howe exclaimed.[5]

The patriot military during the American Revolutionary War was a complex jumble of institutional loyalties and chains of command. The Declaration of Independence had created a confederation of thirteen independent states, not a truly united country. The only central governing body was the Continental Congress, and it had no power to levy taxes or raise military forces on its own authority. It could merely decide how many troops and how much money was needed for a national military, called the "Continental Line" or simply the Continental army, and set quotas for the states to meet in proportion to their population and wealth.

Each state continued to exercise control over its own militia, which competed with congressional agents in obtaining recruits for the patriot army. Unlike volunteers for the Continental army, who had to serve at least three years or for the duration of the war, militiamen had to stay in the ranks for one year at the most, and usually received financial inducements, principally bounties, that compared most favorably with those derived from service in the Continental army. Further complicating matters was the fact that governors and militia leaders tended to regard Continental officers as outsiders, as irritating interlopers, because the states played no role in selecting commanders of the Continental army. That prerogative belonged to Congress alone. This circumstance meant that only those Continental officers who possessed extraordinary skills of diplomacy and cajolery could operate successfully within the labyrinth of jousting military bureaucracies and persuade state officials and militia officers, many of whom possessed preening egos, to cooperate with the Continental army. Unfortunately, Robert Howe was no diplomat.

On November 18, 1778, Howe marched his Continental troops out of Charleston and headed south. After reaching Zulby's Ferry on the Savannah River, about thirty miles above the Georgia capital on November 27, the patriot army moved to the opposite bank and proceeded into Georgia. There they hoped to intercept an enemy force headed by Major Mark Prevost, Augustine Prevost's younger brother, that was collecting cattle and other supplies in the Newport and Midway settlements. "(They) destroy everything they meet in their way. They have burnt all the houses on the other side of Newport Ferry," commented one observer of the foraging redcoats.[6] Unable to catch the younger Prevost before the British returned to Florida, Howe could at least take heart at the news that Colonel Lewis Fuser and a small British force had failed to capture Fort Morris near Sunbury in early December.

With the immediate threat past, Howe placed elements of his army at strategic points along the Georgia coast, especially at the mouths of rivers, to sound the alarm when the British fleet was sighted. The lame duck American commander learned from a British deserter that Campbell had set sail on December 6 and was unquestionably headed for Georgia. When the ships began to arrive off Tybee Island on December 23, Howe knew that Savannah, some eighteen miles upriver from the coast, was the primary objective of the invading redcoats. He also knew that his situation was dire.

Howe's attempts to obtain help from Governor Houstoun and the Georgia militia went largely unheeded. Indeed, the lack of cooperation on the part of state officials in the face of this immediate menace was astounding. The Georgians spurned Howe's offers to repair the few cannon which belonged to the state, ignored his appeals to provide slaves to strengthen defensive works at Sunbury, and even told South Carolina troops whom Howe had summoned to Savannah to go home. Governor Houstoun virtually ignored General Howe, preferring to deal directly with Benjamin Lincoln, who had just arrived in Charleston.

Howe had approximately 600 Continental soldiers at his disposal for the defense of Savannah, comprised of about an equal number of South Carolinians, commanded by General Isaac Huger, and Georgians, headed by General Samuel Elbert. On December 24, Christmas Eve, Governor Houstoun finally agreed to place approximately 100 militia, led by Colonel George Walton, under Continental authority, but the Whig troops would still be outnumbered about four-to-one. A council of war composed of field officers nonetheless advised Howe to mount a vigorous defense of the Georgia capital in hopes that Lincoln, who had arrived in Charleston on December 7, would be able to bring reinforcements before Savannah fell.

The American commander surveyed the landing sites where the British could come ashore and considered where to deploy his soldiers to oppose them. Because there were a dozen places above and below Savannah where the redcoats could disembark, Howe had to hold the majority of his troops in reserve until the point of attack became known. Therefore, the decision as to where the battle would occur belonged to Archibald Campbell, whose invading army included two battalions of the Seventy-first Regiment, two regiments of hessians, a detachment of Royal Artillery, and two Tory contingents—Courtland Skinner's Jersey Volunteers and Oliver DeLancey's New York Provincials. "This formidable army was well trained, experienced, properly equipped, and led by splendid officers," states one authority.[7]

Campbell learned from two captured Georgians that the patriot army defending Savannah, which sits atop a sandy bluff on the southern bank of the Savannah River, could not match his strength. Consequently, the enterprising redcoat abandoned his intention of waiting for General Augustine Prevost to arrive from Florida before moving against Howe. Campbell began putting his troops ashore at daybreak on December 29 at Girardeau's Landing.

Howe realized that engaging the enemy near the river would bring his troops within range of British naval gunners, and he could be easily out-flanked. Therefore, he placed his men astride the road that ran through Fair Lawn Plantation just outside Savannah and waited for the redcoats to attack. At first glance Howe's position looked formidable. His left flank, where General Elbert's Georgians stood ready to defend their native state, reached almost to the river and the extreme right, occupied by Colonel Walton's Georgia militia, was protected by a supposedly impassable swamp. Still, the Whigs were to suffer a humiliating defeat outside Savannah on December 29, 1778.

Unlike many of his fellow officers, who tended to be overly cautious because of their desire to protect their cherished political reputations, Campbell was a bold and aggressive commander who eagerly seized the opportunities that presented themselves on the battlefield. "I thought it expedient, having the day before me, to go in quest of the enemy rather than give them an opportunity of retiring unmolested," he reported to Germain.[8] Fortune smiled on Campbell and his men. A black slave wandered into the British camp and told the redcoats that he could lead them along a "private path through the wooded swamp upon the enemy's right."[9] Campbell immediately grasped that this information was vital and that it would allow him to achieve a decisive victory. The British would be able to fall unexpectedly upon Howe's southern flank; Colonel Walton's Georgia militia would have little hope of resisting an unexpected bayonet charge mounted by disciplined redcoats.

Indeed, when rolling drums and squealing bagpipes announced that the British were moving forward, even the cool winter air could not keep sweat from beading on the foreheads of the outnumbered defenders of the Georgia capital. Campbell, knowing that the patriots believed that their right flank was secure, sent elements of his light infantry toward the river to demonstrate on Howe's left, so that the American commander would conclude that the major British thrust would occur there. Meanwhile, Campbell dispatched the Seventy-first Regiment under Sir James Baird and some of the New York Tories through the swamp on Howe's right and readied his artillery to coordinate its firing with the impending attack of Baird's force upon the unsuspecting Georgia militia.

Colonel Walton and his militiamen were taken by surprise when Baird's troops burst from the swamp and fell mercilessly upon them. Fleeing in complete panic, the Georgians signaled by their precipitous departure that Howe's southern flank had utterly collapsed and, even more ominously, that the British and their allies were proceeding to encircle the patriot army.

The outmaneuvered American commander, under intense pressure from an artillery barrage and a bayonet charge all along his front, had no choice but to order his force to withdraw. By previous arrangement, the patriots, who had anticipated that they would not be able to hold Savannah indefinitely, began to move toward a pass to the south of the town. The Georgia Continentals became confused, however, when General Elbert ordered them to alter their order of march. Breaking ranks, Elbert and his men dashed frantically through the streets of Savannah, paused briefly at the courthouse, and then scampered toward Musgrove Creek just west of town, where they were told that a log bridge would carry them to safety.

When these reports proved to be false and no bridge existed, the Georgia Continentals, with General Elbert ingloriously in the lead, jumped into the cold, murky waters of Musgrove Creek and began to swim toward the opposite bank. This was about 3:00 P.M. Unfortunately, most of Elbert's men, including Mordecai Sheftall and his son Benjamin, were captured before they could enter the stream.

> On our arrival at the creek, after having sustained a very heavy fire of musketry from the light infantry under the Command of Sir James Baird, during the time we were crossing the Common, without any injury to either of us, we found it high water; and my son, not knowing how to swim, and we with about one hundred and eight-six officers and privates, being caught, as it were, in a pen, and the Highlanders keeping up a constant fire on us, it was thought advisable to surrender ourselves prisoners, which we accordingly did, and which was no sooner done than the Highlanders plundered every one amongst us. . . .[10]

The British had achieved a total victory at Savannah. "Eighty-three of the enemy were found dead on the Common, and eleven wounded," Archibald Campbell stated in his report to Germain. "By the accounts received from their prisoners, thirty lost their lives in the swamp, endeavoring to make their escape."[11] British casualties totaled twenty-six: seven killed and nineteen wounded. General Howe, who had had 550 soldiers killed or captured out of 700 effective troops, plus all his artillery and support vehicles destroyed or captured, led the tattered remnant of his army northward across the Savannah River into South Carolina and ordered the two remaining patriot garrisons in Georgia, which were at Sunbury and Augusta, to retreat as well. On January 15, 1779, General Augustine Prevost, who had marched from St. Augustine and captured Fort Morris at Sunbury en route, assumed command of all British forces in Georgia.

At last George Germain and Henry Clinton had captured a major Southern port to which the Tory "hordes" in the region could rally with impunity. This new sanctuary did attract large numbers of the king's supporters, at least at the outset. Archibald Campbell "acted with great policy, in securing the submission of the inhabitants," says an early historian of the American Revolutionary War.[12] Loyalists "flocked by hundreds to the King's officers, and made their peace at the expense of their patriotism," states another source.[13] James Fergus, a South Carolina militiaman who was called up in late 1778 to collar a Tory leader named Captain Coleman, commented that "Coleman and his Tories had gone off to join the British in Georgia."[14]

The Whigs knew that the American Revolution in the South had entered a perilous phase. "I hope we shall drive those gentry on board their vessels," proclaimed William Moultrie, the hero of the Battle of Fort Sullivan, who was encamped with the patriot army across the river from Savannah in January 1779. "We hear their drums beat every morning from our out posts; nay, hear their sentinels cough."[15] Moultrie and his colleagues realized that the next few weeks could be pivotal in determining the durability of patriot resistance in the South now that the British were ashore in considerable numbers.

Up to this point the redcoats had good reason to feel smug about their accomplishments in Georgia, but the real test of the king's ability to embolden the Tories to accept responsibility for defeating the rebellion in the South was yet to come. The crucial trial would not transpire along the coast where the British, at least if the French navy stayed away, possessed overwhelming military superiority. The critical engagements would occur in the backcountry. It was in the pine barrens and upland hardwood forests of the hinterland, in the same general region where the Regulators and the Highland Scots had gathered to begin their ill-fated march to Moore's Creek Bridge, that the viability of Germain's policy would be validated or belied. Clearly, if the Tories in the Georgia and Carolina backcountry stepped forward again to proclaim their allegiance to His Majesty's government only to suffer an ignominious defeat, as Donald MacDonald and his cohorts and the Cherokees had experienced almost three years before, they too would recoil. In that instance, the Tories would likely refuse to shoulder the major burden of subduing the Whigs. As always, the pivotal engagements were not the large, spectacular encounters that happened on or near the coast. The battles that ultimately decided the outcome of the American Revolution in the South were the small, often momentary skirmishes that erupted between Whig and Tory partisans in the woods and meadows of the hinterland.

On January 22, 1779, Archibald Campbell set out from Ebenezer, Georgia, a town about fifteen miles above Savannah, and headed for Augusta, the backcountry patriot stronghold approximately 100 miles upriver to the northwest. "I need not inform Your Lordship, how much I prize the hope of being the first British Officer to rend a Stripe and a Star from the flag of Congress," Campbell wrote to Germain.[16] The mood of his troops was buoyant. Among Campbell's officers was Thomas Brown, the same Tory who had been beaten almost to death and mutilated by his Whig neighbors outside Augusta when the war had begun. Think how Brown must have felt when he realized that he was returning to the scene of that horrible event and would soon be able to mete out revenge on those who had sought to cripple him. Is it any wonder that the blood was hot and the passion fiery as Campbell's men moved inland? Vengeance can be wonderfully sweet.

Campbell's move into the interior was only one component of a complex scheme that the British had devised to conquer the hinterland of Georgia and South Carolina. According to this plan, which was reminiscent of the fanciful strategy that Josiah Martin had conjured up in 1775 for subjugating North Carolina, the Cherokee and Creek Indians would rise up on the Georgia and South Carolina frontier, overpower the local Whigs, and march to join Campbell and the legions of backcountry Tories who were expected to assemble in Augusta. This awesome display of power would then presumably persuade any wavering Tories to come out for the king and convince any recalcitrant rebels to lay down their arms and submit to Royal control.

This tricky invasion plan was totally out of touch with reality. Indeed, it was little more than complete and absolute nonsense. Events soon demonstrated that the British had vastly underestimated the determination of the Whigs to defy the imposition of Royal authority.

On January 26, Brown attempted to capture the patriot stronghold at the Burke County Jail as ordered by Campbell. Brown was repulsed by the Whig militia, and his arm was shattered in the struggle. Although Campbell captured Augusta without a fight on January 31 and welcomed some 1,100 men into his camp over the next two weeks, all of whom swore allegiance to the king, he was unable to prevent the destruction of a large body of Carolina Tories about fifty miles northwest of Augusta at the Battle of Kettle Creek on February 14.

The man who led the patriot partisans to victory at Kettle Creek was Andrew Pickens, a dour Presbyterian elder who grew up in an "atmosphere of rifle and religion."[17] Born on September 19, 1739, in Bucks County, Pennsylvania, Pickens had moved with his family first to the Shenandoah

Valley of Virginia and then, like many Scotch-Irish, migrated farther south, in his case to the Waxhaw community in upper South Carolina, where he had reached manhood. In the mid-1760s, Pickens settled in the Long Canes district of South Carolina, about twenty-two miles west of Ninety Six, where he married and built his home and a blockhouse.

Andrew Pickens prospered in the Indian trade. He was so successful as a merchant that he erected a warehouse across the Savannah River from Augusta to hold the goods that he gathered for transit down river. Like most of the wealthier residents of the hinterland who sought to increase their involvement in commercial agriculture and to own more slaves, Pickens sided with the Whigs partly because he shared common economic interests with the plantation owners in the coastal areas of the Carolinas and Georgia. Determined to protect his substantial economic holdings, this adept Presbyterian elder, his resolute commitment to Christian beliefs notwithstanding, never hesitated to use the methods of social control he had learned in the primitive environment that characterized the southern frontier during the American Revolution. If it would do the job, Pickens would merely whip his enemies or burn down their houses. If necessary, he would kill them.

As for the Indians, they were asked to perform an essentially impossible task. The Creeks and the Cherokees were supposed to conduct an intricate, coordinated campaign against the upcountry patriot militia and then converge on Augusta, where Campbell and his formidable body of troops were waiting to greet them. They were expected to distinguish between Whig and Tory settlers, who looked identical to Native Americans except for the pine sprigs the supporters of the king were told to wear in their hats. The Indians were even given outlandish orders to fight the patriots in Georgia but to spare those in South Carolina until proper legal authority arrived to attack them.

Harassed by Whigs along the frontier and devoid of effective leadership, the Cherokees and Creeks never materialized in significant numbers at Campbell's camp. In a real sense, the Indian uprising, much like the Cherokee rebellion in 1776, in which Andrew Pickens had served as a militia commander, helped the patriots more than the Tories because it enabled the enemies of the king to convince even more backwoodsmen, like the redoubtable Pickens, that only by taking up arms against the king could they work to reduce the threat posed by Native Americans against the farms and settlements of the white man. "As objects of long-standing fear and hostility, the Cherokees were more useful to the whigs as enemies than as allies," asserts Rachel N. Klein.[18]

A pathetic scene played itself out in Augusta early in the morning of February 14, 1779. With no fanfare and no farewells, Archibald Campbell, aware that Benjamin Lincoln was sending a sizeable body of troops inland to attempt to surround the town, marched his troops out of Augusta and headed back toward Savannah. Reverend James Seymour, the local Anglican priest, who only two weeks before had joyously greeted the redcoats as liberators, looked on sullenly as the British moved off into the thick woods. Seymour had good reason to anticipate the worst from the Whigs. "Our Feelings at first on that Occasion cannot be easily described. We expected to be plundered of everything we had, and even that our Lives were in Danger," he declared.[19]

Even though Seymour suffered only imprisonment, he and the other Loyalists in the Georgia and Carolina hinterland had learned a bitter lesson—one which they would not soon forget. Clearly, the ability of the redcoats to protect the supporters of Royal prerogatives remained at best ephemeral, especially in the backcountry. Those colonists who dared to declare their allegiance to the king still risked retribution from their patriot neighbors, and these retaliatory raids occurred not just in battles like Kettle Creek. More common were reprisals carried out by unrelenting bands of grisly partisans, who had learned the skills of bitter conflict in the harsh conditions of the frontier. "A relentless, corrosive, intenecine war between wild bands of Whigs and Tories had torn at the vitals of the Carolinas and Georgia," asserts one authority. "As often as not these irregulars were simply marauders who pillaged and killed their neighbors for gain rather than principle."[20] "After burning a number of the Tories' houses that were gone, we returned home," wrote one Whig militiaman.[21]

On his trek back to the coast, Campbell, who would soon leave Georgia, relinquished command of the expedition to Lieutenant Colonel Mark Prevost, who had just come up from Savannah. On Campbell's advice, Prevost attacked a large body of Whigs, headed by General John Ashe, at Briar Creek on March 3, 1779. Again, the British professionals achieved a decisive victory. Although General Elbert and his Continentals firmly resisted the redcoats, the patriot militia, much like their counterparts outside Savannah the previous December, virtually ran off without firing a shot. The British suffered five killed and eleven wounded at Briar Creek. Between 150 and 200 Whigs lost their lives, including many who drowned trying to escape the redcoats. "Twelve of us got together," explained a South Carolina soldier, "and, as it was moonlight in the night, we formed a small raft of driftwood in the mouth of a lagoon, on which three of us with danger and much difficulty got over the river, after being carried above a mile down before we landed."[22]

The British victory at Briar Creek could not belie the fact that Germain's expectations that the Tories would rise up in great numbers and assume the major share of the burden of defeating the enemies of the king were not being fulfilled. As John Pancake writes in his brilliant analysis of the British campaigns in the South,

> From a military point of view, the campaign ended in a stalemate. But in the context of controlling the Georgia backcountry, the results were disastrous for the British. . . . The pattern was clear. A show of force by the British was useless unless it could be demonstrated that the authority of the crown was permanent. Loyalists who literally or figuratively came out of hiding found themselves abandoned to the retribution of the enemy. The sporadic offensive of Campbell and Prevost had failed to gain any territory and had thoroughly aroused the Whig partisans.[23]

War of Maneuver in the Carolinas

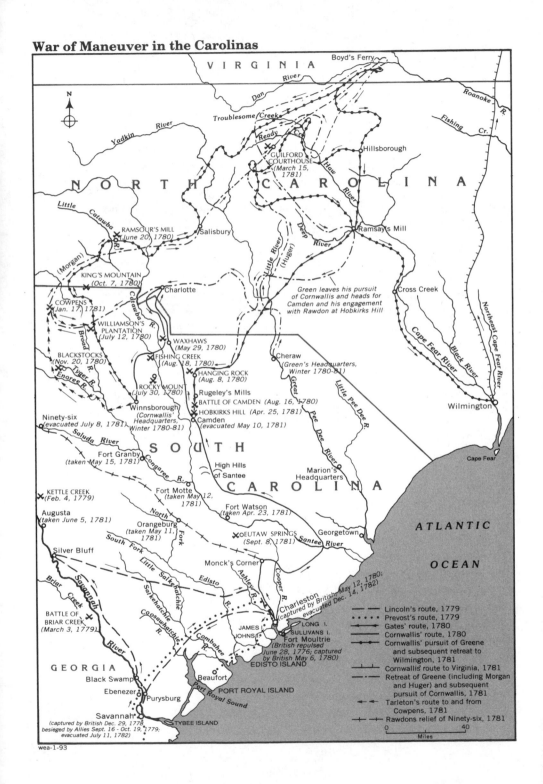

VIRGINIA

Boyd's Ferry

Roanoke R.

Dan River

Fishing Cr.

Troublesome Creek

Ready Cr.

GUILFORD COURTHOUSE
(March 15, 1781)

Hillsborough

Haw River

N O R T H   C A R O L I N A

Yadkin River

Little Catawba R.

RAMSOUR'S MILL
(June 20, 1780)

Salisbury

Ramsay's Mill

Deep River

Little River (Huger)

(Morgan)

KING'S MOUNTAIN
(Oct. 7, 1780)

Charlotte

Cross Creek

Northeast Cape Fear River

COWPENS
(Jan. 17, 1781)

Catawba R.

Green leaves his pursuit
of Cornwallis and heads for
Camden and his engagement
with Rawdon at Hobkirks Hill

WILLIAMSON'S
PLANTATION
(July 12, 1780)

Broad R.

WAXHAWS
(May 29, 1780)

Cape Fear River

Black River

BLACKSTOCKS
(Nov. 20, 1780)

FISHING CREEK
(Aug. 18, 1780)

Cheraw
*(Green's Headquarters,
Winter 1780-81)*

Tyger R.

Enoree R.

ROCKY MOUNT
(July 30, 1780)

HANGING ROCK
(Aug. 8, 1780)

Wilmington

Rugeley's Mills

BATTLE OF CAMDEN (Aug. 16, 1780)

Ninety-six
(evacuated July 8, 1781)

Winnsborough
*(Cornwallis'
Headquarters,
Winter 1780-81)*

HOBKIRKS HILL *(Apr. 25, 1781)*

Camden
(evacuated May 10, 1781)

Great Pee Dee River

Little Pee Dee R.

Saluda River

Fort Granby
(taken May 15, 1781)

S O U T H

Congaree R.

High Hills
of Santee

Marion's
Headquarters

Cape Fear

Fort Motte
*(taken May 12,
1781)*

C A R O L I N A

KETTLE CREEK
(Feb. 4, 1779)

Fort Watson
(taken Apr. 23, 1781)

Pee Dee River

Augusta
(taken June 5, 1781)

North Fork

Orangeburg
*(taken May 11,
1781)*

ATLANTIC

Georgetown

OCEAN

OEUTAW SPRINGS
(Sept. 8, 1781)

Santee River

Silver Bluff

South Fork

Little Salkehatchie

Monck's Corner

Edisto R.

Ashley R.

Cooper R.

Briar Creek

Savannah River

Salkehatchie R.

Coosawhatchie R.

Combahee R.

Charleston *(captured by British May 12, 1780;
evacuated Dec. 14, 1782)*

BATTLE OF
BRIAR CREEK
(March 3, 1779)

JAMES I.

LONG I.

SULLIVANS I.

JOHNS I.

Fort Moultrie
*(British repulsed
June 28, 1776; captured
by British May 6, 1780)*

EDISTO ISLAND

GEORGIA

Black Swamp

Beaufort

PORT ROYAL ISLAND

Ebenezer

Purysburg

Port Royal Sound

Savannah
*(captured by British Dec. 29, 1778
besieged by Allies Sept. 16 - Oct. 19, 1779;
evacuated July 11, 1782)*

TYBEE ISLAND

— — — Lincoln's route, 1779
• • • • • Prevost's route, 1779
◄—— Gates' route, 1780
———— Cornwallis' route, 1780
●—●—● Cornwallis' pursuit of Greene
      and subsequent retreat to
      Wilmington, 1781
—┼—┼— Cornwallis route to Virginia, 1781
—·—·— Retreat of Greene (including Morgan
      and Huger) and subsequent
      pursuit of Cornwallis, 1781
◄—◄— Tarleton's route to and from
      Cowpens, 1781
—┼—┼— Rawdons relief of Ninety-six, 1781

0   40
    Miles

wea-1-93

Chapter Six

Savannah: The Second Time

The next six months saw a series of dramatic military operations in the South, but no significant changes in the overall balance of power between the armies of Benjamin Lincoln and Augustine Prevost. On April 23, 1779, Lincoln, strengthened by the arrival of large numbers of militia who were summoned to active duty by Governor John Rutledge of South Carolina, crossed the Savannah River and marched toward Augusta to interpose himself between the British and their Indian allies on the frontier. To counteract this initiative, on April 29 Augustine Prevost ordered his 2,500-man army to move into South Carolina and threaten General Moultrie and his 1,000 troops who were stationed near Purysburg, a village just upriver and on the opposite shore from Savannah.

Prevost initially planned a limited raid into South Carolina, but when Moultrie refused to offer resistance and retreated steadily toward Charleston, Prevost decided to take advantage of the situation and go all the way to the South Carolina capital. On May 10, the redcoats reached Ashley Ferry on the Ashley River about seven miles northwest of Charleston, crossed to the opposite shore, and mauled a small force of patriot cavalry that Moultrie sent out the next day under Brigadier General Casimir Pulaski to try to delay the British advance toward the town's defenses. Governor Rutledge, knowing that Benjamin Lincoln was on a rapid march from Augusta to relieve Charleston, attempted to delay Prevost's withdrawal by proposing that if the redcoats spared the town, the state would remain neutral during the war. As expected, the redcoat commander wasted little time in rejecting this subterfuge.

On May 12, Prevost intercepted a message sent by Lincoln to Moultrie and learned that the main American army was indeed en route from Augusta. Weighted down with piles of booty that they had gathered since leaving Georgia, the British troops retreated to Ashley Ferry, camped for two weeks, and then, to avoid Lincoln's approaching army, veered southwest to Johns Island, where they stopped at Stono Ferry and fortified the eastern terminus of the ferry with three redoubts, which are enclosed defensive works, and an abatis, a defensive obstacle formed by felled trees with sharpened ends facing the enemy. On June 16, Prevost and the majority of the British force departed by boat, but about 900 redcoats, Loyalists, and hessians remained behind under the command of Lieutenant Colonel John Maitland to protect the British rear.

Benjamin Lincoln, commanding between 5,000 and 7,000 troops now in Charleston, decided to mount a assault against the Royal outpost at Stono Ferry. Unfortunately, the patriot general was able to muster only about 1,200 men for the strike, and many of these combatants were militia. The engagements at Savannah in December 1778 and at Briar Creek in March 1779 had demonstrated that troops of this sort could not match the resolve and discipline of professional soldiers. It is true that Moultrie had been successful in using militia to defend Beaufort, South Carolina against a British attack the previous February, but at Stono Ferry contingents of the North Carolina and Virginia militia were being asked to dislodge seasoned redcoats and hessians from prepared defensive positions.

Lincoln began the attack against the British fortifications at Stono Ferry about 7:00 A.M. on June 20th. His troops, arrayed in two lines approximately 700 yards long, moved through the sparse pine forest in the moist morning air, knowing that they would soon run up against the huffish Hessians and elements of the renowned Seventy-first Regiment. William R. Davie, a Whig officer who was seriously wounded in this brief but fierce engagement, described what happened: "The British reserved their fire till the Americans were within sixty yards when a General discharge of Musquetry and Artillery completely checked the assailants."[1] Cannon thundered, muskets cracked, and bayonets clattered as two companies of the Seventy-first Regiment and Lincoln's Continentals met in ferocious, hand-to-hand combat. Standing on level ground within easy killing range of one another, the two armies poured volley after volley of musket fire into one another's ranks, knocking men down like so many tenpins in a bowling alley. Finally, realizing that he could not oust the enemy, Lincoln broke off the attack about 8:30 A.M. and returned to Charleston.

Casualties were high on both sides at Stono Ferry. The British suffered 26 killed and 103 wounded. The patriots suffered 34 killed, 113 wounded, and 18 missing. His mission of shielding Prevost's retreat accomplished, Maitland marched southward on June 24 and, after an arduous journey through the coastal islands of South Carolina, joined Prevost at Beaufort on Port Royal Island on July 8. Soon thereafter, Prevost took most of his army back to Savannah, but left Maitland in Beaufort as a base from which to launch future invasions of South Carolina. Contrary to his expectations, however, Augustine Prevost soon found himself hard pressed even to maintain control over the territory he still had.

Summers in Savannah are hellish things. Moss droops from the branches of gnarled oaks and time seems suspended in a stuporous routine of suffering. The humidity rises up like some sort of Promethean monster and adheres to the skin like sticky glue. Swarms of sand flies, gnats and mosquitoes thrive in the oppressive heat, and thunderstorms pound the earth with torrential rain.

In this torpid environment Augustine Prevost could lull himself into the belief that all was well, but Governor James Wright, writing to Germain on July 31, 1779, was less confident and more realistic: "I shall look with the utmost Anxiety and Impatience for the Troops from New York," he proclaimed, "and hope they will be in our Neighborhood early in October, for till then, as the Troops that were here are so much Scattered about, I shall not Consider this Province as safe."[2] The significance of October for Wright was that by then the hurricane season would most likely be over, and a powerful French fleet under Vice Admiral d'Estaing in the Caribbean would be able to sail northward, if unchecked by the Royal Navy, and pose an ominous threat to Prevost's command. Clinton, who admitted that he "had not received any certain accounts of the French fleet's operations on the American coast," was almost a thousand miles away.[3] Prevost, if deprived of the ability to receive assistance by sea, would find himself in a most precarious position. He had barely 1,500 men in Savannah, some 900 troops under Lieutenant Colonel Maitland fifty miles north in Beaufort, and approximately 100 Loyalists under Colonel John Harris Cruger in Sunbury, about forty miles south.

Had Governor Wright known what was transpiring between the French and the patriots during that stultifying Georgia summer, he would have been even more concerned. Colonel Bretigny, a Frenchman stationed in Charleston, was endeavoring to persuade d'Estaing to come to the Carolina coast. "All here is in frightful confusion; very few regular troops, no help from the north, a feeble and badly disciplined militia and the greatest friction among the leaders," he asserted.[4] Governor Rutledge, Benjamin Lincoln, and William Moultrie were also greatly troubled about the course of the war in the South. What prospects for survival would the patriots have if the British, reinforced by Clinton and aided by throngs of Tories and Indians in the backcountry, took the offensive in the fall? The Whig leaders virtually begged d'Estaing to come to their rescue. The French vice admiral, who later would describe the campaign against Savannah as a "cruel task," explained that he was told that the "American cause was in great peril and that all hopes were based on my early arrival."[5]

D'Estaing probably should have spurned these entreaties to leave the relative safety of the Caribbean and to venture forth into the Atlantic in the height of the hurricane season, but the prospect of inflicting a decisive blow against the British in North America was irresistible to this proud Frenchman. On September 3, a squadron of three French ships arrived off Charleston with the heartening news that the vice admiral was approaching the Georgia coast with twenty-five sail of the line, twenty frigates and three corvettes and about 4,000 land troops.

The British were caught completely off guard by the arrival of this formidable armada. Nobody "could have thought or believed that a French fleet . . . would have come on the Coast of Georgia in the month of September," Governor Wright exclaimed.[6] Prevost had no hope of challenging the French on the high seas. Indeed, Clinton did not even learn about the coming of d'Estaing to Savannah until October 8, when the battle was at its height. The stark reality for the British was that Augustine Prevost was under siege and would have to depend solely upon his own resources.

On September 5, Benjamin Lincoln and d'Estaing's emissary in Charleston agreed upon a scheme to mount a joint attack against the outnumbered and isolated British garrison in Savannah. Fancy the excitement at patriot headquarters when word went out to the rebel militia and the two available Continental regiments that they should assemble and head for the Georgia capital. Ever since the previous December, when Archibald Campbell had come ashore, the Whigs had had no hope of overwhelming the redcoats or their hessian mercenaries in Georgia or South Carolina. Even at Stono Ferry, where Lincoln had enjoyed a substantial superiority in terms of the size of his army, the enemy had avoided defeat. But now the moment for retribution had arrived, or so the patriots thought. In a dispatch dated September 5, 1779 to Captain Roderick McIntosh in Augusta, Benjamin Lincoln declared:

> You will excuse my pressing the matter in such strong terms—
> I do not mean to call into question your zeal and dispatch, but
> to convey my own ideas how necessary I take the measure—
> Saturday next (the 11th) I have engaged that the Troops shall be
> collected near Ebenezer—the good of my Country and my own
> honor demand from me a fulfillment of the engagement.[7]

It must have been quite a sight. Stretched out along the pine-matted roads of South Carolina and Georgia, like multicolored beads on a seemingly endless string, marched 1,100 patriot militiamen and 1,000 Continentals, "every one cheerful, as if we were sure of success; and no one doubted but that we had nothing more to do, than to march up to Savannah; and demand a surrender."[8] They included such eminent figures as Francis Marion, later immortalized as the Swamp Fox, and Thomas Heyward, Jr., a signer of the Declaration of Independence. Perspiring profusely in the suffocating heat, the temperature rising to ninety-eight, ninety-nine, even a hundred degrees Fahrenheit, the ragtag troops, now and again drinking some liquor to maintain their enthusiasm, bore dramatic testimony to the individualism which permeated colonial society. Their uniforms came in all kinds of shapes and sizes. "Makes them appear more like wild savages than soldiers," commented one exasperated officer.[9] Cocked hats. Round hats. Beaver hats. Leather hats. Straw hats. Uncombed hair and unshaven faces. Buckskin pants. White cloth pants. Black coats trimmed in red. Blue coats edged in white. Deerskin jackets. Moccasins made from animal hides. Yes, a potpourri of men and material headed toward Savannah in September 1779.

Meanwhile, Augustine Prevost, realizing that he would be outgunned and outnumbered, labored frantically to shore up his defenses. "We will defend ourselves as long as we can," Prevost boasted in a message to St. Augustine.[10] He knew that his only chance for survival was to erect or strengthen redoubts, trenches, and abatis so the garrison could withstand a massive assault by the Franco-American army. Prevost also realized that he must succeed in bringing his outposts, especially Maitland's 900 troops at Beaufort, within his lines before the main attack occurred.

The first of these objectives was more directly under the British commander's control. Prevost ordered James Moncrief, a brilliant army engineer, to gather between 400 and 500 slaves and commence constructing a semicircular line of fortifications about 1,200 feet long on the level plain immediately south of the town. In a frenzy of activity, the rigorous task was addressed. "The General," wrote a British seaman, "ever attentive to increase the defences of the town, with Captain Moncrief, our principal engineer, was now, indefatigably, night and day, raising new works and batteries."[11] The barn and other agricultural buildings on Governor Wright's plantation, located just outside Savannah, were quickly dismantled, and the lumber used for platforms from which the defenders could fire upon their assailants. Houses were destroyed at the edge of town so that the attackers would have no cover and would have to cross an open space several hundred yards wide before they reached the British lines. But with only four redoubts and ten or twelve cannon in place when Moncrief began his efforts to buttress the town's defenses, Prevost anticipated that he would not have sufficient time to prepare the garrison for the massive strike he expected.

Lieutenant Colonel Maitland left Beaufort on September 12 and turned his troops southward toward Savannah. That very night d'Estaing began landing his troops at Beaulieu Plantation on the Vernon River about fourteen miles below the Georgia capital. By the morning of September 16, without waiting for the arrival of the main body of patriot soldiers, the vice admiral was approaching the outskirts of Savannah. D'Estaing was encouraged by the fact that the French had yet to encounter any opposition. Convinced that victory was inevitable and that resistance on the part of the redcoats was futile, he dispatched a courier to Prevost's headquarters with a call for the British commander to capitulate:

> Count d'Estaing summons his Excellency, General Prevost, to surrender to the arms of the King of France. He apprises him that he will be personally responsible for all the events and misfortunes that may arise from a defence, which, by the superiority of the force which attacks him, both by sea and land, is rendered manifestly vain and of no effect.[12]

Prevost stalled for time in hopes that Maitland would somehow escape capture by the French or the Americans and get to Savannah with his vital reinforcements. "I hope your Excellency will have a better opinion of me and of British troops," Prevost replied, "than to think either will surrender on general summons, without any specific terms."[13] Believing that there was no reason for haste, the vice admiral agreed on the evening of September 16 to a twenty-four hour truce so that the British could formulate the conditions under which the surrender would be consummated. "But this I know, that what has happened between us this night is a proof that matters will soon come to a decision between us one way or another," d'Estaing declared.[14]

A major reason why the vice admiral was so perfunctory in negotiating with Prevost was his belief that Lieutenant Colonel Maitland was safely bottled up in Beaufort. D'Estaing and his American compatriots had recognized from the very outset of the campaign that it was essential to prevent Maitland from reaching Savannah. "To prevent any sort of junction," the vice admiral proclaimed, "was the basis of the plan."[15]

Almost unbelievably, d'Estaing and Benjamin Lincoln were unclear as to who had ultimate responsibility for carrying out this critical mission. The Americans thought it was the French, and the French thought it was the Americans. The French placed ships outside the mouth of the Broad River, which separates Port Royal Island from Hilton Head Island, but Benjamin Lincoln, convinced that the French presence off shore was sufficient to obstruct Maitland, had nobody in the river itself to forestall the British from sailing behind Hilton Head Island and entering Callibogue Sound.

Crossing Callibogue Sound in small boats, Maitland and his men could see the masts of the French ships that were anchored at the mouth of the Savannah River. All seemed lost, until some black fishermen told Maitland about a narrow passage, called "Wall's Cut," that ran behind Daufuskie Island and emptied into the Savannah River upstream from where the French had placed their ships. Struggling through marsh muck up to their waists, keeping a sharp eye on the "alligators lying in the mud like old Logs," the redcoats, Tories, and hessians inched their way southward toward open water.[16]

Suddenly, on the morning of September 16, Maitland and his men reached the riverbank and realized that their objective was within sight. The first contingents of the Beaufort garrison arrived in Savannah about midday, just a few hours after d'Estaing had issued his call for surrender. "Our men . . . suffered from fatigue and want of rest," a Loyalist lady explained, "but in the height of our despondence Colonel Maitland effected a junction in a wonderful manner . . . thus giving new life and joy to the worn-out troops."[17] Colonel Cruger also succeeded in bringing his Loyalist troops into the Georgia capital.

Bolstered by the appearance of Lieutenant Colonel Maitland and his battle-tested soldiers, Augustine Prevost wasted no time in rejecting d'Estaing's demands that he surrender. The British commander must have taken special delight in sending the following dispatch to the Vice-Admiral on September 17:

> SIR:—In answer to the letter of your Excellency, which I had the honour to receive about twelve last night, I am to acquaint you that having laid the whole correspondence before the King's civil Governor, and the military officers of rank assembled in council of war, the unanimous determination has been, that though we cannot look upon our post as absolutely inexpungable, yet that it may and ought to be defended; therefore, the evening gun to be fired this evening at an hour before sundown, shall be the signal for recommencing hostilities. . . .[18]

Furthering strengthening Prevost's resolve to fight was the fact that

James Moncrief had by then succeeded in fashioning a formidable array of fortifications along the southern edge of Savannah. Consisting mainly of confiscated lumber and piles of sand, they included more than a hundred cannon, thirteen redoubts, and an abatis of cedar and pine across the entire front. Moreover, the British sank several ships in the channel below the town to prevent the French from sailing upriver, and Prevost had a boom placed across the river above Savannah to prevent fire ships from coming down on the current. These preparations meant that whereas the French could have taken the Georgia capital with relative ease if they had moved directly against the town after first coming ashore on September 12, they would now encounter considerable difficulty in breaking through. "Such was Moncrief's ardor, skill, and industry that he made the town able to stand a siege of six weeks," exulted a resident of Savannah.[19]

With the arrival of Benjamin Lincoln's American army on September 16, d'Estaing had about 5,500 troops outside Savannah, while Prevost had only some 2,360 men, about half of them Loyalists from the North, to defend the town. Even though he outnumbered the British more than two to one, the vice admiral scoffed at suggestions that he launch a direct assault upon Moncrief's entrenchments. He issued orders instead to begin hauling heavy artillery from his ships off shore, because he reckoned that Prevost would capitulate if the British garrison was subjected to a massive artillery bombardment.

For six days, October 3–8, the French and Americans relentlessly poured shells into the houses and streets of Savannah. Ironically, it was not the soldiers who suffered most from the fusillade. They could reach safety by crouching behind the fortifications at the edge of town. It was the civilians, especially the women and children, who were in greatest danger. "The Town was torn to pieces," wrote a redcoat officer, "nothing but Shrieks from Women and Children to be heard."[20] "The appearance of the town afforded a melancholy prospect, for there was hardly a house that had not been shot through," commented another British official.[21] One patriot soldier gave an especially gripping account of what a deserter told him was happening in Savannah:

> Poor women & children have already been put to death by our bombs & cannon; a deserter is this moment come out, who gives an account that many of them were killed in their Beds and amongst others, a poor woman with her infant in her arms was destroyed by a Cannon Ball; they all got into Cellars but even there they do not escape the fury of our Bombs, several having been mangled in that supposed place of security.[22]

The carnage unleashed against the civilian population by the French and American batteries had little effect upon the town's defenses. By fashioning fortifications from sand, Moncrief, much like the builders of Fort Sullivan at the entrance to Charleston harbor three years before, had produced defensive works "which were more easily repaired than damaged," as one frustrated Frenchman observed.[23] "I am fully of the opinion that a more determined mode of attack must be adopted before Savannah is ours," declared the portly Benjamin Lincoln.[24] Finally, on October 8, d'Estaing concluded that a massive frontal assault against the town's defenses offered the only hope for a quick victory. He certainly had no intention of attempting to capture Savannah with traditional siege techniques, which would have taken weeks to run their tedious course. The vice admiral was anxious to be done with this place. Supplies were running low, and the French sailors were suffering mightily from scurvy and dysentery aboard ship. Every day between thirty and thirty-five corpses were heaved overboard. There was always the possibility that a powerful storm would come upon the scene or, even worse, the British fleet.

Moments arise in human history when one would prefer to look away. The folly, the foolishness, and the arrogance of mankind can attain truly astounding proportions. Episodes of this sort would be almost laughable if they were not so tragic. Such an event occurred outside Savannah just after dawn on October 9, 1779, when Vice Admiral d'Estaing, largely to protect his own reputation, sent his army head-on against the British garrison. It was to be the bloodiest day in the history of the American Revolution in the South in terms of losses on one side.

Many of d'Estaing's subordinate officers attempted to dissuade the vice admiral from launching a frontal attack against Prevost's strongly fortified position. His chief of staff, Francois Fontanges, argued that the French and Americans lacked the strength needed to dislodge Prevost. D'Estaing refused to heed this or any other caution. "Extreme bravery can conquer everything," he insisted.[25] To reassure his compatriots, the vice admiral announced that he would personally lead his men in the assault. "Monsieur," he proclaimed, "I will march at the head and you will follow me."[26]

Clearly, it was pride alone that prompted d'Estaing to send his men and his American allies into battle. "The honor of the King's arms," he announced, required that he "not raise the siege ignominiously, without striking a vigorous blow."[27]

D'Estaing's battle plan was ill conceived and fundamentally flawed. Its success depended upon the French, who would carry the brunt of the attack, and the Americans catching the British completely unawares. The main assault, which was scheduled to commence at 4:00 A.M., was to be directed at the British right, more specifically against the Spring Hill redoubt on the road to Augusta. A vanguard of French volunteers was supposed to chop its way through the abatis under the cover of darkness and then, supported by a column of about 1,100 troops, storm the defenders and overwhelm the redoubt before the redcoats knew what was happening. A second column of French soldiers would attack the British lines to the west of the Spring Hill redoubt and penetrate to the Savannah River and then turn Prevost's flank, or so it was thought. Finally, in hopes of confusing the enemy, elements of the American militia would launch a sortie against the British left, while a contingent of Frenchmen would test Prevost's center.

D'Estaing either ignored or overlooked the fact that it was impossible to maintain secrecy outside Savannah. One could not distinguish between Whig and Tory militiamen. They dressed alike, and they spoke alike. Moreover, as was the case throughout the American Revolution, deserters moved back and forth between camps with relative ease. Consequently, Augustine Prevost knew hours beforehand that the assault was coming. He did, however, anticipate that it would be against his left, where the ground was "firm and clear."[28]

The vice admiral, whose camp was about a mile from Prevost's lines, had selected the right because he thought the Spring Hill redoubt was defended mostly by militia. Moreover, he calculated that a wide and shallow marsh would provide cover for his men up to about fifty yards from the British works. There were militia at the redoubt, including Thomas Brown, the ferocious Tory who had accompanied Archibald Campbell to Augusta and back, but Lieutenant Colonel Maitland and elements of the Seventy-first Regiment, the Scotsmen who had fought so bravely at Stono Ferry, were also in that area, as were Colonel John Harris Cruger and his Tories. The defenders on the British right were up early on October 9, many playing mournful tunes on their beloved bagpipes.

All hope of commencing the assault at 4:00 A.M. slipped away as the guides provided by Benjamin Lincoln got lost in a dense, pre-dawn fog. The marsh near the Spring Hill redoubt proved to be more helpful to the British than to the French and American allies. The morass confused the attackers and caused them to lose their way and fall behind schedule. Complicating matters even further, d'Estaing insisted that the order of march satisfy the brittle demands of French military etiquette, which stipulated that the placement of regiments in the line of troops moving into battle must correspond to the date of each regiment's establishment.

It was almost 5:30 A.M. before the French troops reached the edge of the woods some 200 yards in front of the Spring Hill redoubt, and even then only the vanguard was ready to attack. D'Estaing, realizing that dawn was just a few minutes away, ordered the first wave forward. The main body of French soldiers was still wandering about trying to get into position for the assault, but the vice admiral announced that the time for maneuvering was over, and the time for fighting had arrived. Decked out in their traditional white uniforms, the French vanguard crept into the open ground and dashed toward the British fortifications.

"The troops waited coolly at their several posts to receive the enemy," Prevost would later explain in his official report to Germain.[29] In the darkness, the British could hear axes hacking away at the abatis. About seventy North Carolina Loyalists who were expert marksmen were placed along the parapet of the redoubt to pick off the French officers as they came into view. Artillery was loaded with grapeshot to catch the attackers in a flanking fire of murderous shrapnel. The crew aboard a British ship anchored in nearby Yamacraw Creek filled canisters with chains, bolts, and scrap of all kind to fire at the American rebels.

Elements of the courageous French vanguard fought their way up the sides of the Spring Hill redoubt and briefly placed their regimental colors atop the berm. When the expected reinforcements did not arrive, however, the French began to fall back and were "mown down by the right battery which took them in flank," wrote a French officer.[30]

D'Estaing, who was urging the main body of troops forward, was shot in the arm and then in the calf of his right leg. Casimir Pulaski, the Polish cavalry officer who served under General Lincoln, was fatally wounded when grapeshot tore into his groin. All was havoc and mayhem in the trenches surrounding the redoubt. The assault became fragmented. French and American troops arrived on the scene only to be destroyed piecemeal by the British and Tory gunners. "By this time the 2d American column . . . arrived at the foot of the Spring Hill Redoubt, and such a scene of confusion as there appeared is not often equalled," declared South Carolinian Thomas Pinckney.[31]

The trenches around the fortress began to fill with dead and dying soldiers. The fighting was ferocious. At a critical moment in the battle, Lieutenant Colonel Maitland ordered a bayonet charge that threw the French and Americans into even greater confusion. Meanwhile, the sorties against the British left and center, never intended to be major assaults, were easily repulsed.

After about an hour of unspeakable suffering, the vice admiral ordered a retreat. "The Almighty and Gracious God did . . . assist us, and we conquered," proclaimed a jubilant Tory.[32] Governor Wright was more worldly in assigning credit for the British victory over the French and their American allies. "Give me leave to mention the great ability of Captain Moncrief, the Chief Engineer who was Indefatigable day & Night and whose Eminent Services contributed vastly to our defence and safety," he told Germain.[33]

Maitland and his men surveyed a ghastly scene when they inspected the ground in front of the Spring Hill redoubt after the battle. Bodies were seemingly everywhere. In places the earth was completely covered with corpses. Augustine Prevost penned a compelling description of this unforgettable spectacle:

> Our loss on this occasion was one captain and fifteen rank and file killed, one captain, three subalterns, and thirty-five rank and file wounded. That of the enemy we do not exaggerate when we set it down from 1000 to 1200 killed and wounded. We buried within and near the abatis 203 on the right, on the left 28, and delivered 116 wounded prisinors, the great part mortally. They themselves, by permission, buried those who lay more distant. Many no doubt were self-buried in the mud of the swamp, and many carried off.[34]

The actual casualty figures were forty British killed, sixty-three wounded, and fifty-two missing. The French and Americans suffered 16 officers and 228 men killed, and 63 officers and 521 men wounded—approximately a fifth of the entire Allied army.

Not surprisingly, d'Estaing was anxious to get out of Georgia. The French troops left their trenches on October 17, returned to their ships, and sailed away. Benjamin Lincoln crossed the Savannah River at Zulby's Ferry and marched his American army back to Charleston. The effort to liberate Georgia had failed. The Royal invasion of South Carolina was about to begin.

Understandably, the British savored their courageous defense of Savannah. "I think that this is the greatest event that has happened the whole war," Henry Clinton proclaimed.[35] "The Siege has rendered famous a sickly hole," wrote Anthony Stokes, the Royal Chief Justice of Georgia.[36] There is no denying the significance of what Augustine Prevost had achieved or, more accurately, what he had prevented. Ceremonial cannon in London were fired to underscore the importance of Prevost's victory. Unquestionably, the loss of Savannah would have been a devastating setback for Germain's Southern strategy. Indeed, it is not improbable that the defeat of Prevost would have intensified opposition in Parliament to the war to such a degree that the king would have been compelled to abandon his quest to subdue the rebellious colonies. Governor Wright minced no words on this point. "The Southern parts of No. America I conceive are now in Your Lordships Power," he told Germain, "whereas had the French got Footing here, I fear they wou'd have been Lost."[37]

The flush of victory, however, could not obscure the fact that Lord North and George Germain could ultimately draw little satisfaction from the events that had transpired in Georgia since Archibald Campbell had come ashore in December 1778. The two premises which were axiomatic to the entire Southern strategy—first, that the Royal Navy would always be able to control the sea, and second, that the Tories in the South would rise up in great numbers if their safety was assured by the presence of British troops—had been called into serious question. Campbell had penetrated more than 100 miles to Augusta only to find himself surrounded and forced to move back toward the coast. Prevost had been cut off by the French navy from his only source of relief, and the failure of d'Estaing to take Savannah was due more to mismanagement on his and Benjamin Lincoln's part than on the valor of the British defenders. John Pancake writes:

> What Clinton obviously failed to appreciate in his euphoria over the successful defense of Savannah was that d'Estaing had landed an overwhelming force on the Georgia coast without the slightest interference by the British navy. Only incredible mismanagement of the allied force and d'Estaing's impatience to return to the West Indies had allowed Prevost's stout defense to save the province. It was a lesson Sir Henry could ill afford to ignore.[38]

Chapter Seven

Charleston: The Second Time

On December 26, 1779, Sir Henry Clinton, convinced that d'Estaing's fleet no longer threatened the North American coast, left New York City aboard a British armada of ninety transports commanded by Admiral Marriot Arbuthnot. The ultimate destination of this formidable invasion force, the largest ever to come south, was Charleston, South Carolina. It consisted of five British infantry regiments, two hessian regiments, five corps of Tories (including Lieutenant Colonel Banastre Tarleton's British Legion and Major Patrick Ferguson's Rangers), plus artillery and cavalry units and 5,000 sailors. After a perilous voyage, during which storms off Cape Hatteras scattered the fleet in all directions, Clinton and his 8,500 men began to gather off Tybee Island on January 30, 1780. "The passage might have been expected to be performed in ten days; but such was the severity of the season that the fleet was very soon separated and driven out of its course by tempestuous weather," recalled Charles Stedman, an officer who came south with the British.[1]

One might assume that Clinton was optimistic when he appeared off the Georgia coast and began making final preparations for the invasion of South Carolina. Governor Wright was in firm control in Savannah and its environs. Although Benjamin Lincoln eventually amassed some 5,500 defenders in the South Carolina capital, about 2,500 of these were militiamen of questionable quality. The French fleet was nowhere to be seen, and Commodore Abraham Whipple, the Whig naval commander at Charleston, had a flotilla of only seven warships, most purchased from France, with which to oppose Arbuthnot's powerful fleet. As for George Washington and the main American army, it was encamped in Morristown, New Jersey, and had no prospect of helping the patriots in the Carolinas and Georgia. Washington could do little more than keep a wary eye on the 15,000-man garrison that Clinton had left in New York City.

Not surprisingly, George Germain, the embattled Secretary of State for the American Department, continued to believe that Tory throngs in

Georgia and the Carolinas were eagerly awaiting the arrival of the British army to protect them so they could feel safe in rallying to the Royal banner. What choice did he have but to hold fast to the assumption that undergirded his entire Southern strategy? "The feeble resistance Major General Prevost met with in his march and retreat through so great a part of South Carolina is an indubitable proof of the indisposition of the inhabitants to support the rebel government," Germain naively proclaimed.[2] "His Lordship," Clinton later affirmed, "seemed also to have cherished very sanguine ideas of the great number of loyalists I should be enabled to embody in the provincial corps."[3]

Despite these reasons for anticipating success, Henry Clinton was not a happy warrior. On August 20, 1779, the British commander in chief told Germain that his own enthusiasm was "worn out by struggling against the consequences of many adverse incidents which . . . have effectually oppressed me." In the same letter, Clinton observed that Lord Charles Cornwallis, an officer of "indefatigable zeal," had just returned to North America, and requested that he "be relieved from a station which nobody acquainted with its condition will suppose to have set light upon me."[4] Clinton urged that Cornwallis, who would be second in command on the Charleston expedition, be elevated to replace him as British commander in chief in North America. Clinton raised this issue again on October 29 when he informed Germain that he was keeping Cornwallis fully informed regarding future military operations in anticipation of "His Majesty's most gracious acquiescence in my prayer to be recalled."[5] Clearly, Henry Clinton had had enough. He wanted to go home.

Germain had responded to Clinton's letter on November 4, although the dispatch did not reach Clinton until March 19, 1780, after the British army had landed in South Carolina and was approaching the Ashley River a few miles northwest of Charleston. Germain had answered,

> I did not omit the earliest opportunity of laying before His Majesty your letter of 20th of August, in which you express your desire of being permitted to return to England and resign the command of the troops to Lord Cornwallis. Though the King has great confidence in His Lordship's abilities, yet His Majesty is too well satisfied with your conduct to wish to see the command of his forces in any other hands.[6]

Henry Clinton, a British aristocrat whose father had served as Royal Governor of New York from 1743 until 1753, was a complex and troublesome human being. A sound strategist and splendid military planner, Clinton nonetheless had faults of personality, especially a marked incapacity to get along with his associates, including Arbuthnot and Cornwallis, that contributed to the eventual outcome of British military operations in the South. "These two breakdowns in human relations, quite as much as the activity of French sea power and the inactivity of the loyalists, were factors in determining the course of Clinton's subsequent command," asserts William B. Willcox, Clinton's biographer.[7] Perhaps Willcox overstates the significance of the personal disputes between Clinton and his associates, but there is no doubt that intense antagonisms existed.

The redcoat commander in chief was an inordinately suspicious human being. "His defects, of which his previous career had given faint hint, were psychological rather than intellectual," Willcox states.[8] Clinton, particularly when he came under severe stress, succeeded in finding signs of treachery everywhere. Almost anything—the twitch of a face, the flare of a nostril, even the slightest change in speech inflection—could provoke his expansive paranoia. "He was haughty, morose, churlish, stupid, and scarcely ever to be spoken with," said Thomas Jones, a leading Loyalist.[9]

One can imagine how Clinton reacted when Cornwallis, upon learning in March that Clinton would unexpectedly remain in command, announced that he no longer wanted to be consulted about future military planning. Clinton knew why Cornwallis did not want to be involved thereafter in devising military strategy. This stance would allow his principal subordinate to escape blame if plans went awry. In the British army of the eighteenth century, where "sound ancestry and connections helped more to secure advancement . . . than sound ideas of strategy," there was no chain of command in the modern sense.[10] Officers like Clinton and Cornwallis were more interested in promoting their own careers than in advancing the overall interests of the Royal military. Subordinates were "ready to criticize their superiors, and quick to flare up at any rebuke from them."[11]

Knowing that Cornwallis was eager to assume command, Clinton, always prone to discover duplicity and disloyalty among his associates, became increasingly estranged from him, especially when Cornwallis befriended Admiral Arbuthnot, whom Clinton despised. The upshot of this situation was that Clinton quit communicating with Cornwallis except by formal memoranda. He "finally came to dislike Cornwallis intensely," writes John Pancake.[12] This was hardly an optimum circumstance within which to commence a complex campaign, particularly when Clinton knew that the possibility of a French naval attack upon New York City would compel him and Arbuthnot to head north and leave Cornwallis in charge in the South once Charleston was taken.

There was a sort of mechanistic inevitability to the process by which Clinton and Arbuthnot captured Charleston. One scholar calls it a "superb example of a beautifully coordinated eighteenth-century joint operation."[13] After repairing sails and rigging, Arbuthnot transported Clinton and 5,000 soldiers to the North Edisto Inlet about thirty miles south of Charleston and began putting them ashore on February 11, 1780. It was a prodigious accomplishment for the British to bring so much military power to bear upon the South Carolina capital. It took two to four months to cross the 3,000 miles of ocean that separated Great Britain from the American colonies, and most of the food and forage for the Royal troops had to come by ship across the Atlantic. But Charleston was worth the effort because of its enormous strategic importance. Privateers sailed from its docks to harass British transports. Ships arrived at its docks from France and Holland, bringing supplies for the Continental army. Moreover, by capturing Charleston, the Royal military would have a base of supply suitable for supporting a major incursion into to the Carolina hinterland, where Germain still hoped to find a multitude of Tories.

Determined to avoid the mistakes which had thwarted his attack upon Fort Sullivan, now renamed Fort Moultrie, Clinton proceeded cautiously. He met no opposition on the beaches, because Major General Benjamin Lincoln and Governor John Rutledge were concentrating their energies upon toughening the patriot defensive works just north of Charleston on the peninsula down which Clinton would have to come to take the city from the landward side. Using the virtual dictatorial powers which he had obtained from the South Carolina legislature, Rutledge assembled 600 slaves to build redoubts, abatis, and dig trenches. Captain Johann Hinrichs, a hessian, said that the American works "like mushrooms . . . sprang from the soil."[14]

Clinton spent weeks making sure that all contingencies were covered before he crossed the Ashley River and undertook classical siege operations against Lincoln's fortifications. Impressed by the defenses which had appeared outside the town, he summoned 1,500 reinforcements from Savannah and another 2,500 troops from New York City, which would bring his total strength to about 10,000 men by mid-April. By March 29, Clinton, still encountering no resistance from Lincoln's army but nonetheless taking care to establish strong points on his line of communications with the North Edisto River, had reached Stono Ferry, had moved from John's Island to James Island, had occupied Fort Johnson on the southern side of the entrance to Charleston Harbor, had crossed Wappoo Cut, a narrow stream that separates James Island from the mainland, and had arrived at Drayton Hall some seven miles northwest of Charleston on the Ashley. Meanwhile, Arbuthnot, having left the British transports at the North Edisto Inlet, had moved with eight British frigates carrying 216 guns north to Five Fathom Hole and had blockaded Charleston Harbor.

The position of Benjamin Lincoln and his 4,000 comrades was becoming untenable. Instead of evacuating the town, however, the patriots foolishly persisted in sending troops into Charleston. Seven hundred North Carolina Continentals, 750 Virginians, and some 700 North Carolina militia came down the eastern bank of the Cooper River, which was Lincoln's only route of supply and reinforcement after Clinton crossed the Ashley on March 29 in a drizzling rain and Arbuthnot sailed past Fort Moultrie and anchored in Charleston Harbor on April 8. "This afternoon . . . the British fleet passed Fort Moultrie . . . and anchored . . . just out of reach of the guns from the town, where they now continue," wrote a Whig observer.[15] This was nothing like the frightful defeat of the British navy in June 1776, when the guns of the palmetto log citadel had repulsed Peter Parker. Admiral Arbuthnot sailed past the patriot batteries with "scorn and disdain," commented Captain Hinrichs.[16] Whipple, the patriot naval commander, did not possess sufficient strength to stop the British frigates, so he sank most of the patriot ships at the mouth of the Cooper River and used them to support a log and chain boom from one bank to the other. At least Arbuthnot could not proceed east of Charleston and shell the town from the river.

On April 10, Clinton summoned Lincoln to surrender. The American commander refused, but he did persuade Governor Rutledge to leave Charleston to assure that civil government would continue if the city fell. The British had been digging zigzag approach trenches and parallels ever since March 31, so that artillery batteries could be brought close enough to breach or knock holes in the patriot ramparts. This technique of siege warfare was slow but unstoppable unless the defender's artillery could silence the attacker's—a feat which was beyond the capacity of the American rebels to accomplish. Benjamin Lincoln should have evacuated Charleston while he and his irreplaceable army could still get out. When the rumor arose that boats were being collected to ferry the Continentals across the Cooper River, however, civil officials said that if the attempt were made they would assist the British in destroying Lincoln's army. Obviously, these were testy times in the South Carolina capital.

The fate of the Charleston garrison was sealed on April 14, 1780, when Lieutenant Colonel James Webster began to move against a force commanded by General Isaac Huger which was stationed at Monck's Corner, thirty-two miles from Charleston, to guard Lincoln's last escape route. Leading a pre-dawn attack against the unsuspecting patriots at nearby Biggin's Bridge was the combative Banastre Tarleton and his Tory Legion of New Yorkers in distinctive green jackets. This mobile force consisted of mounted infantry and cavalry. "The order was executed with the greatest . . . success. The Americans were completely surprised," boasted Tarleton, a 25-year-old native of Liverpool, England who had purchased his commission in the British army.[17]

By April 19, Clinton's zigzag approach trenches were within 250 yards of the patriot fortifications outside Charleston. Recognizing that his situation was hopeless, Lincoln proposed the next day that he surrender on the condition that his army be allowed to march to a destination he selected and that it keep its arms. As expected, Clinton rejected these terms and bombarded the town that night "with greater virulence and fury than ever."[18] William Moultrie observed that among the American defenders "fatigue . . . was so great that, for want of sleep, many faces were so swelled they could scarcely see out of their eyes."[19] "Our men are in good spirits," another Whig soldier had commented the day before, "although it seems to be the general opinion that we must succumb at last."[20]

At 8:00 P.M. on May 9, at the end of a brief truce during which Lincoln had been unsuccessful in persuading Arbuthnot and Clinton to let the militia go home and allow the Continentals to come out of Charleston with flags unfurled and march to drums beating a British tune, a massive artillery duel between the two armies began. "The alterations you propose are all utterly inadmissable; hostilities will in consequence commence afresh at eight o'clock," Clinton and Arbuthnot had proclaimed.[21] Moultrie described what then transpired:

> After receiving the above letter, we remained near an hour silent, all calm and ready, each waiting for the other to begin. At length we fired the first gun and immediately followed a tremendous cannonade, and the mortars from both sides threw out an immense number of shells. It was a glorious sight to see them like meteors crossing each other and bursting in the air; it appeared as if the stars were tumbling down. The fire was incessant almost the whole night; cannon-balls whizzing and shells hissing continually amongst us; ammunition chests and temporary magazines blowing up; great guns bursting, and wounded men groaning along the lines. It was a dreadful night! It was our last great effort, but it availed us nothing.[22]

Finally, even the town leaders of Charleston were ready to submit. "It was a night of horror that broke the spirit of the townsmen, who until now had resisted submission, and they petitioned for a surrender," writes historian Christopher Ward.[23]

At 11:00 A.M. on May 12, 1780, Lincoln, having accepted British terms, brought his troops out with colors furled. One redcoat officer took special delight in the scene that unfolded before his exuberant eyes. "They laid down their arms between their abatis and surrendered prisoners of war," he exclaimed.[24]

The fall of Charleston was a staggering defeat for the patriots. One onlooker said that he saw "tears coursing down the cheeks of General Moultrie."[25] Such an emotional reaction was not inappropriate. Clinton, whose total losses were 76 killed and 189 wounded, had captured 5,466 armed men, 391 artillery pieces, 5,916 muskets, 33,000 rounds of small-arms ammunition, over 8,000 round shot, and 376 barrels of powder. "By this very important acquisition there fell into our hands seven generals and a multitude of other officers, belonging to ten Continental regiments and three battalions of artillery, which, with the militia and sailors doing duty in the siege, amounted to about six thousand men in arms," Clinton declared in his account of the Charleston campaign.[26] Quite simply, there was no effective fighting force left in South Carolina to prevent the redcoats from overrunning the entire state.

Chapter Eight

Bloodshed In the Backcountry

The enormity of the Charleston debacle notwithstanding, the crucial test of whether George Germain and his colleagues would finally be able to elicit widespread popular support and shift the major combat responsibilities to the Loyalists was yet to come. It would occur, as was the case in Georgia, in the hills of the hinterland, not on the flat ground along the coast. This would be to the patriots' advantage, for in the flatlands the British knew how to fight, and could make full use of their superior naval power. Officers like Archibald Campbell and Augustine Prevost had already experienced the vicissitudes associated with fighting in the backcountry of the South. The British were about to encounter similar difficulties in the hinterland of the two Carolinas. The authors of the United States Army's bicentennial history of the American Revolutionary War assert:

> As long as they controlled the sea, the British could land and establish bases at nearly any point on the long American coast line. The many navigable rivers dotting the coast also provided water avenues of invasion well into the interior. But to crush the revolt the British Army had to cut loose from coastal bases and rivers. When it did so its logistical problems multiplied and its lines of communications became vulnerable to constant harassment. British armies almost inevitably came to grief every time they moved very far from the areas where they could be nurtured by supply ships from the homeland.[1]

Before returning to New York City, Henry Clinton sent detachments of redcoats and Tories into the South Carolina backcountry to establish a series of strongholds. They stretched from Georgetown on the coast, up the Pee Dee River to Cheraw, then to Camden, Hanging Rock, and Rocky Mount on the Catawba-Wateree, on to Ninety Six near the Saluda, and finally to Augusta, Georgia on the Savannah River. In Clinton's mind, these fortified positions would serve two purposes: first, they would be havens for the Loyalists; second, and even more importantly, they would serve as bases from which the Royal military, including its Tory allies, could conduct punitive operations against those who continued to defy the king and torment their Loyalist neighbors.

Leaving about two-thirds of his land forces behind, Clinton turned over command in the South to the 43-year-old Charles Cornwallis and sailed north on June 8. As he departed, he was confident that the tide of events was turning the king's way. "The conquest of Charleston, and the consequent submission of South Carolina," Clinton later wrote, "had given such a shock to the measures of the disaffected colonists that Great Britain was well warranted in the flattering expectations she soon entertained of soon seeing the war brought to a favorable issue."[2]

Events were to demonstrate that Clinton's expectations of a quick victory were illusory. A combination of factors worked against the British being able to win the hearts and minds of the people, not the least of which was the inability or unwillingness of Royal officers to maintain proper discipline among their troops. "The great mischief Complain'd of in the prosecution of the war is that relaxation of discipline which disgraces the army and has alienated the Affections of the inhabitants from the Royal Cause," lamented George Germain.[3] "More important was the increasing evidence that the military authorities could not guarantee the protection of lives and property that Clinton had promised," says Pancake.[4]

It is true that the redcoats and their allies, including hessians and Loyalists, sometimes perpetrated undue violence upon their military adversaries and, even more alarmingly, upon the civilian population. Lieutenant Anthony Allaire, a Tory who marched from Savannah to Charleston with Major Patrick Ferguson's corps, told how the troops punished the patriots by "destroying furniture, breaking windows, etc., taking all their horned cattle, horses, mules, sheep, fowls, etc., and their Negroes to drive them."[5] A South Carolina woman described how in June 1780 a band of redcoats rode up to her front door, "bellowing out the most horrid curses imaginable." She continued:

> It was terrible to the last degree; and, what augmented it, they had several armed Negroes with them, who threatened and abused us greatly. They then began to plunder the house of every thing they thought valuable or worth taking; our trunks were split to pieces, and each man, pitiful wretch, crammed his bosom with the contents, which were our apparel, etc., etc., etc.[6]

Admittedly, in many instances the British were simply giving tit for tat. Nevertheless, especially when they were seeking to implement Germain's strategy of convincing former enemies to abandon the patriots and join the Tories instead, the redcoats worked against their own purposes and played into the Whigs' hands when they stole property or were responsible for creating wanton destruction. There were many reasons for this excessive violence and thievery. Many soldiers simply could not resist the temptation of taking what they saw. Frequently they would sell stolen goods to obtain fuel for cooking and heating or liquor. According to one British officer, "Drunkeness & means of Purchasing Liquor . . . are the Cause of most of the Disorders, of which Soldiers are Guilty."[7] "Most pertinently," writes one scholar, "we know that Americans were held to be different because they were rebels . . . and needed to be beaten back to their proper allegiance."[8]

The most infamous practitioner of rampageous behavior in the Royal army during the southern campaign was Banastre Tarleton. The smallish son of a Liverpool slave trader, the lieutenant colonel was a gambler and unrepentant womanizer. He first exhibited at Biggin's Bridge the qualities that were to earn him the shibboleth Bloody Tarleton. Even Pennsylvania Loyalist Charles Stedman was disturbed by the excessive violence that he witnessed during and after this engagement. A Whig major, he reported, "was mangled in the most shocking way. This unfortunate officer lived several hours . . . even in his last moments cursing the British for their barbarity in having refused quarter after he had surrendered."[9] Stedman was also flabbergasted to learn that troops who had "barborously treated" a refined Charleston lady were apprehended but not imprisoned.[10]

It was the battle known hereafter among patriots as "Buford's Massacre" that irrevocably gave Tarleton the reputation, probably undeserved, of being a vicious and cruel butcher. On May 29, 1780, the heat of summer had returned to the Carolinas. Trudging toward the North Carolina border through the pine and hardwood forests of the Waxhaws region of north central South Carolina, their canteens clanking and their wagon wheels squeaking, were 350 to 400 Virginia Continentals, mostly infantry. Commanded by Colonel Abraham Buford, these weary troops, consisting of veterans and raw recruits, had been sent southward to reinforce Benjamin Lincoln but had turned back about thirty miles from Charleston when they had learned that the city had capitulated to the redcoats.

Pathetically, this small force was the largest body of Continentals left in the South. Buford and his men, who were headed for Salisbury, North Carolina, where they were supposed to become the core around which the shattered patriot army would be rebuilt, reckoned that the British were nowhere near; therefore, they were marching along at a leisurely pace under a roasting afternoon sun. Suddenly, shortly before 3:00 P.M., the sound of bugles signaled that danger was unexpectedly at hand. Dispatched inland by Cornwallis to find Buford's men and to destroy them, the British Legion, forcing their horses to gallop ever faster until the poor beasts almost dropped, had covered 150 miles in 54 hours—a truly astounding accomplishment.

Banastre Tarleton and about 270 men, mainly green-jacketed Tories, had been in hot pursuit of the Virginia Continentals since May 27. After resting briefly in Camden, Tarleton had ordered his troops into their saddles at 2:00 A.M. on May 29 and had sent them into the Waxhaws hard on Buford's heels. In the middle of the afternoon the Virginia Continentals finally came into view. This was Tarleton at his best—plunging headlong on horseback toward an isolated enemy, casting all restraint aside, focusing totally on the single objective of fulfilling his mission. When Buford rejected a summons to surrender and continued to move toward the North Carolina border, Tarleton "determined as soon as possible to attack, there being no other expedient to stop their progress and prevent their being reinforced the next day."[11] "I reject your proposals, and shall defend myself to the last extremity," the rebel commander announced.[12]

What followed has been the subject of unending controversy, although there is no question about the outcome of the battle. Tarleton achieved a decisive and overwhelming victory in the Waxhaws on May 29, 1780. He suffered five killed and fourteen wounded. The Whig losses, 113 killed and 150 wounded, many fatally, were appalling. Buford made the crucial mistake at the outset of the engagement of ordering his men to withhold their fire until the Loyalists were only ten yards away. Delivered too late, the patriots' volley did not retard the advance of the Tory horsemen, who rode among Buford's men, screaming and yelling, "hacking with sabers and thrusting with bayonets."[13]

According to patriot accounts, Tarleton kept up the slaughter even after the Whigs had raised the white flag and had asked for quarter. "The demand for quarter, seldom refused to a vanquished foe, was at once found to be in vain," proclaimed Dr. Robert Brownfield, a surgeon who rode with Buford.[14] There were reports that members of the British Legion tossed aside the dead, so they could stab and bludgeon the wounded lying underneath. Tarleton admitted that his troops displayed a "vindictive asperity not easily restrained" but insisted that such excesses had occurred because the Tories mistakenly believed that "they had lost their commanding officer."[15]

It was a grotesque scene. The familiar stench of death was everywhere.

After the battle, women from the Waxhaw Presbyterian Church came to help carry off the wounded in overburdened wagons. Trenches were dug in the red clay earth of the Carolina piedmont to receive piles of mutilated corpses. Eighty-four bodies were buried in one mass grave, and twenty-five in another about 300 yards away. Anybody who wants to retain romantic images of the American Revolution in the South must ignore the accounts given by eyewitnesses of this brief but ferocious battle. Dr. Brownfield gave an especially graphic description of what happened to one unfortunate patriot officer in this sordid engagement:

> Early in the sanguinary conflict he was attacked by a dragoon, who aimed many deadly blows at his head, all of which by the dextrous use of the small sword he easily parried; when another on the right, by one stroke, cut off his right hand through the metacarpal bones. He was then assailed by both, and instinctively attempted to defend his head with his left arm until the forefinger was cut off, and the arm hacked in eight or ten places from the wrist to the shoulder. His head was then laid open almost the whole length of the crown to the eye brows.[16]

No less compelling is the portrayal of the misfortunes suffered by a member of Buford's rear guard:

> In a short time Tarleton's bugle was heard, and a furious attack was made on the rear guard, commanded by Lieut. Pearson. Not a man escaped. Poor Pearson was inhumanely mangled on the face as he lay on his back. His nose and lip were bisected obliquely; several of his teeth were broken out in the upper jaw, and the under completely divided on each side. These wounds were inflicted after he had fallen, with several others on his head, shoulders and arms."[17]

Tarleton's virtual annihilation of Colonel Abraham Buford and his Virginia Continentals "quickly became a symbol of British atrocities against Americans," writes J. Tracy Power in the *South Carolina Historical Magazine*.[18] Hereafter, says historian Don Higginbotham, "'Bloody Tarleton' and 'Tarleton's Quarter' were household epithets in the South."[19] Rational judgment suggests that the commander of the British Legion was most likely innocent of intentionally ignoring Buford's white flag or practicing bloodthirsty tactics. If he were completely insensitive to the accepted conventions of warfare, why, for example, did Tarleton let the wounded patriots go and allow them to be hauled away by the Presbyterian ladies? "Reports that

Tarleton's men bayoneted the wounded are hardly consistent with the fact that the British paroled the wounded" contends John Pancake.[20] Also, aggressive tactics were always appropriate for a cavalry unit operating well in advance of the main British army. But this was a time when emotion, not rationality, swayed public opinion. In a political and social environment characterized by violence and disunity, reports of "Buford's Massacre" exacerbated what was already a volatile situation in the Carolina backcountry. According to Power, "Though the British hoped Buford's defeat would mean the end of effective resistance in the South, the massacre's effect on the population was precisely the opposite. It helped create a climate of revenge and resolve which transformed the war in the Carolinas into a crusade."[21]

Another major obstacle for the British in attempting to win over the Whigs for the king arose when Henry Clinton issued a proclamation on June 3, 1780 which stipulated that anyone who did not actively support the Royal government belonged to the enemy and was outside the protection of British law. This measure angered many patriots, because it replaced a more generous set of terms that Clinton had advanced immediately after Charleston had surrendered. The great majority of Whigs, who had heretofore been permitted to remain neutral and to return to their own farms, where they preferred to remain anyway, now had to take an oath of allegiance to the king or assume the enormous burden of becoming outlaws. The British commander in chief incorrectly assumed that this more restrictive arrangement was a "prudent measure" because under the earlier conditions a "great number of inveterate rebels might remain in the country, and by their underhanded and secret counsel and other mechinations prevent the return of many well disposed persons to their allegiance."[22]

Clinton's biographer calls this change of plan, which was designed to "divide the sheep from the goats," a "bad lapse of judgment."[23] "Compelled to choose between rebellion and collaboration," Higginbotham asserts, "some shouldered arms for the patriots, others subscribed to the oath under duress and consequently felt no obligation to honor it."[24]

The nature of the war in the hinterland of the two Carolinas began to assume the character of a bloodbath in the Summer of 1780, when the cruelty and savagery practiced both by Whigs and Tories reached unprecedented levels. Old grudges gave rise to a virtual orgy of tumult and ruin. Perhaps it was the impact of Tarleton's victory in the Waxhaws, or perhaps it was the techniques local residents had learned in the Indian Wars, but the people lashed out at one another with a viciousness and severity that is difficult to imagine. Part of the answer has to do with the British having the support of "various groups already alienated from the backcountry's leadership," primarily Indians, slaves, and bandits.[25] Consequently, when the British began to send troops inland in relatively large numbers, disgruntled minorities seized the opportunity to intensify the disruptive behavior they were already practicing.

A more or less typical example of this phenomenon is the career of Plundering Sam Brown. Brown, a disreputable character who, among other things, killed his father-in-law's stock when Mrs. Brown left him, lived with a mistress and his sister, Charity, in a large cave in a cliff on the western bank of the Catawba River in what is now Catawba County, North Carolina. The cave had to be big to hold all the booty that Brown had been grabbing and stealing for years from folks who lived in the piedmont of the two Carolinas. Not surprisingly, when British troops began moving into the piedmont after Charleston had fallen, Brown sided with the British, because they were fighting the same people who were attempting to arrest him. "The advent of Colonel Ferguson to the up-country of South Carolina proved a perfect God-send to such hardened wretches as Brown," writes Lyman C. Draper in *King's Mountain And Its Heroes*.[26] Brown was shot dead by some Whigs who ambushed him outside a house near the Tyger River in South Carolina where he had stopped to drink some liquor. Such was the justice of the Southern backcountry.

Also illustrative of the ruthlessness of affairs during the Summer of 1780 was a brief but bloody encounter at Hanging Rock, South Carolina on August 1. The leader of the Whigs was William R. Davie, who by now had recovered from the wounds he had received at Stono Ferry. Davie succeeded in surrounding a detachment of Tory infantrymen who offered no resistance because they thought the Whigs were Loyalists. (Incidents of wrongly identifying the enemy were relatively common in the backcountry.) The Tories were easily overwhelmed and trapped against a fence where they had no chance of escape. Davie, who gave no quarter and took no prisoners, described what happened:

> The astonished Loyalists fled ... and were charged by the dragoons in full gallop and driven back in great confusion; on meeting again the fire of the infantry they all rushed impetuously against the angle of the fence where in a moment they were surrounded by the dragoons who had entered the field and literally

cut to pieces: as this was done under the eye of the whole British camp no prisoners could be safely taken which may apologize for the slaughter that took place on this occasion.[27]

The first large scale battle in the Carolina backcountry during the Summer of 1780 occurred at Ramsour's Mill in south central North Carolina a few miles west of the Catawba River on June 20. It too became a blood-stained affair. John Moore, a Loyalist who had served with the British during the Charleston campaign, returned from South Carolina and summoned large numbers of Tories to join him at his encampment at Ramsour's Mill. By mid-June, some 1,300 men, about three-fourths of whom were armed, had arrived. Griffith Rutherford, the Indian fighter who commanded the patriot militia in this section of North Carolina, decided to attack Moore. But the first Whig troops to reach Moore's camp were 400 militiamen commanded by Colonel Francis Locke of Rowan County, North Carolina. Although outnumbered, Locke decided to attack.

This was an encounter between backwoods farmers, not professional soldiers. Consequently, the fighting lacked discipline and order and quickly lost all semblance of military decorum. It essentially became little more than a savage brawl. The only way the two ragtag armies could tell each other apart was for the Whigs to stick pieces of paper in their hats, which made them easy targets for head shots, and for the Tories to adorn their bonnets with green twigs. Not having bayonets, soldiers on both sides resorted to using their muskets and rifles as clubs, as often bashing the skull of one of their own as hurting somebody on the other side. "In this battle neighbors, near relations and personal friends fought against each other, and as the smoke would from time to time blow off, they would recognize each other," commented a Whig who fought at Ramsour's Mill.[28] Casualties were heavy on both sides. Locke suffered about 150 killed and wounded, and Moore approximately the same number. Technically, the patriots were victorious, because the Tories ran from the field and dispersed.

An especially effective partisan leader for the Whigs was Thomas Sumter. An Indian fighter from Virginia who had moved to the Carolina piedmont in 1764, Sumter had built a store near the Santee River about halfway between Charleston and Camden, married a rich widow, and had established a large plantation. A boisterous and truculent 45-year-old, Sumter, who was nicknamed the Carolina Gamecock, had served as a militia captain and as the commander of a South Carolina Continental regiment. In 1780, however, he was living on his plantation near Nelson's Ferry, having resigned his commission due to disagreements with his military superiors.

Anticipating that the British would arrest him as they moved inland after capturing Charleston, Sumter sent his wife and son to a cottage in the High Hills of the Santee in May 1780. He later rode up the Wateree-Catawba Valley, where he established a camp and began recruiting and training a force of volunteers to conduct hit-and-run raids against British outposts. No doubt contributing to Sumter's decision to take up arms was the fact that on May 27, some of Tarleton's men burned down the cottage where the Carolina Gamecock's wife and son were residing. The redcoats had even carried Mrs. Sumter out of the house in a chair to the front yard, where she had been forced to watch the flames consume the building.

Ironically, Sumter was away from camp obtaining money, men, and supplies when his troops first engaged the enemy. Lieutenant Colonel George Turnbull, who commanded the British outpost at Rocky Mount just below the great falls of the Catawba, sent a detachment of troops under Captain Christian Huck, a Pennsylvania Tory, to "push the rebels."[29] Huck and his horsemen, including thirty-five from Tarleton's British Legion, pushed hard. They proceeded to recruit about 300 Loyalists who lived in the area and burn the houses and plunder the plantations that belonged to the patriots in the Catawba Valley of upper South Carolina. About 500 of Sumter's men broke camp and set out to find and destroy this dangerous band of Tories. Before dawn on July 12, the Whig troops stormed into Huck's overnight camp and caught the Loyalists, who were still asleep, completely by surprise. The Tories were quickly defeated, and Captain Huck, who tried to escape on horseback, received a mortal neck wound and fell from his horse.

Sumter himself led his troops into battle on August 1, when he moved against Turnbull's post at Rocky Mount, South Carolina. The New York Tories who were stationed there, most of whom had fought at Savannah and Charleston, succeeded in repulsing the surprise attack by occupying a fortified house that the patriots could not burn down because of a heavy afternoon rainstorm. The Carolina Gamecock was more successful in a three-hour engagement with several hundred Loyalists at Hanging Rock on August 6. His feisty guerrillas killed and wounded up to 200 Tories and took 73 prisoners. Their victory would have been even more complete if they had not stopped to swig down a large supply of rum and pillage the enemy camp.

No matter how important the contributions of partisan leaders like the Carolina Gamecock might be, the ultimate fate of patriot fortunes in the South also depended upon the presence of regular troops proficient in the techniques of eighteenth century combat, particularly the bayonet charge and the volley firing of muskets. Battles such as Archibald Campbell's capture of Savannah, Mark Prevost's victory at Briar Creek, and John Maitland's defense of Stono Ferry had demonstrated that militiamen were no match for seasoned troops. This truth was even more applicable to partisan bands like those headed by Thomas Sumter. They had little experience beyond knowing how to conduct hit-and-run raids against their Tory neighbors, but help was on the way.

Chapter Nine

Camden

In April 1780, General George Washington dispatched a 59-year-old Bavarian called Baron de Kalb, although his real name was Johannes Kalb, south from Morristown, New Jersey at the head of about 1,400 Maryland and Delaware Continentals to assist Benjamin Lincoln's army in Charleston. This small but excellent fighting force comprised the only regular soldiers still operating below the Potomac after the virtual annihilation of Buford's command by Tarleton's Legion. Unfortunately, this force did not arrive in Hillsborough, which is about 240 miles from Charleston, until June 22, more than a month after the rebel garrison in the South Carolina capital had surrendered to Henry Clinton.

De Kalb was not favorably impressed with the region, including its violent thunderstorms and its pesky insects. "The most disagreeable of these is what is commonly called a tick, . . . which makes it way under the skin, and by its bite produces the most painful irritation and inflamation," he complained.[1] De Kalb was especially disappointed with the meager response he was receiving from the militia of the southern states, who were supposed to rally to his camp and bring provisions. Not unlike Robert Howe in Georgia, de Kalb became increasingly frustrated by the unwillingness of state officials to cooperate. Major General Richard Caswell of Moore's Creek Bridge fame was in the field with a large body of North Carolina militia, but he refused to join the Continentals, preferring instead to maintain an independent command and seek out and punish local Tories who had fled into the forests and swamps.

Obtaining few recruits and fast running out of food, General de Kalb had no thought of challenging Cornwallis except under the most advantageous conditions. A man of vast experience in the French military before coming to America in 1777, de Kalb was bent on keeping his isolated army intact. "I am determined to be on the defensive until reenforcement," he wrote to his superiors.[2] Accordingly, de Kalb marched his troops out of Hillsborough at the end of June and headed west about forty miles to the

Deep River Valley, where he camped and sent out foraging parties to scour the countryside. One soldier grumbled:

> We marched from Hillsborough about the first of July, without an ounce of provision being laid up at any one point, often fasting for several days together, and subsisting frequently upon green apples and peaches; sometimes by detaching parties, we thought ourselves feasted, when by violence we seized a little fresh beef and cut and threshed out a little wheat; yet, under all these difficulties, we had to go forward.[3]

As a foreigner, de Kalb had no prospect of remaining in command of the Southern Department of the Continental army, which technically fell upon him when Benjamin Lincoln was captured. Washington's choice for the position was Nathanael Greene, a former Quaker from Rhode Island who possessed superb abilities as a soldier and diplomat. However, Congress, which had ultimate authority in such matters, selected 52-year-old Horatio Gates, a Virginian and the hero of Saratoga, to assume the leadership of military affairs in the South. Gates arrived in de Kalb's camp at Hollinsworths' Farm on the Deep River on July 25 and took control with proper ceremony. An ambitious and politically savvy officer, Gates was called a "dirty little genious" by Greene.

As the new American leader, Gates had no illusions about the enormous challenges facing him.[4] While traveling south, he wrote to one of his associates, "I feel for myself, who am to succeed to what? To the command of an army without strength—a military chest without money, a department apparently deficient in public spirit and a climate that increases despondency instead of animating the soldier's arm."[5]

Gates was expected to persuade large numbers of militia to join his small and undernourished army and to take them all southward over the wretched, muddy and sandy roads of the piedmont and position them to block Cornwallis's advance into the Carolina hinterland and eventually to recapture Charleston. "He faced a victorious enemy, strong, strongly posted, and planning to spread its conquests wider and wider," states one scholar.[6] A competent administrator, Horatio Gates would prove to be a mediocre tactician and field commander.

Upon assuming command, Gates met and talked individually with his officers and pondered what moves his southern army should take. In addition to de Kalb, his subordinates included William Smallwood and Mordecai Gist, brigade commanders of the Maryland and Delaware Continentals, Colonel Otho Williams, the inspector general of the Maryland Division (whose written account gives us most of the information we know about the campaign), Thomas Pinckney, an aristocrat from Charleston who was to become one of Gates's personal aides, and Lieutenant Colonel Francis Marion, who had luckily escaped from the South Carolina capital just before Lincoln surrendered, and who now rode into camp with a motley band of about twenty horsemen, including some blacks. "Distinguished by small black leather caps and the wretchedness of their attire, their number did not exceed twenty men and boys, some white, some black, and all mounted, but most of them miserably equipped," wrote Otho Williams.[7]

The majority of Gates's officers favored a cautious plan of action. Realizing that the troops remained short on food and other provisions and that no depot of supplies had been established ahead of them, they advised Gates to remain in camp for several days and then march west and turn southward toward the North Carolina towns of Salisbury and Charlotte, where Whig support was strong and the land bountiful. According to this proposal, Gates would proceed into South Carolina down the Catawba-Wateree Valley toward Camden, keeping himself between the British and his main base of supplies in Charlotte, North Carolina. Others, especially South Carolinians Thomas Pinckney and Francis Marion, who were understandably anxious to oust the redcoats from their native state, opposed this plan. They urged Gates to break camp immediately and take his army directly southward through the sparse, Tory-dominated sandhills of North Carolina, cross the Pee Dee River, and move unhesitatingly against the British outpost at Camden.

Gates announced his decision on July 26. He was throwing caution to the wind and moving straight southward through the sandhills. "The Troops will strike their Tents tomorrow at half an hour after 3 o'clock (a.m.) when the baggage is to be loaded and the Whole to march by the right," the orders stated.[8] Several considerations had prompted the American commander to choose this more direct but more difficult route to South Carolina. Taking the fifty mile longer roundabout way through Salisbury and Charlotte, he reasoned, would further discourage the already demoralized Whigs in the South Carolina upcountry. Also, Gates thought that by marching into the sandhills he could increase his chances of inducing Richard Caswell and his militia, who continued to conduct operations in this Tory-infested region, to cooperate with the Continentals and join them on their offensive against the British. Thomas Sumter, who persisted in tormenting redcoat outposts in upper South Carolina, insisted that Lord Francis Rawdon, the 25-year-old commander of the British outpost at Camden, had only about 700 men and could be easily overwhelmed if the Whigs moved forthrightly and attacked him before reinforcements could be sent to strengthen his garrison.

But uppermost in the American commander's mind was his desire to waste no time in bringing further glory to himself by fulfilling his orders to attack the enemy. Otho Williams called Gates's choice a "precipitate and inconsiderate step," that would take the Southern Army into a region "by nature barren, abounding with sandy plains, and very thinly inhabited."[9] It was in this same section of North Carolina that Donald MacDonald and the Highland Scots had assembled in 1776 to begin the march that culminated at Moore's Creek Bridge. Clearly, the patriot army would find few friends and little food as it passed through this hostile territory.

The plight of the patriot army as it stumbled southward in late July and early August 1780 did not bode well for Gates's bold strategy. The heat and humidity continued to be ferocious as the soldiers and their baggage train struggled along at the punishing rate of about eighteen miles a day. Wagons carrying everything from anvils and bellows for the blacksmiths to tool chests for the gunsmiths lumbered behind, their sweat-soaked drivers cracking whips and cursing all the way. Bringing up the rear were women in threadbare dresses, many with small children. These brave women were responsible for laundering and cooking and otherwise giving pleasure to the men, but even they could do little with the scant larder that was available in the sandhills. Otho Williams described the miseries that he and his colleagues endured:

> The distresses of the soldiery daily increased—they were told that the banks of the Pee Dee River were extremely fertile—and so indeed they were; but the preceding crop of corn (the principal article of produce) was exhausted, and the new grain, although luxuriant and fine, was unfit for use. Many of the soldiery, urged by necessity, plucked the green ears and boiled them with the lean beef, which was collected in the woods, made for themselves a repast, not unpalatable to be sure, but which was attended with painful effects. Green peaches also were substituted for bread and had similar consequences. . . . It occurred to some that the hair powder which remained in their bags would thicken soup, and it was actually applied.[10]

It must have been a pathetic scene on the Pee Dee during that sultry summer. De Kalb's Continentals, young warriors from Maryland and Delaware who had already experienced the punishing winters at Valley Forge and Morristown, now found themselves bent over with nausea and diarrhea in the sweltering heat and humidity of the Carolina backcountry. Trying to digest green corn and peaches and soup thickened with hair powder, they were forced again and again to make urgent trips into the pine forests to relieve themselves. Such were the unromantic realities of the American Revolutionary War in the South.

At least Gates did succeed in bringing more troops into his army by marching through the sandhills. On August 7, General Richard Caswell brought 2,100 North Carolina militia into camp; one week later, after the patriot army had crossed the Pee Dee River and moved to Rugeley's Mills, some fifteen miles northwest of Camden, 700 Virginia militia, including Garret Watts of Caroline County, joined Gates. Watts would write a gripping account of his involvement in this ill-fated campaign. "This was not far from Camden, where the British were under Rawdon and Cornwallis," he commented many years later.[11]

Charles Cornwallis faced a formidable task in subduing Whig resistance in South Carolina. By instinct a bold and aggressive military strategist, he had received instructions from Clinton which were ambiguous and difficult to decipher. In keeping with his penchant for giving broad latitude to his subordinates so he could protect his own reputation, Clinton had told Cornwallis that he could act offensively or defensively and that he could place troops where he wished and could act virtually independently as long as he kept his commander in chief informed. "I am persuaded that the slightest reflection on the distance and difficulty of communication between Charleston and New York will point out the propriety . . . of vesting the officer who commanded in the southern district . . . with a discretionary power of acting according to the impulse and urgency of the present moment," Clinton explained.[12] While the British commander in chief had insisted that Royal control of South Carolina and Georgia should not be jeopardized, he had urged Cornwallis to conquer North Carolina and then march into Virginia for operations along the shores of the Chesapeake Bay.

It is easy to see how relations between Cornwallis and Clinton became increasingly strained. Cornwallis, who had been hankering for an independent command for years, was anxious to demonstrate his prowess and thereby strengthen his chances to replace Clinton as the head of British forces in North America. Clinton had left him with only six undermanned British regiments (the Seventh, Twenty-third, Thirty-third, Sixty-third, Sixty-fourth, and Seventy-first), about sixty regular cavalry, two German regiments (the Huyne and Ditfurth), and six provincial or Tory regiments (the British Legion, the Volunteers of Ireland, the New York Volunteers, the Prince of Wales American Regiment, the South Carolina Royalists, and the

North Carolina Volunteers); about 4,000 men in all. Despite this meager force, Cornwallis, who had established direct communication with Germain, was resolute in his determination to achieve a great victory in the South. In a letter written on June 30 he told Clinton,

> I shall now take the liberty of giving my opinion with respect to the practicability and the probable effect of further operations in this quarter, and my own intentions if not otherwise directed by your Excellency. I think that with the force at present under my command . . . I can leave South Carolina in security, and march with a body of troops into the back part of North Carolina with the greatest probability of reducing that province to its duty. . . . . If I am not honored with different directions from Your Excellency before that time, I shall take my measures for beginning the execution of the above plan about the latter part of August or beginning of September. . . .[13]

"I did not in my instructions restrict His Lordship from acting offensively," Clinton admitted.[14]

During June and July, Cornwallis busied himself with establishing the logistical base that would allow the British army and its allies to take the offensive in the Carolina hinterland. This was no small task. Almost totally devoid of cavalry, the redcoat commander was forced to rely almost exclusively upon Tarleton's British Legion to maintain contact with the redcoat garrisons in the interior. Conveying such indispensable items as ammunition, uniforms, and camp equipment to the occupying soldiers was made even more difficult by patriot privateers who would descend upon cargo ships as they crossed the Charleston bar and by Whig partisans who would attack British supply wagons as they traveled inland. Having practically no money with which to buy food from the Loyalists, Cornwallis was compelled to confiscate most of his perishable supplies from the Whigs—a policy hardly designed to gain favor with the local populace. "Cornwallis and his men could win battles, but they were not equipped to win hearts and minds," write Cornwallis's biographers.[15]

On August 9, at his headquarters in Charleston, Cornwallis learned that Horatio Gates was closing in on Camden. Recognizing that Rawdon and his 700 men could not hold the town, the redcoat commander marched at the head of reinforcements and arrived in Camden on August 13. The British had 2,043 men fit for combat. They included 817 regulars, 844 provincials, and 382 militia. Gates had 3,052 troops, but almost two-thirds of his army were militia. Learning from a spy that Gates's army was largely comprised of irregulars, Cornwallis decided to march his troops out of Camden on the night of August 15 in preparation for an attack upon the patriot army the next morning at Rugeley's Mill. Ironically, at exactly the same hour, 10:00 P.M., Gates, expecting the British to retreat toward Charleston, sent his troops down the same sandy road to occupy a defensive position along a ridge about five miles northwest of Camden, where he thought he would be able to keep an eye on the redcoat garrison.

Horatio Gates performed miserably as a field commander at the Battle of Camden. He violated several fundamental principles of the military arts. First, an officer must have a firm understanding and make a careful assessment of the strengths and weaknesses of his men. To expect the Virginia and North Carolina militia to repulse British regulars, especially on a battlefield where the level terrain of widely-spaced pine trees was well suited for traditional eighteenth century tactics, was totally unrealistic. "Others could not imagine," Otho Williams exclaimed, "how it could be conceived that an army, consisting of more than two-thirds militia, and which had never been once exercised in arms together, could form columns and perform other maneuvers in the night and in the face of the enemy. . . ."[16] Second, a commander must know his enemy and plan his own actions accordingly. Nothing in Rawdon's or Cornwallis's careers suggested that they would pull back or seek to avoid the whiff of gun smoke and the clatter of bayonets.

Third, a commanding officer should plan for all potential eventualities. When Gates ordered his troops to undertake a night march toward Camden, he made no provisions for unexpected developments and confounded all logic by overlooking or ignoring the imperative of selecting a place for his army to rendezvous if it were forced to retreat. Vastly overestimating the size of his command and believing that Cornwallis and the main British army were still in Charleston, the hero of Saratoga even went so far as to weaken his force shortly before the battle by dispatching 400 men, including 100 Continentals, across the Wateree to assist Thomas Sumter in blocking a major road to Charleston and by sending about twenty horsemen under Francis Marion down the Santee to harass the British rear, all the while holding to the conviction that Rawdon was alone and would abandon Camden without a fight.

In the early morning hours of August 16, 1780, with a full Carolina moon peeking furtively through fast moving clouds, the two armies gradually came closer together, converging like two giant caterpillars. Luckily, Cornwallis had learned from three prisoners the previous afternoon that Gates was probably going to move that night toward Camden. Consequently, the Royal forces, led by Tarleton's British Legion, were on the alert as they crossed Sanders Creek and headed northwestward on the sandy road that shone ghostly white in the moonlight. Meanwhile, the patriot troops, who were walking down the same road in the opposite direction, were having great difficulty keeping silent because their bowels were once more in turmoil. As a special treat, Gates had arranged for a dessert of dumplings and molasses to be served just before the men set out on their march through the pine forests outside Camden. Otho Williams described the disquieting impact of this syrupy delight.

> The troops . . . had frequently felt the bad consequences of eating bad provisions; but at this time, a hasty meal of quick baked bread and fresh beef, with a desert of molasses, mixed with mush or dumplings, operated so cathartically as to disorder very many of the men, who were breaking the ranks all night and were certainly much debilitated. . . .[17]

The patriot army groped its way southward in the sultry darkness. At the front was the Frenchman Colonel Charles Armand and his dragoons. Shortly before 2:30 A.M., when the Whig cavalry was about to reach Gum Swamp, they peered ahead and could barely make out the forms of several horsemen approaching fast. Not knowing whether they were friend or foe, Armand and his men called out, hoping that they would receive a cordial response. Then suddenly riding out of the early morning mist came forty members of Tarleton's Legion, shouting "Huzza!", twenty mounted infantry firing their muskets, and twenty cavalrymen swinging their sabers. The Battle of Camden had begun.

After a brisk exchange of gunfire between their forward elements, the two armies pulled back into the woods some 500 to 600 yards apart and waited for daylight, when they would resume the fight. From captured redcoats, the patriots learned to their dismay and astonishment that Lord Cornwallis and the entire British army, not just the Camden garrison, were arrayed opposite them. This disconcerting news was immediately taken to Horatio Gates. "The general's astonishment could not be concealed," Otho Williams observed.[18]

Obviously shaken, Gates assembled his principal subordinates and sought their advice. General Edward Stevens of the Virginia militia exclaimed, "Gentlemen, is it not too late now to do anything but fight?"[19] Nobody spoke up to refute this assertion, even though some officers, including de Kalb, privately felt that the army should withdraw. The clash of arms would erupt again at first light.

Baron de Kalb, placing a metal helmet atop his massive German frame, moved quietly among his splendid Continentals. Bayonets glistened in the moonlight as the young men of Maryland and Delaware were told to check to make sure that their powder was dry. Sporadic exchanges of musket fire interrupted the summer stillness. Garret Watts and his fellow militiamen from Virginia and North Carolina tried to remain calm despite having to make frequent trips to makeshift latrines. The crickets droned, and the frogs croaked incessantly. Then, almost imperceptibly at first, the eastern sky began to brighten. Dawn was breaking. The time for waiting was over. The time for fighting had arrived.

The engagement occurred at a place that was well suited for the British. The armies were encamped on a sandy, wooded plateau about 1,200 yards wide with a swamp on either side, which meant that Gates could not use his superior numbers to turn Cornwallis's flanks. "The Ground on which the armies met . . . was perfectly favorable to the inferior numbers of the royal army," proclaimed William R. Davie.[20] The road ran north to south through the middle of the battlefield, and the ground was clear except for the tall pine trees and a few bushes. As was customary, Gates put his best troops, de Kalb's Continentals, on his right, and his less experienced units, the militia, on his left. Cornwallis did likewise. Consequently, opposite the North Carolina and Virginia militia were such crack British outfits as the Royal Welsh Fusiliers and the Twenty-third and Thirty-third Regiments.

Astoundingly, Gates ordered the Virginia militia to open the battle by advancing against the redcoats. "Gates put incredible faith in irregulars to stand resolutely in open combat," says Don Higginbotham.[21] One shudders at the thought of what must have been going through the minds of these unseasoned, part-time soldiers as they came up against some of the most expert fighters in the world. It was no contest. Seeing the redcoats coming toward them with bayonets extended, maintaining absolute discipline and yelling "Huzza!" in unison, the militiamen panicked and began to throw their loaded muskets on the ground and rush pell mell from the battlefield without even firing a shot. Among these terrified souls was Garret Watts. Writing many years later, this contrite Virginian attempted to defend his actions on that fateful morning:

> Amongst other things, I must confess I was amongst the first that fled. The cause of that I cannot tell, except that everyone I saw was about to do the same. It was instantaneous. There was no effort to rally, no encouragement to fight. Officers and men joined in the flight. I threw away my gun. . . .[22]

Otho Williams, who also witnessed this rueful spectacle, offered the following explanation:

> He who has never seen the effect of a panic upon a multitude can have but an imperfect idea of such a thing. The best disciplined troops have been enervated and made cowards by it. Armies have been routed by it, even where no enemy appeared to furnish an excuse. Like electricity, it operates instantaneously—like sympathy, it is irresistible where it touches.[23]

Horatio Gates stood by helplessly as virtually the entire left wing of his once-splendid army evaporated before his disbelieving eyes. Sitting astride his magnificent mount, Gates tried to muster the fleeing militia, but his efforts were in vain. In the meantime, de Kalb and his Continentals, unaware of developments elsewhere, were maintaining a stubborn defense on the American right, but the flight of the patriot militia meant that Cornwallis could now outflank the brave Bavarian. Standing tall in his splendid uniform with gleaming gold epaulets, his horse long since shot out from under him, de Kalb fought like a man possessed, swinging his sword mightily over his head and shouting encouragements to his beleaguered compatriots. Hopelessly outnumbered, the Continentals gradually gave way. After about fifty minutes of ferocious combat, de Kalb, blood oozing from eleven wounds in his massive body, fell to the ground. His injuries were fatal.

The patriot army was crumbling as individuals and small groups waded into the swamps that adjoined the battlefield or hastened north on the same road that they had traveled down the night before. Knowing that Tarleton's dragoons were not far behind, men cut horses loose from the supply wagons and left the women to fend for themselves. "Others were obliged to give up their horses to assist in carrying off the wounded," said Otho Williams, "and the whole road, for many miles, was strewed with signals of distress, confusion and dismay."[24] It was only 6:00 A.M.

Brandishing sabers in the air, the British Legion descended upon the helpless militia, literally cutting to pieces anyone who did not immediately turn about and surrender. "After this last effort of continentals, rout and slaughter ensued in every quarter," Tarleton boasted.[25] As for Horatio Gates, he was already five miles away at Rugeley's Mills, having decided to depart the scene with considerable haste. "By this Time the Militia had taken to the Woods in all directions, and I concluded with General Caswell to retire towards Charlotte," the Whig commander later explained.[26] He covered the sixty-five miles to Charlotte in one day and was in Hillsborough, 180 miles away, in three. "Was there ever such an instance of a general running away . . . from his whole army?" decried Alexander Hamilton when he heard the news.[27]

Charles Cornwallis had won a stupendous victory over the patriot army at Camden. De Kalb was dead, Thomas Pinckney was seriously wounded, and Griffith Rutherford had been captured. Cornwallis was understandably joyous when he wrote to George Germain on August 21,

> A number of prisinors, near 150 wagons, a considerable quantity of military stores, and all the baggage and camp equipment of the rebel army fell into our hands. The loss of the enemy was very considerable. A number of colors and seven pieces of brass cannon, with all their ammunition wagons, were taken. Between eight and nine hundred were killed and about one thousand prisinors, many of them wounded.[28]

On the British side, 88 were killed and 245 wounded.

There was no denying the enormity of the defeat. Sent to block the British advance and to recapture Charleston, Horatio Gates had instead suffered a humiliating setback and had now left his men behind to wander about in small groups with no instructions where to gather. Only about 700 dispirited Continentals, most with no weapons, finally joined Gates in Hillsborough. The Carolina hinterland lay virtually prostrate before the redcoats and their Tory allies. "Gates' defeat was the second major disaster to American armies in the South," asserts John Pancake.[29] "Thus the battle of Camden ended in panic, defeat and disgrace," says Henry Lumpkin in *From Savannah to Yorktown. The American Revolution in the South.*[30] What would the future hold?

Two days later, on August 18, the Whigs suffered another setback. At Fishing Creek, about thirty miles west of Camden, Tarleton and some 350 men surprised and overwhelmed Thomas Sumter and about 700 unsuspecting troops. Many of Sumter's troops were either asleep, swimming in the Catawba River, or just plain drunk. British losses were light—sixteen killed and wounded. The Tory horsemen succeeded in slaying or wounding 150 rebels and capturing 350 more. The only reason Sumter escaped capture was because he was knocked unconscious during the struggle and the British Legion simply overlooked him. "This action was too brilliant to need any comment of mine," Cornwallis was to declare.[31]

The struggle to win independence from Great Britain had reached its nadir in the South in late August 1780. Alarmingly, growing numbers of settlers, whose inclination to be for one side or the other was commonly dictated by immediate self-interest, began to take up arms for the king now that the armies of Benjamin Lincoln and Horatio Gates had been destroyed within thirteen weeks of one another. These converts even included militia units that were on their way to Camden to fight the British. When news arrived that Cornwallis had prevailed, they simply switched sides and began attacking and robbing stragglers from Gates's army as they fled from the battlefield. Otho Williams described what happened to some North Carolina militiamen:

> . . . they met many of their insidious friends, armed, and advancing to join the American army; but learning its fate from the refugees, they acted decidedly in concert with the victors; and, captivating some, plundering others, and maltreating all the fugitives they met, returned, exultingly, home.[32]

Anyone who possesses even a modicum of respect for human life must be repulsed by the rage that continued to sweep over the South. A Swedish officer serving with the French navy described a particularly loathsome incident of debauchery: "On a beautiful estate a pregnant woman was found murdered in her bed through several bayonet stabs," he reported. "The barbarians had opened both of her breasts and written above the bed canopy, 'Thou shalt never give birth to a rebel.'"[33]

Excessive violence occurred on both sides of the struggle, especially during the weeks and months after the British victory at Camden, when partisan leaders like Thomas Sumter and William R. Davie had no army of regulars to protect their interests and had to depend solely upon their own resources. A British historian contends that a Whig colonel performed "extraordinary acts of brutality" on a convoy of sick and wounded redcoats in South Carolina.[34] Moses Hall, a patriot militiamen from Rowan County, North Carolina, thus described a "scene that made a lasting impression" upon his troubled conscience:

> I was invited by some of my comrades to go and see some of the prisoners. We went to where six were standing together. Some discussion taking place, I heard some of our men cry out, "Remember Buford," and the prisoners were immediately hewed to pieces with broadswords. At first I bore the scene without any emotion, but upon a moment's reflection, I felt such horror as I never did before nor have since, and, returning to my quarters and throwing myself upon my blanket, I contemplated the cru-

elties of war until overcome and unmanned by a distressing gloom. . . .[35]

Anthony Allaire's journal of his exploits with Patrick Ferguson, who was laboring to bring order to the Carolina backcountry in the summer of 1780, provides a fascinating glimpse into the nature of everyday life on the Carolina frontier. Seemingly spending most of his time wading through streams, killing rattlesnakes, seeking cover during thunderstorms, and meeting an odd assortment of characters, Allaire could not help but feel the tension and apprehension that gripped the settlers as they decided which side to back in the conflict that engulfed them.[36] "Many good friends of Government have suffered much by the Rebels," Allaire declared.[37] He saw one woman, a mother of five children, who had been "stripped of all their clothes, bedding, and other furniture."[38] In June, while bivouacked with Ferguson in Ninety Six, the New York Tory took special delight at seeing the patriot prisoners in jail, "peeping through the grates, which affords some satisfaction to see them suffer for their folly."[39]

The reasons for someone becoming a Whig or a Tory continued to be complex and highly personal. "While a number of North Carolinians travelled more than a week to reach the British," one scholar asserts, "most joined after the forces reached their home areas."[40] Mark Allen attacked two patriots in Montgomery County, North Carolina, for example, simply because he "had particular business to Settle of his own."[41] A group of disgruntled residents in Chowan County plundered Whig merchants because of their "oppression of trade."[42] (In other words, their prices had been too high.) It was on such fickle issues the decision to be for or against the king often rested.

One might assume that Lord Cornwallis was optimistic and ebullient when he set out from Camden with about 2,300 men on September 8, 1780. He had won a smashing victory over Gates, Tarleton had sent Sumter and his partisans scurrying at Fishing Creek, Ferguson had succeeded in recruiting and instructing a large force of Tory militia in the South Carolina backcountry, and the closest regular troops the enemy had were over 150 miles away in Hillsborough. Badly bruised and utterly fatigued, Gates's Continentals numbered less than 1,000 and were in no position to challenge the British advance into North Carolina.

Counterbalancing these reasons for optimism, however, were troublesome realities that could not be overlooked or easily discarded by Cornwallis. The Royal military had suffered heavy casualties at Camden, and the redcoats had had 800 soldiers hospitalized by illness before the battle had even begun. The Thirty-third Regiment had lost a stunning 36% of its men and 50% of its officers on August 16, and these seasoned troops could not be easily replaced. Meanwhile, Francis Marion, who was fast earning his reputation as the Swamp Fox, was leading his small but ferocious band of partisans on daring raids, swooping down upon British patrols and supply trains as they traveled between interior garrisons and the coast. "The Disaffection . . . of the Country East of the Santee is so great, that the Account of our Victory could not penetrate it—any person daring to speak of it being threatened with Death," Cornwallis wrote to Clinton on August 23.[43]

Thomas Brown, the hotheaded commander of the British outpost at Augusta, was so heavy-handed in his treatment of the local citizens that he quickly pricked the ire of Colonel Elijah Clarke, a veteran of the Indian wars. Clarke sent word to Isaac Shelby and John Sevier, old comrades who lived in the Watauga settlements, to march over the mountains and join him in operations against the British and the Tories. On August 18, at Musgrove's Mill north of Ninety Six, Clarke and Shelby ambushed and severely defeated a force of Loyalists headed by Colonel Alexander Innes. Clarke was wounded in this brief but bloody engagement and retired to his plantation in Georgia. Shelby marched his men back into what is now Tennessee. The patriots had demonstrated that they were still capable of inflicting considerable harm upon the advancing redcoats.

The initial British objective in North Carolina was Charlotte, the seat of Mecklenburg County, where numerous grist mills would enable Cornwallis to replenish his supplies before proceeding on to Salisbury and eventually to Hillsborough. Despite enjoying overwhelming superiority in men and firepower, the redcoats and their allies encountered difficulty as they marched out of Camden and headed up the left bank of the Catawba River into North Carolina. William Lee Davidson, who became commander of the militia in western North Carolina after Griffith Rutherford was captured at Camden, was determined to resist the British advance. He dispatched William R. Davie toward the Waxhaws with a band of mounted infantry and instructed him to torment Cornwallis. Davie did just that. At daylight on September 20, he led his men on a daring strike against elements of the British Legion and the Seventy-first Regiment at Wahab's Plantation. Using tactics reminiscent of those he had employed at Hanging Rock, Davie explained that "the vicinity of British quarters, and the danger of pursuit satisfactorily account for no prisoners being taken."[44]

Retribution by the redcoats was swift and unforgiving. "The British commanding officer out of pique or a mistaken & cruel policy immediately ordered the improvements of the plantation to be set on fire, . . . altho' there were three families of women & children living there," Davie reported.[45]

At Charlotte on September 26, Davie gathered his men at the court-house and fired upon Cornwallis's army as it occupied the town. "Charlotte was taken possession of after a slight resistance," wrote Charles Stedman, the main army's commissary.[46] When the redcoats sent foraging parties into the surrounding countryside, however, they found that the Whigs were still defiant. Stedman explained,

> So inveterate was their rancour that the messengers with expresses for the commander-in-chief were frequently murdered; and the inhabitants . . . make it a practice to waylay the British foraging parties, fire their rifles from concealed places and then fly into the woods.[47]

Chapter Ten

Kings Mountain

Patrick Ferguson, an athletic man of slight build with a kindly, oval-shaped face, was one of the best professional soldiers in the British army. Having purchased a commission in the military with family money at age fifteen, Ferguson served with distinction throughout his career. He enjoyed the respect and admiration of the men who served under him, including the fiercely independent Tory militiamen he recruited and trained in the Carolina hinterland in 1780. An expert marksman even after his right arm was rendered almost useless by an elbow wound at the Battle of Brandywine, Ferguson had a congenial and affable disposition. "He was brave and humane, and an agreeable companion," proclaimed Anthony Allaire.[1] Nathanael Greene agreed that Ferguson had a pleasant disposition. "It was his peculiar characteristic to gain the affections of the men under his command," said the famous Rhode Islander, who would soon succeed Horatio Gates as head of the Continental army in the South.[2]

These amiable qualities made this resourceful and enterprising Scotsman a superb propagandist and teacher. He spent countless hours under the blazing summer sun, patiently showing the backwoodsmen how to load and fire their weapons and fix bayonets (although many had to make do with whittled-down butcher knives jabbed into the ends of their musket barrels). A dutiful instructor, Ferguson would blow on a shrill silver whistle each time his recruits were supposed to respond to a specific command. By summer's end, Ferguson had organized seven battalions of Tory militia and had put a force of about 1,000 men into the field. He wrongly assumed that these frontiersmen, having learned how to fight like professional soldiers and move about the battlefield like obedient robots, would be able to overwhelm any troops the enemy dared to send against them. It was to be a fatal miscalculation.

At first glance, it seemed that Patrick Ferguson was finally fulfilling the expectations that George Germain had had for the South since 1778, when he first told Henry Clinton to send troops to Georgia. "Five hundred subjects came in," declared Allaire on September 24, the day after he and his compatriots occupied Gilbert Town, now Rutherfordton, North Carolina, at the edge of the Blue Ridge Mountains.[3] "The poor, deluded people of this Province begin to be sensible of their error, and come in very fast," Allaire boasted on another occasion.[4] Clearly, this was the optimum moment for the Tories to come forward. Unlike Archibald Campbell, who had to march inland from Savannah to Augusta in early 1779 with relatively few troops, and Donald MacDonald, who in 1776 had little else to depend on other than the prospect that British troops would soon land on the lower Cape Fear River, Ferguson could embolden his recruits by reminding them that Cornwallis's army was firmly entrenched close by in Charlotte. If, under these favorable circumstances, the redcoats could still not entice the Tories to flock to and protect the Royal standard, what hopes for success would Lord Germain's policy ever have in the South? The answer was not long in coming.

Ferguson was caught on the horns of a dilemma. On the one hand, the indefatigable Scotsman was endeavoring to win the support of the rank-and-file citizens of the Carolina backcounty, which meant that he had to avoid being unduly provocative. On the other hand, he had to be sufficiently forceful to suppress the unrest that continued to flourish in the impassioned political and social environment of the southern hinterland.

Anthony Allaire's journal is replete with examples of lawlessness on the part of patriot partisans. "This settlement is composed of the most violent Rebels I ever saw, particularly the young ladies," he observed on September 15.[5] To illustrate the savagery that could occur on the frontier, Allaire described what happened to a "very decent woman" who was attacked by Indians the year before. "They scalped and tomahawked her several times in the head," he declared.[6]

Ferguson, who had recently been elevated to the rank of lieutenant colonel, although he was yet to receive news of the promotion, was no brute. Greene called him "a fit associate for Tarleton in hardy, scrambling, partisan enterprise; equally intrepid and determined, but cooler and more open to impulses of humanity."[7] But Ferguson did not shrink from the consequences of attempting to pacify a region dominated by wolfish Whigs. When he failed to prevent Elijah Clarke, who had assembled a force of about 300 men and had attacked Thomas Brown in Augusta in mid-September, from taking refuge in the Watauga settlements, Ferguson released a prisoner and sent him over the mountains with an understandably stern warning to Shelby and his fellow frontiersmen. Ferguson told the over the mountain men that unless they desisted from defying British authority, he "would march his army over and lay waste their country."[8]

The white pioneers, or Wataugans, who lived along the Holston, Watauga, and Nolichucky Rivers had demonstrated in 1776 what they would do when threatened. These feisty folks believed in the doctrine of preventive warfare. Consequently, they were prone to take up arms and attack their enemies before their enemies could attack them. Ferguson's message had just such an effect upon Isaac Shelby, who was a native of Maryland and the son of a distinguished Indian fighter. Writing in the third person, Shelby later explained, "It required no further taunt to rouse the patriotic indignation of Col. Shelby. He determined to make an effort to raise a force, in connection with other officers which should surprise and defeat Fergurson."[9]

On September 25, 1780, a large band of backwoodsmen assembled at Sycamore Shoals on the Watauga River. Among the hundreds of grisly frontiersmen testing their rifles that day were Colonel Shelby and 240 men from Sullivan County, North Carolina; Colonel Charles McDowell, who had brought 160 men over the mountains from Burke and Rutherford counties in North Carolina; Colonel John Sevier and 240 troops from Washington County, North Carolina; and Colonel William Campbell, with 400 men from Washington County, Virginia. They would later be joined at Quaker Meadows on the Catawba River by 350 men from Wilkes and Surry counties, North Carolina, led by Major Joseph Winston and Colonel Benjamin Cleveland, and subsequently by other smaller contingents, including troops from Georgia and South Carolina.

The principal firearm used by these frontiersmen was the Deckard or Dickert rifle, from 43 to 54 caliber. "Men who did not know who Horatio Gates was, or care much about what had happened at Camden, were taking down their rifles from their fireplaces," declares Charles Bracelen Flood in *Rise, and Fight Again.*[10] Unlike the musket, which was designed as a combat weapon, the so-called long rifle was essentially used for hunting, which meant that accuracy rather than rate of fire was its most important attribute. Even an expert marksman could not expect to fire more than a single round in a minute, but the spinning bullet shot by a rifle had a killing range of up to 300 yards, more than three times as far as the Brown Bess musket. Muskets were more suited than long rifles for organized military operations because they were easier and cost less to manufacture, could take greater abuse, and accepted standard ammunition.

On September 26, this motley band of frontiersmen, motivated by the desire to safeguard their homes and families, mounted their horses, headed up the Doe River, and began their ascent to the top of the Blue Ridge Mountains, knowing that Ferguson and his band of Tories were somewhere out ahead. To the summit of Roan Mountain they marched, where even in late September they encountered a blanket of snow. On a broad, verdant meadow more than 5,000 feet high, Shelby and his compatriots, bedecked in typical backwoodsmen's garb of fur-skin caps, hunting shirts, and trousers made from homespun, held a full-dress parade. Around each man's waist was a belt holding a knife, a shot bag, a pouch full of parched corn, and usually a tin cup. Powder horns hung from the men's necks, and their long rifles were slung over their shoulders. These militiamen were grim and pitiless warriors. "Many of these men were Indian fighters, whose idea of warfare was as ruthless as that of their forest opponents," writes one scholar.[11]

Although organized into regiments, these forbidding troops fought as individuals, not as members of disciplined groups. They depended upon their own marksmanship, not upon firing volleys in preparation for a bay-onet charge. They didn't have bayonets, because their rifles had no sockets to hold them. These resolute soldiers had learned from the Cherokees to hide behind trees or rocks and pick off the enemy one by one, not infre-quently with head shots. On level, open ground, like at Camden or outside Charleston, these tactics would be ineffectual and no match for the tradi-tional European battle techniques employed by the redcoats and their allies, but the final encounter between the over the mountain men and Ferguson would occur at a site more suited to the backwoodsmen's combat techniques.

On September 30, Ferguson learned from two deserters that the over the mountain men were stalking him. Knowing that he was in jeopardy and that it was imperative that supporters of the king come to his aid as never before, the wily Scotsman began retreating eastward toward Charlotte. He sent couriers to ask Cornwallis in Charlotte and Cruger in Ninety Six for reinforcements, and issued a stirring and ardent proclamation to the Tories. He minced no words. It was now or never—the critical hour had arrived.

> Gentlemen:
> Unless you wish to be eat up by an inundation of barbarians, who have begun by murdering an unarmed son before the aged father, and afterwards lopped off his arms, and who by their shocking cruelties and irregularities, give the best proof of their cowardice and want of discipline; I say, if you wish to be pinioned, robbed,

and murdered, and see your wives and daughters, in four days, abused by the dregs of mankind—in short, if you wish or deserve to live and bear the name of men, grasp your arms in a moment and run to camp.

The Backwater men have crossed the mountains; McDowell, Hampton, Shelby and Cleveland are at their head, so that you know what you have to depend upon. If you choose to be pissed upon forever and ever by a set of mongrels, say so at once and let your women turn their backs upon you, and look out for real men to protect them.[12]

The response of the Tories to this dramatic summons was disappointing. Moreover, Cornwallis did not receive word of Ferguson's plight until it was too late to find the Scotsman and make a major effort to assist him. Cruger did answer, but informed Ferguson that he could not spare any troops, because Ninety Six was also under threat of attack. On October 5, Ferguson sent a dispatch to Cornwallis which revealed how apprehensive the Scotsman had come to feel about the unfolding course of events. "I should hope for success against them myself; but numbers compared, that must be doubtful," he observed. He went on to urge Cornwallis to send 300 or 400 "good soldiers, part dragoons," who would "finish the business."[13] Despite these expressions of concern, Ferguson did not proceed to Charlotte, but stopped retreating and prepared for battle.

Considerable controversy surrounds the question of why Patrick Ferguson did not march his men to Charlotte where their safety would have been assured. Charles Flood contends that Ferguson feared that he could not reach Cornwallis without being attacked and that he preferred to select a place suited for defensive operations rather than risk being assaulted on open ground. Some argue that Ferguson, hearing that Loyalist units were finally responding to his so-called "pissing" summons, stopped at Kings Mountain in the belief that the Tories could easily find him there. According to Hank Messick, the Scotsman was motivated by less rational and more personal considerations. Ferguson, he claims, was jealous of the fame that Banastre Tarleton had come to enjoy and was determined to avoid the ignominious fate of having to flee for cover. "A proud man was Ferguson and he had no intention of scurrying into Charlotte with his tail between his legs no matter how many Backwater Men came after him."[14] Henry Lumpkin shares the view that arrogance and pride played significant roles in persuading Ferguson to stand and fight rather than taking the more prudent course of proceeding to Charlotte, which was only thirty-five miles away. "He was a keen sportsman and well-born Scottish gentleman, professionally frustrated, mistrusted, deeply ambitious, and therefore anxious for personal glory," Lumpkin contends.[15]

The site Ferguson chose to turn about and face his unrelenting pursuers was a puzzling choice for an experienced British officer. "Got in motion at four o'clock in the morning, and marched sixteen miles to Little King's Mountain, where we took up our ground," wrote Anthony Allaire on October 6th.[16] Kings Mountain was really a high ridge that rose only some sixty feet above the surrounding countryside about a mile and a half below the North Carolina line. Approximately 250 yards wide from one base to the other, this rocky hill, which at the time of the battle had no trees on the top, extended about 600 yards in a general northeast to southwest direction. Ferguson and his 1,125 Tories encamped near the northeast end of the summit. There they erected their tents, parked their supply wagons in a semicircle, and waited for Loyalist reinforcements or maybe the over the mountain men to arrive. Apparently because he had such a low regard for the military abilities of his adversaries, whom he frequently called "mongrels," "banditti," or "backwater barbarians," Ferguson did not even take such customary precautions as clearing a field of fire down the steep, wooded slopes of Kings Mountain, making sure that he had a supply of water within his lines, or erecting barricades and an abatis to retard an attacking enemy. "I arrived today at Kings Mountain & have taken a post where I do not think I can be forced by a stronger enemy than that against us," he boasted.[17]

During the previous week, the over the mountain men had made final preparations for the chase. On October 2, encamped about a day's march from Gilbert Town, where they had thought they would find Ferguson, the troops had selected Colonel William Campbell to be their commanding officer, although his real job in the democratic arrangements that governed their affairs was "to execute the plans adopted by the commandants of the regiments, who assembled in council to determine the orders of the day."[18] When the rifle-toting frontiersmen discovered that Ferguson had left Gilbert Town and had retreated southward, possibly toward Ninety Six, they decided to form their best-armed men with the fastest horses into a special strike force which would ride out ahead of the main body of troops and overtake the Scotsman and his Loyalists. "We accordingly started about light the next morning with 910 men," Shelby explained.[19] On October 6, the same day that Ferguson moved his men atop Kings Mountain, the over the mountain men crossed into South Carolina and arrived that evening at

Cowpens, an area about six miles below the Broad River where farmers brought their cattle to graze and to be separated into pens for sale. Upon learning that Ferguson was retreating toward Charlotte, the strike force, then containing about 1,300 men because of the recent arrival of some 400 troops from the Carolinas and Georgia, set out on a night-long ride in a fine drizzling rain.

Early on the morning of October 7, Campbell and his fellow frontiersmen crossed the Cherokee Ford on the Broad River and continued their pursuit of the allusive Scotsman. Informed by spies that Kings Mountain was where they would find their adversary, the backwoodsmen pressed on doggedly in the rain. "The day was showery, and they were obliged to use their blankets, and their great coats, to protect their arms from wet," one officer reported.[20] "The forenoon of the day was wet," wrote another participant.[21] Over the undulating terrain of the piedmont they rode, peering expectantly toward the horizon, "exhausted by fatigue, hunger, cold and wet," now and again passing an isolated farmstead in the otherwise unending forest.[22] The pugnacious frontiersmen drew energy from the fact that with each weary step, they came closer and closer to the hill where the abominable Ferguson and his Loyalist cohorts were encamped.

The same soaking drizzle was falling atop Kings Mountain that fateful October day. Ferguson and his 1,125 men, about 100 of whom, including Anthony Allaire, were New York or New Jersey Provincials commanded by Captain Abraham de Peyster, spent an enjoyable morning resting from the rigors of dashing from one trouble-spot to another, which had largely been their fate since marching into North Carolina in early September. Except for pickets sent to the bottom of the hill to keep watch, the troops lounged about in their tents, hauled supplies from their wagons, or cleaned their weapons. In mid-afternoon, Captain Alexander Chesney, a South Carolina Tory, rode among the pickets and returned to the summit of Kings Mountain to report to Ferguson that all was well. The proud Scotsman remained confident that his militiamen, if ordered to march down the steep slopes that encircled them with muskets and bayonets extended, would be able to meet all eventualities and repulse the "backwater barbarians," who knew nothing about traditional battlefield tactics. Events would soon demonstrate with murderous consequences that Ferguson's assumptions were invalid.

Shortly before 3:00 P.M., the patriot strike force arrived, "tied all their loose baggage to their saddles, fastened their horses, and left them under charge of a few men, and then prepared for an immediate attack," said Isaac Shelby.[23] One officer, no doubt aware of how the militia had discarded their guns and run away in humiliation at Camden, carefully instructed his troops on how they should conduct themselves when they came up against a bayonet charge:

> I will show you by my example how to fight. . . . Fire as quick as you can, and stand your ground as long as you can. When you can do no better, get behind trees, or retreat; but I beg you not to run quite off. If we are repulsed, let us make a point of returning and renewing the fight. Perhaps we may have better luck in the second attempt than the first.[24]

The regiments scurried quietly to the base of Kings Mountain in four columns, each man placing slugs in his mouth so he could reload quickly. Imagine how the over the mountain men must have felt: Joyous that they had finally overtaken their prey, they nonetheless must have moved forward with stomachs made queasy by anxiety and excitement. Among them was 16-year-old James Collins. "Here I confess I would willingly have been excused . . . but I could not swallow the appellation of coward," he declared many years later.[25]

The attackers had agreed to coordinate their advance up the hill by shouting bloodcurdling Indian whoops to one another. Isaac Shelby and William Campbell took their troops to the narrow or southwestern end of Kings Mountain, while the remainder of the men, including those under Benjamin Cleveland, Charles McDowell, and John Sevier, surrounded the base of the broad or northeastern part of the hill. Ferguson's pickets were caught completely by surprise and gave no warning. Shrill cries rang out; Abraham de Peyster, who had fought at Musgrove's Mill, knew this sound only too well. "Things are ominous," he told Ferguson. "These are the same yelling devils."[26] Their respite over, the Tories on the treeless summit grabbed their muskets and began to line up to prepare for battle just like Ferguson had taught them to do.

The hour-long conflict that unfolded at Kings Mountain on October 7, 1780 was a bloody but fascinating engagement. It was fundamentally a contest between two divergent military stratagems—one essentially European, the other distinctively American. Patrick Ferguson, riding his white horse from one side of the summit to the other, blowing constantly on his shrill silver whistle, sent his disciplined militiamen down the steep slopes to hurl back the grisly frontiersmen. The same deadly pattern occurred over and over again. Firing volleys and then sticking their makeshift bayonets into the ends of their muskets, the Tories would repeatedly repulse the enemy. "As either column would approach the summit," Shelby explained,

"Ferguson would order a charge with fixed bayonet, which was always successful."[27]

But the attackers refused to quit, partly because they were ably led, and partly because the Loyalists tended to aim too high and shoot over the heads of their whooping, stealthy adversaries. "The shot of the enemy soon began to pass over us like hail," James Collins remembered.[28] "Their great elevation above us," he continued, "had proved their ruin; they overshot us altogether."[29]

Even more significantly, because the slopes fell off precipitously and had a thick cover of trees, the Tories could not press their initial advantage. As the Tories fell back toward the summit, the concealed patriots had ample time to load and fire their long rifles, with devastating results. "I stood behind one tree and fired until the bark was nearly all knocked off and my eyes pretty well filled with it," said Thomas Young, a patriot private.[30] According to Alexander Chesney, "King's Mountain, from its height, would have enabled us to oppose a superior force with advantage, had it not been covered with wood, which sheltered the enemy and enabled them to fight in the favorite manner."[31]

Gradually, with over the mountain men coming at him from all sides, Ferguson began to give way. Hearing incessant shrieks from the Scotsman's silver whistle as they climbed upward, growing numbers of attackers succeeded in gaining the summit, where they stood at the edge of the tree line, well out of range of the Tories' muskets, and let loose with their long rifles upon the helpless enemy. De Peyster, who was ordered by Ferguson to shore up one particularly vulnerable spot, found to "his astonishment when he arrived at the place, he had almost no men, being exposed in that short distance to the constant fire of their rifles."[32] Captain Chesney explained that the rebels "were able to advance to the crest . . . until they took post and opened an irregular but destructive fire from behind trees and other cover."[33]

Finally sensing the inevitability of defeat, Ferguson attempted to fight his way though the encircling enemy. Atop his white horse with a hunting shirt over his jacket and brandishing a sword in his only good hand, the intrepid Scotsman was an easy target. Rifles discharged seemingly from everywhere, propelling slugs into Ferguson's slender body. One bullet ripped into his thigh; another shattered his already crippled right arm. The fatal shot penetrated the Scotsman's skull and sent blood splattering across his previously handsome face. With one foot hung up in a stirrup, the dutiful instructor of Tory militiamen was dragged like a side of beef into the trees at the northeastern end of Kings Mountain where he soon expired.

After viewing the corpse a few minutes later, James Collins wrote, "On examining the body of their great chief, it appeared that almost fifty rifles must have been leveled at him at the same time. Seven rifle balls had passed through his body, both his arms were broken, and his hat and clothing were literally shot to pieces."[34]

The Tories were ready to surrender now that Ferguson was no longer there to encourage and direct them. De Peyster, who had assumed command of the Tories, ordered the defenders to raise the white flag and submit. But passions were running hot among the bearded and near breathless frontiersmen as they charged triumphantly across the summit of Kings Mountain that October afternoon. Unable to restrain their fury, many patriot militiamen repeatedly fired at point blank range into a crowd of Loyalists who had gathered in a small depression near the upper end of the hilltop. The carnage continued even after most of the Tories had thrown down their muskets and were begging for quarter. Yelling "Tarleton's Quarter," the over the mountain men persisted in discharging their long rifles at the defenseless enemy. Even James Collins could not overlook what many of his colleagues were doing: "The dead lay in heaps on all sides, while the groans of the wounded were heard in every direction. I could not help turning away from the scene before me, with horror, and though exulting in victory, could not refrain from shedding tears."[35]

Another disgusting event occurred nearby. Ferguson's dead body, stripped naked by plunderers, was subjected to one final act of despicable humiliation. Remembering that the proud Scotsman had warned the residents of the piedmont that the over the mountain men would "piss" on them, a lusty bunch of patriot militiamen, imbued with the euphoria of victory, urinated on Ferguson's bare corpse.

"And why not?," asks Hank Messick in his sympathetic study of the Whigs who fought at Kings Mountain. "These mountaineers were not professional soldiers, trained to observe a code of warfare."[36] One must admit that such behavior, especially in light of occurrences that had already transpired at places like Ramsour's Mill, Hanging Rock, and Wahab's Plantation, was not surprising. Such was the character of fratricidal conflict in the South during the American Revolution.

That night the triumphant rebels camped atop Kings Mountain. The next morning, expecting Tarleton's dragoons to appear at any moment, the patriots prepared to leave with their 698 prisoners, including New York Tory Anthony Allaire. The Loyalists had suffered 157 killed and 163 so badly wounded that the Whigs simply left them to die. "They thought it necessary to move us sixteen miles," Allaire reported on October 8 in his daily journal.[37]

Before departing with his compatriots, the youthful James Collins witnessed the horrible aftermath of battle, when the women came forward to find their loved ones. The next morning, which was Sunday, the families of the Tories came in great numbers. Their husbands, fathers and brothers lay dead in heaps, while others lay wounded or dying.

> We proceeded to bury the dead, but it was badly done. They were thrown into convenient piles and covered with old logs, the bark of old trees, and rocks; yet not so as to secure them from becoming prey to the beasts of the forest or the vultures of the air. And the wolves became so plenty that it was dangerous for anyone to be out at night, for several miles around. Also, the hogs in the neighborhood gathered into the place to devour the flesh of men. . . . [38]

The destruction of Ferguson and his entire command was a devastating setback for the British. Indeed, it was the turning point in the American Revolution in the south. Even though the redcoats continued to pursue the elusive goal of quelling the rebellion in the two Carolinas and Virginia for two more years, the fate of the King's fortunes in the South had been sealed by the utter annihilation of the Loyalist militia at Kings Mountain. "Much had been expected from the exertions of Major Ferguson . . . and by his unfortunate fall and the slaughter, captivity or dispersion of his whole corps the plan of the expedition into North Carolina was entirely deranged," commented Charles Stedman, who was in Charlotte with Cornwallis's army when word arrived that the Tories had been crushed.[39]

Henry Clinton stated in his account of the American Revolutionary War that the defeat at Kings Mountain "unhappily proved the first link in a chain of evils that followed each other in regular succession until they at last ended in the total loss of America."[40] "The hopes of Cornwallis had hinged upon that battle," write Cornwallis's biographers.[41] Christopher Ward could not be more resolute in his assessment of the significance of what the over the mountain men had accomplished: "The effect of the victory at King's Mountain was instantaneous and of great importance. It turned the tide of the war in the south."[42]

The history of the American Revolution published by the United States Army's Center of Military History states that "King's Mountain was as fatal to Cornwallis' plans as Bennington had been to those of Burgoyne."[43] Henry Clinton recognized that the prospect of inducing the supporters of the king to take up arms and fight their neighbors, never an easy task, would now become increasingly difficult, if not impossible.

> And, surely, never was the trite apothegm *that the greatest events often proceed from little causes* more fatally confirmed than by the present check—which, though in itself confessedly trifling, overset in a moment all the happy effects of our successes at Charleston and His Lordship's glorious victory at Camden, and so encouraged that spirit of rebellion in both Carolinas that it never could be after humbled. For no sooner had the news of it spread through the country than multitudes of disaffected flew to arms all parts, and menaced every British post on both frontiers, 'carrying terror even to the gates of Charleston.' "[44]

Never again would as many Tories gather under the Royal banner as had come forth for Patrick Ferguson during the weeks preceding the Battle of Kings Mountain, and the snorting hogs, circling buzzards, and howling wolves that infested the macabre hilltop the day after this horrific engagement sent a terrifying but unmistakable warning to many a Loyalist's home. Charles Cornwallis reported from his headquarters in Winnsborough, South Carolina, to which he was compelled to retreat in October, that the militia in the Tory stronghold of Ninety Six and its environs "was so totally disheartened by the defeat of Ferguson that of that whole district we could with difficulty assemble one hundred."[45] "Kings Mountain appeared to mark the beginning of the end of Cornwallis's offensive in the South," proclaims one scholar. "The next encounter between organized forces would confirm that beginning."[46]

Chapter Eleven

Nathanael Greene Assumes Command

On October 14, 1780, one week after Ferguson's demise at Kings Mountain, 39-year-old Major General Nathanael Greene was chosen to assume command of the Continental army in the South. The actual transfer of authority in the field did not occur until December 3 in Charlotte. The Continental Congress, which had appointed Greene's predecessors, including Robert Howe, Benjamin Lincoln, and Horatio Gates, had finally come to realize that military considerations should be paramount in choosing the man who they hoped would rescue the deplorable situation that still existed below the Potomac. Therefore, Congress deferred to Washington's judgment in elevating Greene to head of the Continental forces in the South.

A Rhode Islander who had never been farther south than Maryland, Greene was vigorous and ingenious, if sometimes melancholy. He also had an array of skills and abilities that would enable him to transform the military fortunes of the regular forces in the Carolinas to eventually win a decisive, if not dramatic, strategic victory.

Greene was born into a somber and provincial middle class Quaker family on July 27, 1742 in the village of Potowomut. He spent his childhood under the watchful eye of his father, also Nathanael, who was considered the spiritual leader of the surrounding East Greenwich Quaker community. In this stern but compassionate environment, Greene developed the habits of mind and thought that were to guide his actions and shape his attitudes throughout his adult life. Like thousands of other young and impressionable Quakers who gathered every Sunday in meetinghouses large and small, Greene was taught that human beings should strive to glorify God by living upright, sober, and, above all else, *useful* lives. Not surprisingly, especially when one considers the nature of his upbringing, Nathanael Greene was a man of impeccable character.

Unlike many Rhode Island youngsters of the time, Nathanael Greene was gregarious. He moved easily among people and was able to speak and listen with equal ease. He had a boisterous laugh and enjoyed a good joke, as long as it was not irreverent. This sociability helped Nathanael prosper in the family business.

In 1770, Greene moved to Coventry, Rhode Island, where he took charge of the family's ironworks. A large industrial enterprise for its day, the ironworks manufactured anchors, chains, and other items used in the maritime trade. As a businessman responsible for overseeing the operations of the factory, Nathanael began to refine the administrative skills which were to serve him so effectively as a military strategist during the American Revolution. He understood and appreciated the importance of meticulous planning, of systematic analysis, of having the requisite supplies on hand, and of foreseeing problems and working unceasingly to solve them. Workers had to be hired, fired, and trained. Customers had to be contacted and served. M. F. Treacy in his *Prelude To Yorktown* writes,

> Nathanael Greene's military abilities were not of the romantic kind in which the dashing leader gallops up on a white charger or a black stallion and cries, 'Follow me!' or 'Come on, you sons of bitches, do you want to live forever?' His genius lay rather in an infinite capacity for taking pains in advance.[1]

"No man was more familiarized to dispassionate and minute research than was General Greene," proclaimed one of his subordinate officers in the South.[2]

The transformation of Nathanael Greene from Quaker to renowned military commander occurred over several years. Excluded from his religious community in 1774 because he volunteered for the Rhode Island militia, Greene was selected the following year to lead his state's troops to assist the residents of Boston and its environs during the turmoil that followed the now famous battles at Lexington and Concord. Elevated to the rank of brigadier general, he met General George Washington in July 1775. The two men, so dissimilar in background and training, nonetheless established a relationship of mutual trust and confidence that was to persist throughout the war. "He is beyond doubt a first-rate military genius, and one in whose opinions the General places the utmost confidence," proclaimed Tench Tilghman, an aide to General Washington.[3] From his very first days outside the Massachusetts capital, Greene exhibited the qualities of leadership that were to carry him so far, especially those associated with being a strict but just disciplinarian and a stickler for details. He ordered every soldier to be "neatly dressed" and insisted that "during the march no soldier be permitted to talk."[4]

After William Howe and the British evacuated Boston in March 1776, the Rhode Island blacksmith marched southward with Washington's army. When they arrived in New York on April 17, Greene was placed in charge of the defenses of Long Island. Unable to lead his men into battle in August because he was ill, probably from asthma, Greene returned to active duty in September and thereafter participated in every major battle General Washington fought over the next three years. He retreated across New Jersey and into Pennsylvania after New York fell to the redcoats and Howe sent Cornwallis in pursuit of the American army; he re-crossed the Delaware River with Washington on Christmas Day of 1776 and commanded troops in the patriot victory over the hessian garrison at Trenton, New Jersey. Greene spent the second winter of the war with Washington at Morristown, New Jersey, and the third with the commander in chief at Valley Forge, Pennsylvania. He was on the battlefield at Brandywine, Pennsylvania on September 11, 1777, where he directly opposed Cornwallis, and at Germantown on October 4 of the same year. He again faced Cornwallis at the Battle of Monmouth Court House on June 28, 1778, and was the temporary commander of the strategic post at West Point on the Hudson when he was summoned to take charge of military operations in the South.

Most importantly, at least in terms of preparing him for the challenges he would eventually encounter in the Carolinas, Greene was appointed quartermaster general of Washington's army in 1778. "No one ever heard of a quartermaster in history," he declared in a letter to his brother.[5] "There is a great difference between being raised to an office and descending to one which is my case," he told General Washington.[6]

His lamentations notwithstanding, Nathanael Greene benefitted enormously from occupying this position. Securing supplies was an awesomely complicated task. Overseeing a staff of about 3,000 men, which included deputy quartermasters, wagonmasters, foragemasters, auditors, and clerks, the former Quaker was responsible for securing and transporting a vast array of goods for use by the military.

Greene performed his responsibilities with characteristic dispatch and verve. Boats and wagons were built to transport goods across the upper Delaware and over the roads of Pennsylvania and New Jersey. Crews went to work repairing bridges and upgrading thoroughfares and byways. "The work of the quartermaster embraced a multiplicity of duties," writes Theodore Thayer in *Nathanael Greene. Strategist of the American Revolution.*[7]

It fell to Greene to select the camp sites for the army, which meant that he had to become especially sensitive to such factors as the availability of water, wood, drainage and suitability for defense. Moreover, to secure the money and the goods necessary to keep the army fed, clothed, and housed, he had to persuade politicians to respond favorably to his requests. Consequently, Greene gained firsthand knowledge of the fact that the effort to defeat Great Britain was a coalition enterprise between a weak Continental Congress and the legislatures of thirteen powerful and virtually independent states. Accordingly, the new commander of the patriot army in the South understood only too well that skills of diplomacy and cajolery were fundamental to being a successful general in the American Revolutionary War. William Moultrie, who was imprisoned in Charleston when Greene came south, wrote, "His military abilities, his active spirit, his great resources when reduced to difficulties in the field, his having been quarter-master-general . . . all these qualities combined together rendered him a proper officer to collect and to organize an army that was broken up and dispersed."[8]

Greene conferred with General Washington at Preakness, New York, just before departing for the Carolinas on October 23, 1780. In lengthy discussions with the commander in chief he learned that Baron Von Steuben, the Prussian officer who had developed a standard training manual for the Continental army, would be assigned to his command, as would Lieutenant Colonel "Light Horse Harry" Lee and his superb unit of dragoons and mounted infantry. No doubt this latter piece of news was particularly pleasing to Greene because he, unlike Horatio Gates, reckoned that cavalry could play a critical role in military operations below the Potomac. Greene, who anticipated that Cornwallis's army would greatly outnumber his, at least in terms of seasoned troops, devised a strategy for the South that would employ Lee's Legion as the core of a "flying army of about eight hundred horse and one thousand infantry."[9]

Lee was supremely suited for the role that Greene wanted him to play. He "enjoyed independent action: the raid, the ambush, the skirmish, the rapid march, the surprise attack, the siege of an isolated enemy outpost and an ultimatum to the enemy commander," says Lee's biographer.[10]

Greene secured General Washington's approval for a scheme that would call upon the restructured Continental forces in the Carolinas to practice hit-and-run tactics similar to the unorthodox, guerrilla maneuvers that Sumter, Clarke, Davie, and other partisan leaders in the South had been using with murderous effect. "His primary campaign plan was to initiate harassing and nuisance raids to such an extent that the enemy would be rendered immobile and forced to defend its current positions rather than beginning new conquests," explains historian Hugh F. Rankin.[11]

Washington, aware that the success of such nettlesome tactics would hinge upon the ability of the Continental forces to move freely in a region which was crisscrossed by a series of treacherous creeks and rivers, most notably the Catawba-Wateree, the Broad, the Yadkin-Pee Dee, and the Dan, advised Greene to "direct particular attention to the boats."[12] Greene, ever the prudent planner, would not disappoint him.

Greene realized that the fate of the Loyalists who had served under Patrick Ferguson would dissuade most Tories from taking up arms for the king and that Cornwallis would have to depend almost exclusively upon regular troops to subdue the Carolinas. After Kings Mountain, the only hope for a British conquest of the South lay in Cornwallis's ability to inflict a dramatic defeat upon Greene and thereby induce substantial numbers of Loyalists to return to the British camp and, even more crucially, to enforce the peace once the Royal military had departed. But the Fighting Quaker was determined to avoid making the same colossal blunders that Benjamin Lincoln and Horatio Gates had committed at Charleston and Camden respectively. He was not going to repeat their mistake of challenging the British in a major battle. Greene would be willing to throw down the gauntlet only if the circumstances surrounding the pivotal battle with Cornwallis were overwhelmingly on the side of the patriots. Otherwise, the Fighting Quaker would be content to restrict his operations to the more limited objective of nipping at the enemy's heels. It would prove to be a brilliant strategy.

The first stop on Greene's journey to the Carolinas was Philadelphia, where the former blacksmith gave the Continental Congress a letter from General Washington naming him as Gates's successor and where Congress cited financial reasons for refusing to provide Greene with supplies for his beleaguered southern army. Knowing that the states alone had the power to levy taxes, the Rhode Islander sought assistance from Governor Joseph Reed of Pennsylvania, who provided 1,500 stands of arms instead of the 5,000 that had been promised. The Maryland legislature, which luckily was in session when Greene passed though Annapolis, was even more unresponsive. Greene was told to look elsewhere for help because Maryland "had neither money nor credit."[13]

After visiting Mount Vernon, the new commander of Continental troops in the South proceeded to Richmond, where he met with Thomas Jefferson, Virginia's legendary red-headed governor. Greene was appalled by what he observed. The citizens of Virginia, he exclaimed, were a "lifeless and inanimate mass, without direction, or spirit to employ . . . for their own security."[14] He and Jefferson did, however, come up with an ingenious scheme that would eventually have a profound impact upon Greene's fortunes against Cornwallis. It involved building light portable boats that were designed to fit on wheels for easy transport as the patriot army advanced and retreated in the Carolinas.

Greene appointed von Steuben to the post of military commander in Virginia and ordered the famous Prussian to dispatch southward whatever supplies he could find. Greene then set out for Hillsborough, North Carolina, where he expected to join his army. Arriving on November 27, Greene learned that Gates had marched his troops to Salisbury in hopes of finding supplies of food. After dispatching letters to Governor Abner Nash of North Carolina explaining the needs of his army and, unfortunately, once more being rebuffed, Greene left for Salisbury and soon discovered that Gates had moved on to Charlotte.

Nathanael Greene finally caught up with his ragtag army of some 2,300 men, only about 1,500 of whom were fit for duty, when he rode into Charlotte, a crossroads town of about twenty houses and a log courthouse, on December 2. The Rhode Islander assumed command from Gates amid formal ceremonies the next day. In a letter to Joseph Reed of Pennsylvania, Greene depicted the sad fate that had befallen the Continental forces and their militia allies in the South:

> I overtook the army at Charlotte, to which place General Gates had advanced. The appearance of the troops was wretched beyond description, and their distress, on account of provisions, was little less than their sufferings for want of clothing and other necessities.[15]

Greene reported to General Washington that many of his men were "literally, naked; and a great part totally unfit for any kind of duty, and must remain so until clothing can be had from the northward."[16]

Especially alarming to the pragmatic new commander was the lack of self-control he found among the soldiers he observed in Charlotte. "General Gates had lost the confidence of the officers," Greene explained, "and the troops all their discipline, and they have been so addicted to plundering that they were a terror to the inhabitants."[17]

Not surprisingly, Greene moved quickly to rectify the situation. In keeping with his Quaker upbringing, the Rhode Islander held firmly to the conviction that individual officers could have a profound effect upon the course of military affairs. "It has been my opinion for a long time that personal influence must supply the defects of civil constitution, but I have never been so fully convinced of it as on this journey," he stated in a letter to General Washington.[18] To demonstrate his resolve to restore proper comportment among his troops, Greene had a wayward soldier publicly hanged in the town square of Charlotte as an example to the others. "New lords, new laws," said one eyewitness.[19]

In this as in so many other instances, this remarkable patriot general demonstrated the diligence and attention to detail which were to be basic in enabling him finally to win out over the Royal army in the South. As Banastre Tarleton had already so graphically demonstrated, the propensity of soldiers to destroy private property and murder civilians was decisive in determining where the rank-and-file population of the Carolinas ultimately placed their trust and allegiance. Greene appreciated that it was on the results of countless such decisions, not on the outcome of this or that particular skirmish or battle, no matter how dramatic or bloody it might be, that the course of the war in the South essentially depended. That's why his policy of maintaining tight discipline among his troops and his strategy of avoiding a major defeat at all costs was so inventive. As long as Greene's army remained in the field, darting here and there like a pesky fly, the redcoats could not create a political climate that was conducive to persuading the Loyalists to come out for the King. The reason? The fear of retribution by patriot partisans remained pandemic. Even the most optimistic British officials, especially George Germain, knew that if the Tories did not rally to the Royal standard in substantial numbers, the prospects for a British victory were minuscule.

Part of the reason for his success in the South was that Greene, unlike his predecessors, was empowered to issue orders without having to consult his fellow officers beforehand. In other words, the patriot general could act decisively, because the determination of what the Continental army would or would not do was his alone. Having this prerogative did not mean that Greene discounted the views of his compatriots. Indeed, the initial days of his command were largely devoted to talking individually with his principal subordinates to learn their assessments of the overall situation and to solicit their advice regarding possible courses of action.

In December 1780, an impressive coterie of combatants walked up the courthouse stairs in Charlotte, their swords clanking against the wooden risers. There was Colonel William Washington, second cousin of George Washington, who had led a Continental cavalry unit in the South since 1779 and whose cavalrymen had clashed with Tarleton's green-jacketed dragoons in several sharp engagements, including Monck's Corner outside Charleston. Greene also conversed with Colonel John Eager Howard, whose Maryland brigade had suffered heavy casualties at Camden. He met Major General Isaac Huger (pronounced "u-gee"), the South Carolinian who had been fighting the British since the beginning of the war. He sat down with

Major William R. Davie, whom he named to the significant but not glamorous post of commissary general, meaning that the fiery cavalry commander would now have to oversee the business affairs of the army. Greene reasoned that Davie would have "extensive influence among the inhabitants" and that his reputation as a capable leader of troops would make him "much respected in the army."[20]

Greene selected Lieutenant Colonel Edward Carrington as quartermaster general for the Southern Department. The capacity to pick the right man for the right job was another of Greene's admirable traits. Even before reaching Charlotte, the prudent new commander, remembering Washington's admonition "to direct particular attention to the boats," had ordered Carrington and General Edward Stevens, the Virginia militia officer who had served under Gates at Camden, to survey the rivers of the piedmont. He sent the following instructions to Stevens:

> Lieutenant-Colonel Carrington is exploring the Dan River, in order to perform transportation up the Roanoke . . . and I want you to appoint a good & intelligent officer with 3 privates to go up the Yadkin . . . to explore carefully the River, the Depth of the Water, the Current & the Rocks, & every other Obstruction that will impede the Business of Transportation.[21]

Again, it was his capacity to take care of the particulars while retaining the ability to see the big picture that provided Greene with the critical margin of victory in the South.

The most famous of Greene's subordinate officers at Charlotte was the volatile but unsurpassed tactician Brigadier General Daniel Morgan. A resident of the Virginia frontier, Morgan had joined Gates's army soon after the calamitous defeat at Camden. A boisterous, coarse, irreverent, and rowdy backwoodsman, Morgan became locally famous as a ferocious fighter even in the raucous and unrefined social environment of Winchester, Virginia, where he settled as a young man in 1753 and soon thereafter became a teamster. "Outsiders in particular found Morgan a dangerous man to cross," writes Don Higginbotham. In one "mass brawl," the Old Waggoner and his friends overpowered their adversaries by "resorting to kicking, biting, and gouging."[22]

Selected to lead a company of "expert riflemen" at the outset of the war, Morgan served the patriot cause with distinction and unflagging energy. Like Greene, he had marched north to Massachusetts in 1775 and joined Washington's army outside Boston. He participated in the ill-fated invasion of Canada later that year and was captured by the British when he and his valiant troops were surrounded and overtaken by the redcoats in the streets of Quebec. Exchanged for British prisoners the following spring, the redoubtable Morgan rejoined General Washington, for whom he had undying admiration, and served continuously under his fellow Virginian until 1779, except for a brief period in 1777 when he was sent to assist Horatio Gates on the upper Hudson.

Daniel Morgan made substantial contributions to the decisive American victories over Burgoyne's redcoats at Freeman's Farm on September 19 and Bemis Heights on October 7. Miffed at not being selected to command a newly-formed corps of light infantry, the volatile frontiersman resigned from the army and returned home to Winchester in 1779. But Morgan was never content to sit serenely by the hearth. He returned to military service in 1780, when his old compatriot Horatio Gates asked him to join the patriot forces defending the South. Morgan's presence in the American camp at Charlotte was a godsend for Greene.

The talents of his regular officers notwithstanding, the Fighting Quaker knew that the Continental army alone was not strong enough to deal with Cornwallis, who was still at his winter camp in Winnsborough, South Carolina, some ninety miles south of Charlotte, with about 2,500 seasoned troops. On December 4, his first full day in command, Greene sent a dispatch to Francis Marion, "the Swamp Fox," who throughout the fall had been disrupting British supply columns between Camden and Charleston and attacking enemy outposts between the Pee Dee and the Santee.

On September 29, Marion and about fifty of his peppery cohorts had defeated a small body of Loyalists at Black Mingo Creek. On October 26, the Swamp Fox had again demonstrated his prowess as a partisan leader when his little band of ruffians routed a Tory force at Tearcourt Swamp, killing three and wounding fourteen while taking no casualties themselves. "I have not the honor of your acquaintance but am no stranger to your character and merit," Greene told Marion. The patriot general went on to tell his wily compatriot to remain where he was and to continue "awing the Tories and preventing the enemy from extending their limits."[23]

Greene also reached out to Thomas Sumter in hopes of convincing the flamboyant but cantankerous South Carolinian to put aside his petty jealousies and cooperate with the Continental army. Appreciating that the Carolina Gamecock, like the vast majority of non-Continental officers, preferred to operate on his own without interference from anybody, Greene attempted to convince Sumter that the militia should coordinate its operations with those undertaken by regular troops.

The Fighting Quaker was not about to make the same strategic miscalculation which some analysts contend had foredoomed the British hopes for victory from the moment that Henry Clinton had sent Archibald Campbell south. In Greene's eyes, primary responsibility for defeating the enemy belonged to the Continental army, not to militia or partisans. "It requires more than double the number of militia to be kept in the field, attended with infinitely more waste and expense than should be necessary to give full security to the country with a regular and permanent army," he asserted.[24] Greene proceeded to tell Sumter:

> The salvation of this army does not depend upon little strokes, nor should the great business of establishing a permanent army be neglected to pursue them. Partisan strokes in war are like garnishings on a table, they give splendor to the army and reputation to the officers; but they afford no substantial national security. They are matters which should not be neglected, and yet, they should not be pursued to the prejudice of more important concerns. You may strike a hundred strokes, and reap little benefit from them, unless you have a good army to take advantage of them.[25]

Sumter, who had whipped a force of about 140 Loyalists and redcoats on November 9, 1780 at Fishdam Ford, South Carolina, was severely wounded in a sharp engagement with Tarleton's Legion eleven days later at Blackstocks, South Carolina, on the south bank of the Tyger River. Despite inflicting a serious defeat upon the dreaded Tory dragoons, who had foolishly rushed pell-mell into Sumter's strong defenses, the Carolina Gamecock was in no condition to mount a horse and ride into the general's camp. On December 8, Greene, always the adept diplomat, set out from Charlotte to visit Sumter, who was convalescing in a rock house near the Tuckaseegee Ford on the Catawba River. Sumter informed Greene that substantial reinforcements were on their way to Cornwallis's camp in Winnsborough, and urged the Continental commander to move boldly against the British. Greene agreed to give this venturesome proposition due consideration, and directed the illustrious partisan leader "to keep up a communication of intelligence, and of any changes of their disposition that may take place."[26]

Chapter Twelve

Cowpens

Returning to Charlotte after visiting with Sumter, Nathanael Greene sat down with his officers and finalized his plan of operations. An excellent military strategist does the right thing at the right time. A brilliant military strategist does the *wrong* thing at the right time. Nathanael Greene was a brilliant military strategist.

Defying the dictum that one should never divide an army in the face of a superior enemy, the Fighting Quaker left Charlotte with the larger part of his army on December 16 and marched to a new camp just across the Pee Dee River from Cheraw, South Carolina. He placed the rest of his troops, including 320 of Howard's Maryland and Delaware Continentals and 100 of William Washington's cavalry, under the control of the always resourceful Daniel Morgan. The Old Waggoner led his soldiers out of Charlotte on December 20 and headed westward across the Catawba and Broad Rivers toward Kings Mountain and Cowpens in upper South Carolina, where militia units began to join him.

Greene realized that he could not remain in Rowan and Mecklenburg counties because troops from both sides had already picked the countryside clean. He calculated that by dividing his army, he would enable his ravenous troops to forage in more fertile territory. Moreover, Greene reasoned that by bisecting his army, he would put pressure upon Cornwallis by threatening the major British outposts at Camden, Ninety Six, and Augusta. The American general explained,

> It makes the most of my inferior force, for it compels my adversary to divide his, and holds him in doubt as to his line of conduct. He cannot leave Morgan behind him to come at me, or his posts at Ninety-Six and Augusta would be exposed. And he cannot chase Morgan far, or prosecute his views upon Virginia while I can have the whole country open before me. I am as near to

Charleston as he is, and as near Hillsborough as I was at Charlotte; so I am in no danger of being cut off from my reinforcements.[1]

Consistent with his intention of keeping the British off balance, Greene sent Light Horse Harry Lee and his green-jacketed dragoons and mounted infantry down the Pee Dee to find Marion, so they could help the Swamp Fox make trouble for the redcoats. On December 28, this audacious pair descended upon the British garrison at Georgetown, South Carolina, captured the commandant, and then rode inland to assault Fort Watson, an enemy outpost on the Santee. But the more telling blows against Cornwallis were taking place beyond the Catawba and the Broad, in upcountry South Carolina, where Daniel Morgan and his polyglot army of regulars and militia were succeeding in bedeviling the British. Two days after Marion and Lee had attacked Georgetown, Colonel William Washington and his cavalrymen virtually annihilated a band of Georgia Loyalists whom they overtook at Hammond's Store, South Carolina. The patriot horsemen then moved farther south and threatened the enemy outpost at Williamson's Plantation, only fifteen miles from Ninety Six.

Thomas Sumter was right. Substantial reinforcements were on their way to Cornwallis's winter headquarters at Winnsborough. With the tragic loss of Patrick Ferguson's corps at Kings Mountain in October, Cornwallis had requested that Henry Clinton send more regular troops to the South. By January 1781, Major General Alexander Leslie, on Cornwallis's instructions, had finally arrived from the Chesapeake and was slogging his way through the swamps and swollen streams between Charleston and Winnsborough with 1,530 experienced soldiers. The British Lord would have preferred to remain in camp until Leslie's men arrived, but he felt compelled, especially after the bloody setbacks at Hammond's Store and Williamson's Plantation, to dispatch Tarleton at the head of a small but powerful army of some 1,100 troops to protect Ninety Six. On New Year's Day, Tarleton was ordered to move westward from Winnsborough with the British Legion of 550 men, the first battalion of the Seventy-first Regiment, 200 men from the Seventh Regiment, fifty men from the Seventeenth Light Dragoons, and a detachment of Royal Artillery with two field guns. (The guns were called "grasshoppers" because they jumped off the ground when they were fired.) "If Morgan is still at Williams's, or any where within your reach, I should wish you push him to the utmost," Cornwallis told his combative subordinate.[2]

After determining that Ninety Six was not under immediate threat, Tarleton turned his attention to the task of catching the Old Waggoner and destroying him. The leader of the British Legion proposed to Cornwallis that the main army march up the east side of the Broad River in the direction of Kings Mountain and cut off Morgan's line of retreat, while Tarleton and his men pushed northward from Ninety Six directly toward the Old Waggoner, striking, if you will, like a hammer against Cornwallis's anvil. The British commander in chief approved this bold initiative, telling his fiery, young compatriot: "You have done exactly what I wished you to do, and understood my intentions exactly."[3]

Cornwallis, anticipating that he and Tarleton would achieve a decisive victory over Morgan, left Winnsborough on January 7, 1781, and proceeded slowly in hopes that Leslie's reinforcements would overtake him. Cornwallis headed toward Kings Mountain in absolute confidence that the British would prevail. He wrote, "The . . . quality of the corps (of about eleven hundred men) under Lieutenant-Colonel Tarleton's command, and his great superiority in cavalry, left him no room to doubt of the most brilliant success."[4]

Greene, who was more than 140 miles away at Cheraw, warned Morgan that Tarleton was on the prowl. "Colonel Tarleton is said to be on his way to pay you a visit," he wrote in a dispatch sent in early January. "I doubt not but he will have a decent reception and a proper dismission."[5] The Old Waggoner realized that his militia, many of whom were commanded by Andrew Pickens, the phlegmatic Presbyterian who had returned to the ranks after Tories destroyed his South Carolina home, needed time to prepare for battle, especially when they were being asked to fight professional soldiers. Therefore Morgan, who was becoming increasingly anxious, placed scouts and other small contingents of soldiers at the fords on the Pacolet River to resist the enemy and to warn him when Tarleton was approaching. The Old Waggoner knew that Cornwallis was marching up the opposite bank of the Broad to cut off his line of retreat. One can imagine the apprehension that even the fearless Virginian must have felt as he fell back in the face of this ominous British advance.

On the morning of January 16, couriers rode into Morgan's camp with the startling news that Tarleton had bypassed the Whigs' outer defenses, had crossed the Pacolet, and was headed straight for the patriot army. In great pain because of the arthritis that afflicted his otherwise powerful physique, the Old Waggoner recognized that his isolated band of troops was in great peril. Consequently, he ordered the men to break camp immediately, even though they were in the midst of eating breakfast. The day was bitterly cold. Hoping to cross the Broad River and wait for the advancing redcoats on the rough terrain at Thicketty Mountain, Morgan moved up and down the ranks of his retreating army, bellowing orders to the teamsters and exhorting his shivering soldiers to move ever faster.

At dusk the Old Waggoner and his men arrived at Cowpens, the same spot where Isaac Shelby and the over the mountain men had rendezvoused four months earlier. The patriot army was still five miles south of the Broad River. Cowpens, a sparse, open woodland of red oak, hickory, and pine, seemed inappropriate as a place to do battle with Banastre Tarleton. Unlike Camden or Stono Ferry, Cowpens had no swamps or rivers to impede the enemy from attacking its flanks. The absence of bushes and thickets meant that the British would be able to maneuver their cavalry with ease. If defeated, the patriots would have no ready avenue of retreat due to the presence of the Broad River behind them, much like Robert Howe's defenders at Savannah who had been outflanked by Archibald Campbell. Even Tarleton called it "certainly as proper a place for action as Lieutenant colonel Tarleton could desire."[6]

Why did Morgan choose this site? In later years he defended his decision by contending that he "would not have a swamp in the view of my militia," because "they would have made for it, and nothing could have detained them from it."[7] The Old Waggoner went so far as to claim that he *wanted* Tarleton to attack his flanks. "It would have been better," he proclaimed, "than placing my own men in the rear to shoot down those who broke from the ranks."[8]

The real reason that Morgan selected Cowpens as the battlefield was that he had no real choice. Like Patrick Ferguson, he did not want to be attacked as he marched across country and certainly not when his troops were crossing a major river. Also, Cowpens was similar to Kings Mountain in that it was well known among the inhabitants of the region and would be an easy place for friendly militia to assemble. Some irregulars did wander into camp in the hours just preceding the battle, bringing Morgan's total strength to about 1,100 men, roughly the same as Tarleton's. Morgan also figured that by spending the night south of the Broad River, he could give his weary troops a chance to rest and have a hearty meal. All along the gentle slopes at Cowpens on that frigid January night, seasoned soldiers and militiamen joined together in jumping up and down and beating their arms against their sides to keep warm, while campfires glistened and kettles bubbled beneath a star-lit sky.

His selection of a place to tangle with Tarleton notwithstanding, Daniel Morgan was no Patrick Ferguson. The ill-fated Scotsman had suffered a disastrous defeat at Kings Mountain because he had not appreciated the talents of his enemy and because his own troops had not been properly prepared to fight a battle they had been expected to win. The Old Waggoner was just the opposite kind of leader. "It was upon this occasion I was more perfectly convinced of General's Morgan's qualifications to command militia than I had ever before been," said Major Thomas Young, who served under Colonel William Washington.[9] A frontiersman himself, Daniel Morgan spent the night squatting by campfires and talking with small groups of men, especially the militia. "I don't believe he slept a wink that night," reported cavalryman Young.[10]

The largest body of irregulars was Pickens's South Carolinians. Also present were Charles McDowell's North Carolinians, including James Collins and others who had fought at Kings Mountain, a contingent of Virginians, the majority of whom were former Continentals, and some Georgia partisans. Thomas Sumter did not stand with the Old Waggoner at Cowpens. Ever prickly, the Carolina Gamecock had been deeply offended when his brigade had been placed by Greene under Morgan's authority without first consulting South Carolina officials. Thomas Sumter and his men decided to sit out the fight.

Morgan knew what had happened to the patriot left wing at Camden. Coming up against grunting redcoats with bayonets extended, the irregulars had panicked and run away, thereby assuring the destruction of de Kalb's Continentals. The Old Waggoner was determined that no such calamity would befall his army when Tarleton predictably sent his troops charging forward in a bayonet attack the next day. The crafty Virginian conceived an unorthodox but masterful tactical plan that would use the militia in a way that would maximize their strengths. Anticipating that Tarleton would make a direct, frontal assault, just as he had against Buford in the Waxhaws and Sumter at Blackstocks, Morgan took the unusual step of placing his most inexperienced troops at the very front of his army. He instructed a contingent of riflemen to hide behind trees some 300 yards downhill from Lieutenant Colonel Howard's Delaware and Maryland Continentals and shoot the British officers when Tarleton sent them forward. "Look for the epaulets! Pick off the epaulets!"[11]

About 150 yards behind the sharpshooters was the main body of militia under Pickens. The dour Presbyterian was told to hold his fire until he could see the whites of the enemy's eyes. Convinced that the militia would do their duty if they understood precisely what was expected of them, the Old Waggoner explained that he wanted them to fire two volleys and then retreat around the left flank of Howard's Continentals. "Just hold up your heads, boys," Thomas Young reported Morgan as saying, "and then when you return to your homes, how the old folks will bless you, and the girls kiss you for your gallant conduct."[12] Finally, to protect the retreating militia from the kind of slashing onslaught for which Tarleton's dragoons were famous, Morgan instructed Colonel William Washington to attack the British right with the patriot calvary when Pickens's irregulars began to retire.

At the crest of the gentle slope that extended from north to south for about 800 yards at Cowpens stood the Maryland and Delaware Continentals, commanded by Colonel John Eager Howard. Many had fought valiantly at de Kalb's side in the intense heat and humidity at Camden and were thoroughly familiar with Bloody Tarleton and his methods. The Virginia militiamen, who formerly were Continentals, were on Howard's right, and Virginia and Georgia irregulars occupied his left flank. Having been told that Tarleton was not bringing untested militia, the Continentals and Pickens's militia knew they would have to face some of the best troops that Great Britain commanded in the South, including the highlanders of the first battalion of the Seventy-first Regiment.

About an hour before dawn on January 17, 1781, the waiting was over. When couriers rode into camp telling him that Tarleton was within five miles of Cowpens and closing fast, the Old Waggoner mounted his horse and rode among his men, yelling all the while, "Boys, get up! Benny is coming. . . ."[13] For roughly the next two hours, while the defenders deployed to their assigned positions and watched the night gradually give way to dawn, Morgan bolstered the spirits of his men and assured them that victory would be theirs if they would simply follow his instructions. Unlike Horatio Gates, who at Camden had stayed far to the rear, the Old Waggoner was right up front at Cowpens. The legendary Virginian gave impassioned speeches and pounded his fist into his palm to punctuate the importance of his remarks. To the militia he said, "Let me see which are most entitled to the credit of brave men, the boys of Carolina or those of Georgia."[14] To Howard's Continentals he exclaimed, "My friends, in arms, my dear boys, I request you to remember Saratoga, Monmouth, Paoli, Brandywine, and this day you must play your parts for your honor & liberty's cause."[15] It was truly a virtuoso performance.

Suddenly, at about 7:00 A.M., green-jacketed dragoons and the Royal infantry in scarlet and white began to appear in the woods at the far end of the meadow. The sharpshooters took ramrods from their holders and rammed shot and wadding down the barrels of their long rifles and tapped powder into their priming pans. Pickens's militia and Howard's Continentals spit balls down the barrels of their muskets and prepared to deliver volleys. The din of drums, fifes, and bagpipes announced that the time for talking was over. The time for fighting had arrived.

Banastre Tarleton performed badly at Cowpens. A dauntless cavalry-man, he had demonstrated at places like Biggin's Bridge and Blackstocks that he was totally devoid of tactical expertise and finesse. According to one disgruntled British officer, "the best troops in the service had been put under *that boy* to be sacrificed."[16]

The only thing Tarleton knew how to do well was to hurl his troops unabashedly at the enemy. His men, who had been on a fast march since 3:00 A.M. over roads that in many places were almost impassable, were exhausted. A mature, experienced officer would have understood that there was no reason to attack immediately. Where were Morgan and his men going to go? If they had marched toward the Broad River, Tarleton could have pursued and pounced upon the patriots at the most opportune moment, slashing and ripping them to bits. The British had artillery. The Old Waggoner did not. And even though William Washington and his cavalry, augmented by about 100 volunteers from the militia, were stationed in a swale at the rear of the American army, they would have had great difficulty in preventing Tarleton's dragoons from turning Morgan's flanks if the commander of the British Legion had had sense enough to employ such tactics.

Bloody Tarleton gave no thought to postponing his attack. Determined to charge directly toward the Whigs in a broad, frontal assault, he sent a detachment of dragoons into the open to test the strength of Morgan's forward positions. The sharpshooters let loose with their long rifles, emptying 15 saddles before the stunned cavalrymen returned to the woods. Undeterred, Tarleton enjoined his troops to form a line and prepare to advance up the hill toward the Americans. "The enemy drew up in a single line of battle, four hundred yards in front of our advanced corps," stated Daniel Morgan in a dispatch he sent to Greene two days after the battle.[17] "About sunrise, the British line advanced at a sort of trot with a loud halloo," wrote Thomas Young. "It was the most beautiful line I ever saw."[18]

Tarleton placed his light infantry on the right, the infantry of the British Legion and the two "grasshoppers" in the middle, the Seventh Regiment on the left, and fifty dragoons on each flank. The troops from the Seventy-first Regiment and the bulk of the calvary were stationed some 180 yards to the rear of the main line as a strategic reserve.

Tarleton knew that roughly half of Morgan's army was militia. With considerable justification, the audacious British commander reasoned that these backwoods farmers would scamper away like terrified puppies at the first glimpse of redcoat steel. After all, that's what they had always done. Why should Cowpens be any different? Up the hill at a steady trot the green and scarlet line moved, giving forth with the same yell that the patriot militia had heard at dawn outside Camden: "Hurrah! Hurrah!" They "Raised a prodigious yell, and came running at us as if they Intended to eat us up," Morgan remarked.[19] Realizing that all depended upon the militia holding their ground and delivering two volleys, the Old Waggoner instructed his troops to "give them the Indian whoop."[20]

Pickens, welcoming the sharpshooters who, as planned, now fell back into his ranks, instructed his compatriots to hold their fire until the enemy was within range. "Every officer was crying, 'Don't fire!' for it was a hard matter to keep us from it," remembered one patriot soldier.[21] Meanwhile, the British artillery belched forth with deadly effect.

To Tarleton's surprise, Pickens's militia held their ground and delivered two ragged but potent volleys at the grunting redcoats. Predictably, when the British regulars fired in unison "like one sheet of flame" and rushed forward with fixed bayonets, the patriot irregulars, as instructed by Morgan, began an orderly retreat, but they did not panic or run away.[22]

When some of Tarleton's infamous dragoons arrived, brandishing their sabers and making ready to attack the militiamen, William Washington and his patriot cavalry came upon the scene, engaged the British Legion, drove them off and pursued them down the hill. "In a few moments Col. Washington's cavalry was among them like a whirlwind, and the poor fellows began to keel from their horses without being able to remount," observed James Collins.[23]

Almost instinctively, most of the militia headed for their horses, because they believed their participation in the battle was over. Morgan rode after them, screaming, "Form, form, my brave fellows. . . . Old Morgan was never beaten."[24] With Pickens's help, the Old Waggoner managed to stop most of the irregulars and to assemble them just behind Howard's Continentals.

The British regulars and the infantry of the British Legion extended across the meadow at Cowpens like a string of green and scarlet marbles. Standing no more than fifty yards apart, the two armies poured volley after volley into one another's ranks, each waiting for the slightest hint of the other's giving way. Great clouds of gun smoke billowed into the frigid morning air.

The redcoats were convinced that the rebels would start scampering away at any moment. Frustrated that he was not breaking through, Tarleton ordered the troops of the Seventy-first Regiment, his strategic reserve, to join the fray by attacking Howard's right. To meet this threat, the commander of the Continentals instructed the Virginians opposite the Seventy-first to pull back over the brow of a small hill and pivot to the right to meet the onrushing Highlanders and to protect Morgan's western flank. "In doing this, some confusion ensued, and first a part and then the whole of the company commenced a retreat," Howard observed.[25]

Inexplicably, especially when one considers their level of training, the redcoats broke formation and started dashing after the patriot soldiers, apparently convinced that the rout of the rebel troops had finally begun. Daniel Morgan sensed that this breakdown in discipline on the part of the enemy gave him the opportunity to achieve a decisive victory. The redcoats no longer had the ability to form up and deliver volleys. Grasping the import of this unexpected development, the Old Waggoner rode ahead of Howard's men and pointed to the spot where he wanted the Continentals to face about and fire a fusillade into the advancing British and Tory troops. Coming over the rise in complete confidence that they would witness the same scene of mayhem and disorder that they had seen so many times before, the Seventy-first Regiment was greeted instead by a devastating volley. At that very moment, when the redcoats were stumbling about in utter confusion, Pickens and his militia, urged on by Morgan, turned the British left flank; William Washington, returning from pursuing elements of the cavalry of the British Legion, overwhelmed Tarleton's right. "The result was a double envelopment, perfectly timed," says Don Higginbotham.[26]

The end came quickly. Howard sent a detachment of men forward to seize the "grasshoppers" and ordered the remainder of his troops to launch a bayonet attack against the almost surrounded redcoats. "They began to throw down their arms and surrender themselves prisinors of war," James Collins remarked.[27] Captain Roderick Mackenzie of the Seventy-first Regiment, who later would bitterly refer to Tarleton as a "rash, foolish boy," explained that the sight of so many troops capitulating "communicated a panic to others, which soon became general: a total rout ensued."[28]

Tarleton, who was still at the bottom of the hill with the majority of his cavalry, sat stunned in his saddle. He must have realized the enormity of his defeat and what it portended for the future of British fortunes in the South. Simply put, the king could not afford to lose the services of so many skilled, professional soldiers. Who could replace them? Certainly not the Tories from the Carolinas. Unlike Morgan, who had hundreds of irregulars with him, including some who had come into camp the night before the battle, Tarleton had almost no local Tories in his army. Indeed, the largest contingent of Carolina Loyalists had remained with the British supply wagons, and they were demonstrating their "devotion" to the Royal cause by stealing provisions at the very moment when redcoats were fighting and dying a few miles away at Cowpens.

Tarleton attempted to commit his reserve dragoons to the battle in hopes that they could somehow rescue the situation, but his efforts were futile. The great majority of cavalry, witnessing the slaughter that was unfolding before their very eyes, ignored or defied his order to charge. They wisely chose to ride away instead. "Above two hundred dragoons forsook their leader, and left the field of battle," Tarleton lamented.[29]

The commander of the British Legion did manage to rally some forty horsemen and fourteen officers. This small band skirmished with Washington's calvary as it rode toward the bottom of the hill at the southern end of the battlefield and, as if to provide a fit climax to this dramatic day, Tarleton and Washington actually engaged briefly in one-on-one combat. Realizing that all hope was lost, Tarleton broke off the fight after killing the patriot colonel's horse with two misplaced pistol shots. Telling the dragoons who remained to follow him, Tarleton rode into the woods and headed for the Pacolet. "He was pursued twenty-four miles," Morgan reported to Greene, "but, owing to our having taken a wrong trail at first, we never could overtake him."[30] The Battle of Cowpens was over.

The Old Waggoner, admittedly aided by plenty of good fortune, had achieved an astounding victory at Cowpens. Overjoyed by the results of the engagement, Morgan hoisted his drummer boy into the air and kissed him on both cheeks. The pugnacious Virginian told a friend that the American army had given Tarleton a "devil of a whipping."[31] "The troops I have the honor to command have been so fortunate as to obtain a complete victory over a detachment from the British army, commanded by Lieut. Col. Tarleton," Morgan wrote in a more sedate dispatch to Greene.[32] The reaction of the British and the Tories was predictably glum. William Moultrie wrote,

> This defeat of Colonel Tarleton's . . . chagrined and disappointed
> the British officers and Tories in Charleston exceedingly. . . . I
> saw them standing on the streets in small circles talking over the
> affair with very grave faces. . . . This great victory . . . changed
> the face of American affairs. . . . In two actions, soon after each
> other, the British lost about two thousand men. . . ."[33]

One witness reported that when Cornwallis learned what had transpired at Cowpens, he "leaned forward on his sword as he listened . . . and . . . pressed so hard that the sword snapped in two."[34]

The aftermath at Cowpens in no way resembled the bloody scene which had transpired atop Kings Mountain the previous October. Cries of "Tarleton's Quarter" were quickly quashed by the Continentals, who protected the redcoats and the men of the British Legion from harm once they had surrendered. In the roughly hour-long battle, Tarleton, in addition to losing substantial amounts of supplies, ammunition, and weapons, had suffered 100 killed, including 39 officers, and 229 wounded. Approximately 600 soldiers, including 27 officers, had been captured. "Two standards, two field-pieces, thirty-five wagons, a travelling forge and all their music are ours," Morgan exulted.[35] Cowpens was "Camden-in-reverse." It was truly a British disaster.

This early nineteenth century law office in Salisbury, North Carolina is similar to the buildings that stood in the town when Nathanael Greene and Daniel Morgan passed through on their way to the Trading Ford on the nearby Yadkin River during the "Race to the Dan."

Chapter Thirteen

The Race to the Dan

The events that unfolded during the two months that followed Morgan's victory over Tarleton at Cowpens were to be pivotally important in determining the outcome of the revolutionary war in the South. Although this period witnessed only one major engagement in the Carolinas—the Battle of Guilford Court House on March 15, 1781, which Cornwallis technically won—it doomed the king to ultimate defeat in America because it destroyed any reasonable expectations that the British could establish and maintain a firm grip on the southern hinterland. "It led—indeed, forced—Cornwallis to Yorktown, where the power of Britain in the American states was shattered," contends Christopher Ward.[1] With no enduring British presence in the backcountry, the vast majority of Tories would keep silent, thereby assuring the demise of George Germain's entire southern strategy for winning the war. Countless Royal officials, like Donald MacDonald or Archibald Campbell, could attest to this fundamental truth.

The lion's share of the credit for the momentous achievement of enfeebling the most powerful British army that had ever invaded the Carolina backcountry belongs to Nathanael Greene. Never an outstanding tactician, the Fighting Quaker displayed throughout his masterful retreat across North Carolina and into Virginia and during his return to Guilford Court House those qualities of foresight and industriousness that were so essential to his being a superb military strategist. Alexander Hamilton was effusive in his praise of what Greene accomplished in January and February 1781:

> To have effected a retreat in the face of so ardent a pursuit, through so great an extent of country, through a country offering every obstacle, affording scarcely any resource; with troops destitute of every thing, who a great part of the way, left the vestiges of their march in their own blood—to have done all this, I say, without loss of any kind, may, without exaggeration, be denominated a masterpiece of military skill and exertion.[2]

Learning six days after the Battle of Cowpens that the Old Waggoner had beaten Tarleton, Greene wasted no time in making preparations to take his 1,500 troops, many of whom had neither shoes nor adequate uniforms, northward from near Cheraw, South Carolina to link up with Morgan's 1,100 men, who were also falling back rapidly into North Carolina. "Our prospects are gloomy notwithstanding these flashes of success," he stated in a letter to John Matthews, a member of Congress.[3] Greene ordered Edward Stevens, the Virginia militia general, to escort prisoners to his native state and to see to it that foragers and quartermasters gathered supplies and placed them along the probable line of march. He instructed Lieutenant Colonel Edward Carrington, his quartermaster general, to send boats to the Dan and the Yadkin Rivers. He asked Governor Abner Nash to muster additional militia and provide them with arms.

The Fighting Quaker knew the patriots could not rest upon their laurels and savor their triumph. He was thoroughly familiar with Cornwallis and knew that his adversary was an aggressive and combative commander. Greene anticipated that the redcoat general would advance without delay and attempt to destroy Morgan's isolated force before the two halves of the patriot army could come together. Then Cornwallis, having dealt with the Old Waggoner, would turn upon him, the Fighting Quaker insisted. "Greene's problem, then, was twofold," writes John Pancake. "He must reunite with Morgan and then take the combined force to safety."[4]

From the very outset of assuming command in the South, Greene had envisioned his army as being a highly mobile force, one that could move easily from place to place and thereby deny victory to the more sedentary redcoats, who in typical European fashion took huge supply trains along with them wherever they went. In January 1781, Greene encountered the first serious test of this unorthodox strategy. To survive, he would have to outmaneuver Cornwallis while the entire southern army was in full retreat.

Contrary to popular belief, an orderly and skillful withdrawal, while not manifestly heroic, is among the most difficult movements even a professional army can be asked to make, and the patriot troops in the South could hardly be classified as professional. Continentals comprised barely half of Greene's command. The remainder were partisans or militia, who were notoriously skittish when retreating. Moreover, the two wings of the American army were more than 100 miles apart, and three major rivers—the Catawba, the Yadkin, and the Dan—were at their rear.

Nathanael Greene was correct in predicting that Cornwallis would go on the offensive to redeem his military reputation. The British earl still had a well-trained, powerful army at his disposal. After the arrival of Leslie's

This romantic rendering of early settlers moving through the Cumberland Gap on their way to establish homesteads in Indian territory bears no relationship to the harsh realities.

This obelisk in one of Savannah's elegant squares marks the original burial site of the remains of General Nathanael Greene.

This grand plantation house in Beaufort, South Carolina, the town from which Lieutenant Colonel John Maitland set out on his hazardous voyage to Savannah, bears testimony to the enormous wealth produced by the cultivation of rice and indigo in the South Carolina lowcountry.

George Washington, the commander in chief of the Continental Army, did not come South until 1781, when he joined with the French in defeating Cornwallis at Yorktown. The influence of this remarkable human being had been felt before, however, especially when he had selected Nathanael Greene in 1780 to assume command in the South.

Benjamin Lincoln of Massachusetts headed the Southern patriot army during the abortive attack against Savannah in 1779 and the disastrous capitulation at Charleston in 1780. George Washington appropriately selected Lincoln to accept the sword from the British at Yorktown in October, 1781.

Crude abatis fashioned from logs retarded the advance of the Franco-American Army against the British defenses outside Savannah.

Casimir Pulaski served as a cavalry officer in Benjamin Lincoln's ill-fated Southern army. This dashing Polish soldier became a martyr for the cause of American independence after he was fatally wounded during Comte d'Estaing's direct assult against the Spring Hill Redoubt at Savannah on October 9, 1779.

This crude rock wall outlines a mass grave where the mangled bodies of 84 patriots who were killed at "Buford's Massacre" on May 29, 1780, are buried. It is a somber site.

William R. Davie, a resident of the Waxhaws district of upper South Carolina, was a determined and able leader of Whig partisans. In addition to his military exploits, which included Stono Ferry, the first battle at Hanging Rock, Wahab's Plantation, and the Battle of Charlotte, Davie was appointed by Nathanael Greene to serve as commissary general of the Southern Army.

Lieutenant Colonel Banastre Tarleton rode with his dragoons into the Carolina backcountry in 1780, searching out and attempting to destroy pockets of patriot resistance.

Thomas Sumter, nicknamed the Carolina Gamecock, was a skillful but bothersome leader of partisans in the South Carolina backcountry during Cornwallis's campaign to end the rebellion in the South. Especially disquieting was his unwillingness to cooperate with Continental troops, including Nathanael Greene and Daniel Morgan.

Horatio Gates, the Hero of Saratoga, assumed command of the Southern Continental Army on July 25, 1780. Called a "dirty little genius" by Nathanael Greene, Gates led his troops, mainly militia, against Cornwallis's seasoned redcoats outside Camden, South Carolina on August 16, 1780. The result was a major British victory.

Baron de Kalb, a self-proclaimed nobleman, came south in 1780 and led the Maryland and Delaware Continentals into battle at Camden, South Carolina on August 16th. Surrounded by redcoats, hessians, and Tories, he finally succumbed and fell to the ground with wounds that proved to be fatal.

Otho Holland Williams, the chronicler of the Camden campaign and commander of the 6th Maryland, participated in almost every major battle in the Carolinas in 1780–81. Camden. The Race to the Dan. Guilford Court House. Hobkirk Hill. Eutaw Springs.

Alexander Hamilton admired Nathanael Greene from afar, especially the "Fighthing Quaker's" strategic withdrawel across North Carolina and into Virginia in January and February, 1781. But he felt nothing but disdain and scorn for Horatio Gates when the Hero of Saratoga scampered away from the battlefield at Camden and left his overwhelmed compatriots to fend for themseleves in August, 1780.

Friedrich Wilhelm Augustus von Steuben was ordered by Nathanael Greene to gather arms and supplies in Virginia in 1780–81 for use in the two Carolinas. A Prussian drill master, von Steuben had gained fame for writing training manuals which brought greater discipline to Continental troops and helped them stand up against British regulars.

Andrew Jackson was a teenager in the Waxhaws of upper South Carolina and lower North Carolina when the tide of war swept over the region in 1780–81. Incarcerated in Camden by the British, Jackson reportedly watched the Battle of Hobkirk's Hill through a slit in the jail's log walls.

"Light Horse Harry" or Henry Lee, the father of Robert E. Lee, was a dashing cavalry officer in Nathanael Greene's army as it marched to and fro in the Carolinas in 1780–81. Lamenting the level of violence he encountered. "Light Horse Harry" nonetheless oversaw the murderous slaughter at "Pyle's Hacking Match" in February 1781.

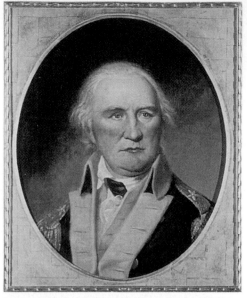

Daniel Morgan, a feisty backwoodsman from near Winchester, Virginia, emerged as one of the outstanding tacticians in the Continental Army. In addition to his noteworthy accomplishments in the North, Morgan achieved fame for his decisive victory over Banastre Tarleton at Cowpens, South Carolina in January, 1781.

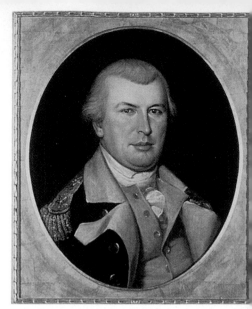

Nathanael Greene, the "Fighting Quaker" from Rhode Island, arrived in Charlotte, North Carolina on December 2, 1780, and took control of the Southern Army the next day. A man of exceptional acumen and ability, Greene devised a strategy of flexible defense which repeatedly frustrated the designs of the British to embolden the tories in the Carolinas and Virginia.

Colonel John Eager Howard and his Maryland Continentals fought in virtually every major engagement except Yorktown after coming south with Baron de Kalb in 1780. Howard's men contributed mightily to Daniel Morgan's victory over Banastre Tarleton at the Cowpens. Indeed, it was they who formed the core of the impenetrable third line on that fateful January morning.

Thaddeus Kosciuszko was a Polish patriot and expert military engineer who devised the classical siege operations which Nathanael Greene employed against John Harris Cruger at Ninety Six, South Carolina in May and June, 1781, until Greene learned that the British were bringing a relief expedition from Charleston.

William Washington fought tirelessly as a cavalry officer in the South. George Washington's cousin, he played the pivotal role in turning Tarleton's right flank at Cowpens in January, 1781. William Washington was wounded and captured at Eutaw Springs the following September.

The Marquis de Lafayette, the young Frenchman who gained great renown for his military exploits in America, was sent to Virginia in early 1781 but soon found himself outnumbered by the British under Charles Cornwallis. Keeping a watchful eye on the redcoats, Lafayette eventually participated in the campaign which culminated in Cornwallis's calamitous surrender at Yorktown on October 19th.

General Anthony Wayne arrived in Virginia in June, 1781, and joined with Lafayette in maneuvering against the more powerful Cornwallis. Always a venturesome fighter, Wayne attacked the British army at Greenspring Planation near Jamestown on July 9th and was sharply repulsed.

General Jean Baptiste de Rocohambeau brought his French army from Newport, Rhode Island and joined George Washington's troops on the Hudson in July, 1781. On August 19th, he set out with the Americans on the 400 mile march to Yorktown, Virginia, where they cooperated with the French fleet in trapping Cornwallis.

The fall of the British Redoubts on October 14, 1781, sealed Cornwallis's fate at Yorktown, Virginia and led to the surrender of his entire command on October 19, 1781.

This equestrian statue of General Nathanael Greene stands at Guilford Court House. The famous Rhode Islander faces southeast, waiting for Cornwallis and his Hessians and redcoats to arrive.

This historic highway marker, located amid gasoline stations and fast food restaurants, is the only reminder of the ghastly carnage that transpired nearby at "Pyle's Massacre."

1,530 troops in mid-January, which included a brigade of the guards commanded by Brigadier General Charles O'Hara and the German Regiment Bose, he possessed a force of about 2,400 British and hessian regulars. This force could easily have crushed Greene and Morgan, either singly or together, especially in view of the fact that many of Greene's militiamen were heading home because their six-month terms of service had ended.

Although Cornwallis's army had suffered severe losses at Cowpens, especially the elimination of a mobile force that could gather intelligence, protect the flanks of marching columns, and hunt down and destroy Whig partisans, the British earl remained steadfast in his determination to prevail. He was bent on destroying the Old Waggoner, freeing the 600 British prisoners Morgan had captured at Cowpens, and then overwhelming Greene. Admitting in a dispatch dated January 18 to Henry Clinton that Tarleton's defeat had been an "unexpected, & extraordinary event," Cornwallis went on to inform Clinton that he should "be assured, that nothing but the most absolute necessity shall induce me to give up the important object of the Winter's Campaign."[5]

Clearly, Nathanael Greene faced an awesome challenge in early 1781. The pace of the retrograde movement of his troops would be determined by the *slowest* elements in the American army, while the speed of Cornwallis's advance would be determined by the *fastest* components in the British army. Ultimately, the outcome of the so-called "Race to the Dan" would hinge upon whether Greene and Morgan could unite their armies and ferry their men across the principal rivers that lay astride their line of retreat before Cornwallis and the redcoats arrived on the same riverbanks in strength. The first crucial test would occur on the Catawba. Could Morgan get his army across that formidable stream before the British came upon its muddy shores?

Happily for the patriot cause, the Old Waggoner was able to reach the Catawba well ahead of the redcoats. He crossed at Sherrill's Ford about thirty miles northwest of Charlotte on January 22. Soon after the last Whig soldier reached the far shore, heavy rains began to fall which turned the already crude roads into squishy quagmires and raised the water level so high that it was impossible for Cornwallis, who arrived at Ramsour's Mill on January 23, to continue the chase for over a week. But Morgan did not benefit from this delay because his troops also had to stop. They were utterly exhausted and needed time to regain their strength before continuing. After all, the Old Waggoner had brought his men 100 miles in five days—a truly ferocious pace. Morgan used this respite to have his troops block Sherrill's Ford and nearby Beattie's Ford with felled trees.

Two factors were paramount in slowing Cornwallis's advance and per-
mitting Daniel Morgan to get across the Catawba. The first was impossible
for the earl to control. He was at a great disadvantage because he no longer
had a Ferguson or a Tarleton at full strength who could range far ahead of
his lines, search out the enemy, and provide intelligence about where his
opponents were headed. Lurching forward like a half-blind bull, the British
army had been able only to guess at Morgan's exact line of retreat. Assuming
that the Old Waggoner was marching toward Ninety Six or staying at
Cowpens, Cornwallis headed west on January 19, which allowed his quarry
to elude him and gain precious time before the mistake was discovered.

Cornwallis did have the power to eliminate the second major imped-
iment to the speed of his advance, and the redcoat general did not hesitate
to act while encamped at Ramsour's Mill. In direct violation of standard
European military practice, he directed that all his army's excess baggage,
including substantial supplies of rum, be destroyed by fire. "He ordered all
the army's wagons burned, beginning with his own," asserts Thomas E.
Baker in *Another Such Victory*. "Only those vehicles that carried salt, ammunition, or hospital stores were spared from the flames."[6] Having essentially transformed his entire army into a mobile or light force, Cornwallis
broke camp on January 27 and headed for the Catawba, which was eleven
miles away. The race to catch Morgan was on again.

Subsequent events were to demonstrate that Cornwallis had made a
critical mistake at Ramsour's Mill. Brigadier General Charles O'Hara of the
British army questioned the wisdom of the earl's decision to destroy vast
stores of his own supplies. The 41-year-old British officer explained:

> In this situation, without baggage, necessaries, or provisions of
> any sort for officer or soldier, in the most barren, inhospitable,
> unhealthy part of North America, opposed to the most savage,
> inveterate, perfidious, cruel enemy, with zeal and bayonets only,
> it was resolved to follow Greene's army to the end of the world.[7]

Henry Clinton, who had lost contact with Cornwallis and who had no
clear understanding for weeks as to how matters were progressing in North
Carolina, would also later criticize the earl for having taken this unconven-
tional step. Indeed, the British commander in chief went so far as to insist
that Cornwallis had subjected his troops to undue hardships and had greatly
weakened their effectiveness as a fighting force by stripping them of their
provisions. Clinton wrote:

> Nor can too much be said in commendation of the firm alacrity

with which the troops under him bore up against and surmounted difficulties not frequently the lot of a superior army—being often without provisions and ever without covering, or even rum, to comfort them under the hardships of a long fatiguing march through all the inclemencies of a cold and rainy winter.[8]

Don Higginbotham is more forgiving of Cornwallis, stating that the earl was "not hidebound by convention, and . . . differed from his fellow British generals, who seldom improvised."[9] Other scholars contend that the redcoat general was guilty of "dangerously risking the future efficiency of his army."[10] Pancake calls it a "a daring gamble."[11]

On balance, one wonders how Cornwallis could have rationally come to the conclusion that he could transform the essential nature of his army in the midst of a hazardous campaign and expect it to maintain battle effectiveness, much less envision that his men could gather enough provisions to sustain themselves as they marched through territory that was overwhelmingly inimical to the king. The redcoat general confounded all logic when he told his officers that they could look for Loyalists to have bounteous stores of supplies waiting for the British army when it occupied Hillsborough, his ultimate objective. On what reasonable basis could he make such a claim? Maybe during the previous summer, when the redcoats were winning battle after battle, Cornwallis could have expected large numbers of Tories to proclaim their allegiance to the king and assist the British army. But in January 1781, horrific visions of Kings Mountain and Cowpens were still too fresh in the minds of the Loyalists. They were not about to step forward in sufficient numbers to tip the balance in Cornwallis's favor.

It is difficult to avoid the conclusion that Charles Cornwallis had become a man possessed, a man motivated primarily by anger and not by prudent military judgment. "My situation is most critical," he confided to Francis Rawdon, whom he had left in charge of a 700-man garrison in Camden, South Carolina. "I see infinite danger in proceeding, but certain ruin in retreating. I am therefore determined to go on. . . ."[12]

The initial plan had been for the British army to function in the Carolinas rather like a plough. It would move carefully and systematically across the countryside, unearthing and nurturing wellsprings of support. At Ramsour's Mill, Cornwallis changed his army into something like a bowling ball. Potent and fast, it could knock over anything that stood in its way, but it had no capacity to penetrate below the surface, to affect the social and political landscape of the Carolinas. Greene himself called Cornwallis's strategy a "mad scheme of pushing through the country."[13] Learning that

Cornwallis had destroyed his supply wagons, Greene is reported to have proclaimed, "Then, he is ours!"[14] The redcoat general, like the vast majority of British officers who served in the American Revolution, never grasped the essential truth that destroying armies would yield nothing unless the king could win the sympathies of the rank-and-file population of the South.

Nathanael Greene, who had ridden with an aide and two cavalrymen through 120 miles of Tory-infested territory, arrived in Morgan's camp on January 30. On the same day, the waters of the Catawba receded enough to allow Cornwallis to begin making plans to cross the river. Unlike Morgan, who wanted to take his army into the Blue Ridge Mountains, the Fighting Quaker insisted that the troops should continue to retreat northeastward to Salisbury and across the Yadkin, where they would eventually unite with the other half of the American army, which was marching northward from Cheraw under the temporary command of Brigadier General Isaac Huger.

The ultimate compliment a military commander can receive is for his enemy to adopt his strategy. Cornwallis had done just that. The British army was a brittle institution, and it had no practice in fighting a guerrilla-like campaign that called upon the troops to sleep without tents or blankets and endure the hardships of war without being able to drink plenty of rum. As for Greene, he recognized that the farther he retreated, the more extended the British supply lines would become. The only hope for victory the redcoats retained was for the Tories to rally to the Royal standard in substantial numbers, or for the Fighting Quaker to blunder and allow his army to be caught before it could get across the Yadkin and Dan Rivers.

On January 31, as the waters of the Catawba continued to recede and scouts from Cornwallis's army began to appear on the opposite shore, Greene ordered the militia general William Lee Davidson to delay the British advance while Morgan and his army dashed for Salisbury and the Trading Ford on the Yadkin. Davidson, a 35-year-old former Indian fighter, had seen extensive service in the Continental army under General Washington in the North before returning to Rowan County, North Carolina in 1780. During the past several days he had been visiting the Scotch Irish settlements in the region to recruit troops, but had been disappointed by the number of men who had refused to take up arms because they feared retribution from the advancing British army, especially from Bloody Tarleton. After conferring with General Greene, Davidson dispatched troops to guard four crossings on the Catawba: Tool's Ford, Tuckaseegee Ford, Beattie's Ford, where he expected the major push to occur, and M'Cowan's Ford, a remote, Y-shaped crossing about four miles below Beattie's Ford. On the

afternoon of January 31, as he rode toward M'Cowan's Ford, Davidson told
Major Joseph Graham, his cavalry commander, "that though General Greene
had never seen the Catawba before, he appeared to know more about it than
those who were raised on it."[15]

About halfway across the river at M'Cowan's Ford, the more shallow
horse ford branched off to the right at about a forty-five degree angle and
reached the eastern bank of the Catawba several hundred yards below the
deeper wagon ford. Because the former was the more logical route for troops
to take, Davidson placed the majority of his infantry assigned to M'Cowan's
Ford at the edge of the river at this point and sent only about thirty pickets
to guard the spot upstream where the wagon ford left the Catawba. Among
them was Robert Henry, a 16-year-old who had already been wounded at
Kings Mountain. He and his cohorts, believing that there was virtually no
chance that Cornwallis and his redcoats would come their way, spent much
of the night eating potatoes and drinking whiskey. Davidson ordered Graham's calvary, some 300 farmers atop draft horses, to occupy a small knoll
several hundred yards back from the river so that they could protect the
militia's rear and move to the critical point of the British attack.

Coincidentally, Cornwallis did select M'Cowan's Ford as the site for
his initial crossing of the Catawba. Once gaining the far bank, these troops
were to protect the flank of the major body of redcoats, who would cross at
Beattie's Ford. Shortly before dawn on February 1, 1781, the British earl
rode out into the river and summoned his troops into the bitterly cold water.
At mid-stream, the Tory guide mistakenly led the redcoats to the left along
the wagon ford, which meant that they soon found themselves wading across
a rocky bottom though water almost up to their shoulders. With their
cartridge boxes tied around their necks and their muskets held high over
their heads, the British troops were incapable of firing their weapons until
they reached the shore on the eastern side of the river. Only the lingering
darkness and a heavy mist offered protection for Cornwallis's men.

Joel Jetton, a patriot militiaman, awoke suddenly when he heard the
whinnying of horses and the sloshing of water somewhere out on the river.
Grabbing his rifle, he ran to the edge of the water and peered into the misty
half-light of dawn. Almost unbelievably, coming straight at him were three
mounted British officers in resplendent scarlet and white uniforms—Cornwallis, Leslie, and O'Hara—and hundreds of redcoats. "The British! The
British!" Jetton yelled as he scurried up the bank and awoke his startled
compatriots.[16]

Dousing his face with water to gain his senses, Robert Henry took
position and began firing at the heads and arms sticking out of the river.

The teenager remarked that he "heard the British splashing and making a noise as if drowning."[17] The muddy Catawba began to turn red with British blood. Unable to stop the British because the redcoats possessed considerable superiority in numbers, the patriot militia began to give up the fight and run to the rear toward Salisbury. They moved so fast that they "made straight shirt tails," commented one observer.[18]

The gunfire caused General Davidson to rush to the wagon ford, where he began rallying the militia and organizing reinforcements. The British, who had now gained the shore in sufficient strength to deliver volleys, fired their muskets at the patriot militia. A musket ball penetrated Davidson's chest, killing him instantly. Thereafter, any semblance of resistance on the part of the militia evaporated, as young and old alike fled for their lives. The British officially claimed that they suffered three killed and thirty-six wounded at M'Cowan's Ford. The actual figures were probably considerably higher. Robert Henry stated, "A great number of the British dead were found on Thompson's fish dam, and in his trap, and numbers lodged on brush. . . . The river stunk with dead carcasses, the British could not have lost less than one hundred men."[19]

Davidson's ultimate sacrifice paid great dividends for Greene and Morgan. It gave the patriot army the critical head start it needed to reach the Yadkin at the Trading Ford, seven miles beyond Salisbury, and get across the river in boats before the first elements of the Cornwallis's army, commanded by Charles O'Hara, arrived there on the night of February 3. Frustrated because the river was out of its banks and because he had no boats to cross it, Cornwallis, who got to the Trading Ford on February 4, could do little more than fire an occasional artillery shell at Greene's camp, which he could clearly make out with an unaided eye on the opposite shore of the Yadkin.

Cornwallis had no choice but to persist in his efforts to catch Greene. On February 6, after the pelting rains had finally stopped and the water had receded, he marched his army twenty-five miles upstream and crossed the Yadkin at Shallow Ford on February 8. The redcoat general took his army in this northwesterly direction because he calculated that Greene would not have enough boats to ferry his entire army across the lower Dan River but would have to cross at one of the upper fords instead. By crossing at Shallow Ford, Cornwallis had a more direct route to the upper Dan. The earl stopped briefly at the Moravian settlement of Salem to acquire some bread and meal and then continued his march.

Meanwhile, Greene and Morgan broke camp and traveled northeastward forty-seven miles from the Trading Ford to Guilford Court House, where they reunited with Isaac Huger and the other half of the southern army on February 8, the same day that Cornwallis got across the Yadkin. Now having a force of about 2,000 men, the redoubtable Rhode Islander assembled his officers to discuss the prospect of remaining at Guilford Court House and doing battle with Cornwallis, who had roughly the same number of troops. Reckoning that the terrain was well-disposed for defensive operations, Greene sensed that the British army was becoming increasingly vulnerable, as its supply lines lengthened to over 200 miles and its soldiers became more and more exhausted. But the other participants in this meeting, Daniel Morgan, Isaac Huger, Light Horse Harry Lee, William Washington, Otho Williams, and John Eager Howard, adamantly insisted that the patriot army was still too weak to take on the British and that the retreat should continue. Only in Virginia could Greene obtain the rest, good food, and reinforcements that he and his troops so desperately needed.

In an attempt to trick Cornwallis into thinking that the American army was indeed headed for the upper Dan, Greene organized a screening force of approximately 700 men, including 350 cavalry under William Washington and Light Horse Harry Lee, and dispatched it westward to make contact with the main British army.

Not surprisingly, he offered the command of this diversionary group to Daniel Morgan. The Old Waggoner reluctantly declined, however, and explained that he could no longer remain in camp but must return to his home in Virginia because of ill health. What Cornwallis and Tarleton could not accomplish, sciatica and hemorrhoids had. Racked with pain and almost incapable of sitting in his saddle, Daniel Morgan, the great hero of Cowpens, left Guilford Court House on February 10. "Great generals are scarce—there are few Morgans to be found," said Nathanael Greene after the Old Waggoner had departed—a fitting tribute to an extraordinary tactician.[20]

Greene broke camp later the same day and began marching toward Irwin's Ferry on the Dan, which was seventy miles away. The weather was miserable. The troops trudged along as snow and freezing rain turned the ground into a sea of crusty mud. Meanwhile, the soldiers in the screening force, commanded by Otho Williams in Morgan's stead, stayed just out of Cornwallis's reach, but close enough to convince the redcoat general that they were the rear guard of the main American army. Washington and Lee nipped at the earl's heels, and then rode ahead to lure him onward. Finally, on February 12, Cornwallis realized that Greene had fooled him again, and he turned eastward toward the lower Dan.

Using boats-on-wheels that Quartermaster Carrington had brought to the site, Greene took the main army across the Dan at Irwin's Ferry on

February 13. Williams and his men followed the next day. Greene had won the "Race to the Dan." Cornwallis, having no boats and being unable to cross the river by foot, had no choice but to head for Hillsborough, "where I erected the King's Standard and invited by proclamation all loyal subjects to repair to it and to . . . take an active part in assisting me to restore order and consitutional government."[21]

Chapter Fourteen

Guilford Court House

Nathanael Greene could take solace from the fact that he had succeeded in extricating himself from the Carolinas with his army intact and had prevented Cornwallis from destroying the Continentals. "The army was evidently the object of the enemy, and while we can keep that together the country never can be conquered—disperse it, and the people are subjugated," wrote Lewis Morris, Jr., a Continental soldier serving under Greene.[1]

The Fighting Quaker took advantage of being north of the Dan to strengthen his body of troops, knowing he would have to march his army back into North Carolina in the very near future. Convinced more than ever that cavalry units were indispensable for screening his own movements and for finding out what the enemy was doing, he obtained fresh mounts for his horse soldiers. "The consequence was, the British dragoons were mounted upon small weak horses: those of the Legion on stout, active horses," reported Light Horse Harry Lee.[2] Hundreds of recruits, including 400 riflemen under Colonel William Campbell of Kings Mountain fame, and 700 militia led by General Edward Stevens, whose Virginians had fled at Camden and who were now eager to redeem themselves, joined Greene at his headquarters at Halifax Court House. Supplies and even some new uniforms were distributed to the men.

The arrival of these reinforcements notwithstanding, Greene understood that the support of the backcountry Carolinians for the patriot cause was not absolute. Repeatedly during his recent retreat he had been disappointed by the refusal of many residents to take up arms and join his endangered army. "The militia in Carolina gave us no assistance," claimed Lewis Morris, Jr. "They were more intent upon saving their property by flight than by embodying to protect it."[3]

Greene was also harsh in his assessment of the minimal role the militia had played during the hazardous campaign he had just completed in North Carolina. In a letter to Joseph Reed of Pennsylvania, he stated,

Our force was so small and Lord Cornwallis's movements so rapid that we got no reinforcements of militia, and therefore were obliged to retire out of State, upon which the spirits of the people sunk, and almost all classes of the inhabitants gave themselves up for lost. They would not believe themselves in danger until they found ruin at their doors. The foolish prejudice of the formidableness of the militia being a sufficient barrier against any attempts of the enemy prevented the Legislature from making any exertions equal to their critical and dangerous situation. Experience has convinced them of their false security.

It is astonishing to me how these people could place such a confidence in a militia scattered over the face of the whole earth, and generally destitute of everything necessary for their defence. The militia in the back country are formidable, the others are not, and all are ungovernable and difficult to keep together. As they generally come out, twenty thousand might be in motion, and not five hundred in the field.[4]

The Fighting Quaker became especially disturbed when he learned that droves of hitherto covert Tories began to join Cornwallis in Hillsborough: ". . . the people began to flock to it from all quarters, either for protection or to engage in their service," Greene lamented.[5] The earl, pleased by the response he was obtaining to his summons, noted in a dispatch to Germain that "many hundred inhabitants of the surrounding districts rode into the British camp, to inquire . . . the news of the day and take a view of the King's troops."[6] This level of support, even in the area between the Deep and Haw Rivers, which was known to be a hotbed of Loyalism, was surprising because the redcoats had not hesitated to plunder friend and foe alike as they had marched through the Carolina countryside.

Even the peaceful Moravians had suffered at the hands of stragglers from the Royal army. "The British found the Moravians mild and inoffensive folk," says Pancake. "But as the army moved on, its backwash of camp followers looted the village."[7] "The war had created lawless bands of brutal men who roamed regions disrupted by the armies and used the conflict as a cover to steal, destroy, and kill," adds another scholar.[8] This cutthroat behavior persisted in and around Hillsborough, which prompted Cornwallis to have the following notice posted in the town:

It is with great concern that Lord Cornwallis hears every day reports of the soldiers being taken by the enemy, in consequence of their straggling out of camp in search of whiskey. He strictly enjoins all officers and non-commissioned officers commanding the outposts and pickets of the army to do their utmost to prevent any soldier from passing them.[9]

On February 18, Greene sent the first patriot troops back across the Dan and into the Carolina piedmont. Made up of Lee's Legion of mounted infantry and cavalry, two companies of Maryland Continentals, plus a regiment of South Carolina militia, all under the command of Andrew Pickens, this force was to gather intelligence and, even more importantly, discourage Tories from gathering and marching toward Cornwallis's camp in Hillsborough. It was in performing this latter function that Light Horse Harry Lee and his legion were to perpetrate an act of wanton violence which has gone down in history as "Pyle's Hacking Match."

Admittedly, the disheartenment of Loyalists was vitally important to Greene's overall plan for defeating the British. "Lieuteunant Colonel Lee's falling in with the Tories upon the Haw almost put a total stop to their recruiting service," the Fighting Quaker proclaimed.[10] Perhaps, but what happened on February 25 about two miles west of the modern town of Graham, North Carolina exceeded the bounds of civilized behavior, even within the context of the savage civil war that was raging throughout the Carolina backcountry. Inevitably, certain events in history underscore the outrageous cruelty of war; one such event occurred on February 25, 1781, at "Pyle's Hacking Match."

Dr. John Pyle, a Tory militia colonel who lived in the country east of the Haw River, had raised a force of 300 to 400 of his neighbors, mostly young men and teenagers, and set out for Cornwallis's headquarters in Hillsborough. Caught up in the youthful euphoria of going to war, these lads, many of whom were surfeited with rum and other intoxicants, lustily sang and joked with one another as they marched through the dense forests and crossed the fast-running streams of the piedmont. Knowing that Cornwallis had sent Banastre Tarleton to escort them into camp, Pyle and his compatriots were on the lookout for the famous green-jacketed dragoons. Light Horse Harry Lee and his legion, who also wore green jackets, happened to be in the neighborhood. Two Tories spotted Lee's men and mistakenly believed that they were Tarleton's. The pair told Light Horse Harry where Pyle was and rode off to tell the good doctor that Tarleton was coming.

No doubt in awe at the prospect of meeting Cornwallis's illustrious cavalry commander, Pyle and his band of backwoodsmen spiffed up their "uniforms" and stood at attention in a long, straight row beside the road with rifles on their shoulders to welcome the "friends of the king." Looming over them on horseback come the patriots, riding slowing along with eyes fixed on the young Loyalists and with sabers in their hands.

Without warning, Lee's Legion pounced upon the unsuspecting Loyalists. The patriot dragoons slaughtered their fellow Americans with sabers, bayonets, and rifles fired at point-blank range. Screams of agony and consternation filled the wintry air. The results tell the tale. This was no "match." It was a one-sided bloodbath. It was an execution. Light Horse Harry Lee, who lost not a single man in this grotesque incident, was ultimately responsible for killing upwards of 100 Tories and wounding and maiming about 200 others.

In later years, Lee would claim that he only intended to disband Pyle's Tories and that the ghastly results of his ruse were unintentional and transpired because some of the Tories finally realized their mistake and opened fire. The evidence suggests otherwise. "Colonel Lee knew what he was about," stated one Whig militiaman.[11]

Historian Christopher Ward contends that "the bloody results of the attack are, in themselves, sufficient proof of its relentless ferocity."[12] Tory Charles Stedman condemned Lee, saying that "humanity shudders at the recital of so foul a massacre."[13] Unlike the backwoodsmen who had committed atrocities atop Kings Mountain the previous October, Lee's cavalry were among the best trained troops in Greene's army. The war in the South had sunk to new levels of savagery.

Cornwallis's situation was becoming increasingly perilous. He was starting to feel the full impact of his rash decision to destroy and discard supplies at Ramsour's Mill. Contrary to his expectations, there was precious little food available in and around Hillsborough as the patriots had almost picked the place clean. This circumstance compelled the redcoats to resort to the locally unpopular practice of slaughtering farm animals, including some belonging to Loyalists.

Unable to procure sufficient supplies to sustain his troops and learning that Greene had brought the remainder of his army across the Dan the day before, the earl marched out of Hillsborough on February 25 and ordered his men to forage in the countryside. One British soldier described in decidedly unenthusiastic terms the diet that he and his compatriots were compelled to eat:

> Sometimes we had turnips served out for food when we came to
> a turnip field; or arriving at a field of corn, we converted our
> canteens into rasps and ground our Indian corn for bread; when

we could get no Indian corn, we were compelled to eat liver as a substitute for bread, with our lean beef.[14]

British soldiers were not trained to live under such harsh conditions. Inadequately fed, sleeping outdoors in the cold with no cover other than a single blanket, forced to march over twenty miles daily for weeks on end, obtaining practically no assistance from the Loyalists, and harassed and hounded by the patriot dragoons, the redcoats began to get sick in alarming numbers. In February alone, Cornwallis lost 227 men due to illness or as a result of casualties suffered in combat. The earl understood that there was little prospect that these soldiers would be replaced by reinforcements. (In another tragic instance of mistaken identity a few days after "Pyle's Hacking Match," Tarleton attacked and severely crippled a group of about seventy Rowan County Tories, who were also headed for Cornwallis's camp. Such incidents robbed the British of any hope that the Loyalists would come forward in significant numbers.)

Meanwhile, the overall strength of the earl's army had dwindled to about 2,200 men. Cornwallis recognized that his troops, who were approaching the limits of even their legendary endurance, would soon have to head for the coast, where they could be protected by the Royal navy and could obtain adequate provisions. Clearly, if the redcoat general was going to succeed in destroying Greene's elusive army and thereby encouraging the local citizenry to stand up for the king, he had to find the Fighting Quaker and attack him soon. In short, time was fast running out for the British. The window of opportunity in the Carolina hinterland was about to close.

"When both parties are agreed in a matter, all obstacles are soon removed," Greene wrote to General Washington.[15] Ever since his first visit to Guilford Court House, Nathanael Greene had been flirting with the idea of doing battle with Cornwallis. Like a skillful boxer who knows when to deliver a punishing body blow, the Fighting Quaker recognized that a decisive defeat would compel the redcoat general to abandon the piedmont, thereby dousing any enthusiasm that might persist among the Loyalists as well as jeopardizing such backcountry strongholds as Camden and Ninety Six.

Until March 11, however, when he received a large number of reinforcements to replace Pickens's South Carolinians, who had left for home because their terms of service were up, Greene persisted in avoiding large scale combat with the British. "It was certain I could not fight him in a general action without almost certain ruin," the Rhode Islander told Joseph Reed.[16] Thus the patriots continued their strategy of launching hit-and-run

raids upon isolated elements of Cornwallis's army. That is why, when Cornwallis attacked at dawn on March 6 and attempted to trap Otho Williams
at Wetzell's Mill near the Haw River, Greene ordered his army to retreat
westward rather than submit to a general engagement with the enemy.

Matters underwent a momentous change during the second week of
March. Greene's acquisition on March 11 of 1,000 Virginia militia commanded by Robert Lawson, 1,000 North Carolina militia under Generals
John Butler and Thomas Eaton, and 530 Virginia Continentals tipped the
balance of power for the first time decisively in the patriot's favor. The
Fighting Quaker now had 4,400 men to Cornwallis's 2,200-a ratio of two
to one. Clearly, the most opportune moment to meet the earl head-on in
combat had arrived. "Our force being now much more considerable than it
had been and upon a more permanent footing, I took the determination of
giving the enemy battle without loss of time and made the necessary dis-
positions accordingly," Greene later explained.[17]

On the afternoon of March 14, the patriot army arrived at Guilford
Court House, and the Fighting Quaker began making preparations to assault
Cornwallis's camp the next morning. The earl was bivouacked twelve miles
southwest at the Deep River Friends Meeting House.

At first light on the morning of March 15, 1781, with frost still
blanketing the forest floor, the British army marched up the New Garden
Road directly toward Greene's camp. Learning the day before that the Fighting Quaker was at Guilford Court House, Cornwallis seized the initiative
and decided to attack first. Soon the sounds of drums and fifes would an-
nounce that death was at hand. Ironically, the two and one-half hour engagement at Guilford Court House was to occur in a region where members
of the Society of Friends predominated. No doubt many of these peaceful
Quakers were aghast at the prospect that one of their own was about to
send young men into the carnage of bloody conflict on that beautiful Spring
day.

The landscape at Guilford Court House was well suited for defensive
operations. The New Garden Road, the main route from Salisbury to Hillsborough, crossed a small stream, named Little Horsepen Creek, about a mile
and a half west of the courthouse and then rose in a gradual slope as it
bisected the battlefield. The first 800 yards or so east of the creek were
largely made up of open fields, principally planted in corn. Thereafter, except for a cleared area around the courthouse itself, the slope was heavily
wooded, which meant that the redcoats would be unable to maintain a solid
line while advancing en masse with bayonets. Rough terrain protected the
patriot army's flanks.

Knowing that the earl had attacked at dawn at places like Camden, M'Cowan's Ford, and Wetzell's Mill, Greene ordered Light Horse Harry Lee to take his legion and about 100 Virginia riflemen a few miles down the New Garden Road in the middle of the night to keep an eye out for any untoward developments. Lee, in turn, sent a small contingent of cavalry under Lieutenant James Heard to the vicinity of Cornwallis's camp "to report from time to time such occurences as might happen."[18]

About 4:00 A.M., Heard reported that he could detect the rumbling of a large number of wagon wheels, which suggested that the entire redcoat army was on the move. When Greene received this same report some time later, he woke his men and instructed them to "take breakfast as quickly as possible."[19]

Nathanael Greene, never an adroit tactician, followed Daniel Morgan's advice in deploying his troops for battle. "If the militia fights," the "Old Waggoner" had written in a recent letter, "you will beat Cornwallis; if not, he will beat you, and perhaps cut your regulars to pieces."[20] With an army twice as large as Cornwallis's but consisting of approximately 1,600 Continentals and 2,800 militia, the Fighting Quaker knew that Morgan's assessment of the situation was fundamentally sound. The irregulars had to be willing to resist the British thrust.

Just as the "Old Waggoner" had done at Cowpens, Greene placed his least seasoned troops, the 1,000 North Carolina militia under Butler and Eaton, at his most exposed position. He ordered them to occupy a fence line some 400 yards uphill from the woods just east of Little Horsepen Creek. The fence ran along the edge of a corn field but, being early in the growing season, the corn was newly planted and would afford no cover for the British. From this vantage point, the Tar Heel militiamen, steadying their firearms on the top fence rail, would have a clear shot at the redcoats as they came forward. Solid woods began just to the rear of the patriots' location.

The skirmish line of North Carolinians, most of whom had never seen battle, extended into the woods on both sides and bent slightly forward, so the militia stationed there could shoot into the enemy's flanks. Protecting the flanks of the patriots who occupied this most forward position on the battlefield were riflemen and dragoons, with those on the right commanded by William Washington.

Some 300 yards east of the first line of defenders, in the midst of the dense woods, were two brigades of Virginia militia, approximately 1,200 men in all. General Robert Lawson's troops were south of the New Garden Road. General Edward Stevens, whose men had performed so badly at Camden, stood with his brigade on the north side of the road. Determined that his militiamen would stand and fight this time, Stevens placed marksmen behind his troops and gave them instructions to kill anyone who broke and ran. In doing so, he was following the instructions of Daniel Morgan, who, commenting upon the reliability of irregulars, had advised Greene to put some "picked troops in their rear with orders to shoot down the first man that runs."[21]

Finally, a little over 500 yards east of the second line, standing on the face of a hillside just west of the courthouse and north of the New Garden Road, were the best troops in Greene's army, his 1,400 Maryland, Delaware, and Virginia Continentals. To the immediate front of these seasoned soldiers, who would be the last to feel the brunt of the British attack, was a gully, a natural amphitheater, which extended about 1,000 yards north to south and 250 yards east and west. Covered with broom sedge and occasional scrub pines, this ravine would be the place where the climatic moments of the engagement would occur. The Continentals who fought at Guilford Court House included Colonel Benjamin Ford's Second Maryland Regiment on the patriot left, Colonel John Gunby's First Maryland Regiment in the center, and the Virginia regiments of Lieutenant Colonel Samuel Hawes and Colonel John Green on the right.

Again taking his lead from Morgan, Greene carefully instructed the militia, especially the untested North Carolinians, on what they were expected to do. "Three rounds, my boys, and then you may fall back," the Fighting Quaker shouted.[22] Light Horse Harry Lee, who occupied the left flank of the first line after he had skirmished with Tarleton's Legion in the late morning as Cornwallis was advancing his army toward Little Horsepen Creek, "rode along the front line from one end to the other, exhorting them to stand firm and not be afraid of the British."[23]

At mid-day, the North Carolinians began to hear the beat of the redcoat drums down the New Garden Road somewhere beyond the distant tree line. The young soldiers, armed with an odd assortment of muskets, rifles, and fowling pieces, were understandably jumpy. Little more than farmers, they were about to come up against some of the finest professional soldiers in the world. "It is scarcely possible to paint the agitations of my mind," wrote Major Richard Harrison to his wife.[24]

It was around noon when the leading elements of the British army arrived at the edge of the woods and looked across the corn field at Butler's and Eaton's men squatting behind the fence on the far side. Lord Cornwallis had little knowledge of the topography at Guilford Court House and was generally ignorant of the exact disposition of the patriot army. Only the middle portion of the enemy's first line was out in the open where the redcoat general could see it. He knew that Greene outnumbered him, but Cornwallis anticipated that his splendid troops would be able to carry the day. Similar to what he had done the previous August at Camden, the earl decided to concentrate his attack on the patriot left. No doubt flashing through his imagination were visions of how the patriot militia had failed to put up any kind of fight at Camden, of how de Kalb and his Continentals had been surrounded and pummeled, and of how Tarleton had ridden up the road toward the Waxhaws, slashing and mutilating the remnants of Gates's army. Cornwallis may have thought that achieving the same results against Greene would make King George the indisputable master of the Carolinas.

The Battle of Guilford Court House opened with a thirty minute long artillery duel. The American 6-pounders and the British 3-pounders hurled cannon balls enshrouded in sulfurous smoke through the afternoon air. The thunderous clamor of the guns and the screeching of the shells as they shattered and splintered tree limbs served as a suitable overture for the main event. Using the forests to conceal his movements, Cornwallis began to organize his troops for a massive, frontal assault against the rebel militiamen who were waiting behind the fence on the other side of the corn field.

On the British right were the blue-coated hessians and Lieutenant Colonel Duncan McPherson's Scottish Highlanders of the Seventy-first Regiment of Foot, all under the command of Major General Alexander Leslie. On the north side of the New Garden Road were the Twenty-third and Thirty-third Regiments of Foot headed by Lieutenant Colonel James Webster, who would die from the wounds he would suffer this day. The British reserve consisted of 250 men of the Second Battalion of Guards under Charles O'Hara, plus Tarleton's dragoons.

Even before the attack began, the American sharpshooters took careful aim with their long rifles and fired upon the British officers who were milling about at the edge of the woods some 400 yards downhill from the patriot position. Cornwallis surveyed his splendid troops, who stood poised in two solid lines that stretched for about 1,000 yards along the western edge of the corn field. He ordered the drums and the fifes to set the pace and instructed his officers to unfurl their regimental banners.

The order to advance was given. It was just after 1:00 P.M. Charles Stedman stated that the British and the hessians "moved forward with that steady and guarded but firm and determined resolution which discipline alone can confer."[25] Slogging slightly uphill over the muddy terrain, with tender shoots of corn sticking a few inches out of the ground, Cornwallis's men had no cover whatsoever for upwards of 400 yards.

The patriot riflemen continued to fire with great effect. One British officer, a Captain Maynard, was hit in the leg and was unable to continue walking. He was in the act of mounting a horse which he had borrowed "when . . . another shot went through his lungs."[26] As soldiers in the first row crumpled into the mud, replacements from the second row filled in the gap. Meanwhile, the main body of Eaton's and Butler's North Carolinians were told to hold their fire until the enemy came into range. Greene, who was stationed far to the rear near the courthouse with the Continentals, would have been relieved to know that the irregulars did not throw down their weapons and run.

The redcoats, shouting and grunting as they moved forward, hesitated about forty yards from the eastern edge of the corn field when they saw hundreds of firearms resting on the fence rail, pointed straight at them. It was an extraordinary moment. Captain Roger Lamb, a member of the Royal Welsh Fusiliers, described what transpired:

> The colonel rode on to the front and gave the word 'Charge!' Instantly the movement was made in excellent order in a smart run. . . . When arrived within forty yards of the enemy's line, it was perceived that their whole force had their arms . . . resting on a rail fence. . . . At this awful period a general pause took place. Both parties surveyed each other for the moment with the most anxious suspense. . . . Colonel Webster rode forward . . . and said . . . 'Come on my brave Fusiliers!' This acted like an inspiring voice. They rushed forward amidst the enemy's fire. Dreadful was the havoc on both sides.[27]

First the Americans and then the British let loose with thunderous volleys. Great clouds of black smoke rose into the air as the redcoats and the hessians fixed bayonets and prepared to assault the militia who were feverishly laboring to reload their weapons. Bullets from the second patriot fusillade ripped into the Royal army. "One half of the Highlanders dropped on that spot," reported Captain Dugald Stuart of the Seventy-first Regiment.[28] William Montgomery, looking out at the corn field from behind the American position, said that the British dead and wounded resembled "the scattering stalks in a wheat field, when the harvest man has passed over it with his cradle."[29]

The North Carolinians had done their job. After firing three volleys and seeing that the British and the hessians were about to reach the fence with their bayonets, the Tar Heel irregulars began to scamper into the woods toward the Virginians. "The enemy did not wait the shock, but retreated behind the second line," said Stedman.[30] The losses he had sustained while crossing the corn field compelled Cornwallis to commit his reserves to the fight before moving into the woods to attack Lawson's and Stevens's militiamen. As the first line gave way, the American left under Light Horse Harry Lee veered off to the southeast and was closely pursued by the hessians and the First Battalion of Guards. For the remainder of the battle, these troops fought an engagement which was totally detached from the others. William Washington, whose dragoons were on the American right, retreated into the woods and scrimmaged alongside the Virginians, who comprised Greene's second line of defense.

Cornwallis did not wait to regroup before dispatching his soldiers into the thick forest to press their advantage, but the British army could no longer maintain the discipline and order of an orchestrated advance. Small clusters of redcoats stumbled through the woods, searching for enemy troops and endeavoring to kill them.

The British were to learn that this was to be no repetition of the easy victory they had won in the pine forests outside Camden. The militia, many of whom hid behind trees and underbrush and fought like Indians, clung tenaciously to their positions. "Posted in the woods and covering themselves with trees," Stedman explained, "they kept up for a considerable time a galling fire which did great execution."[31] The struggle in the woods with the Virginians became so intense, Tarleton stated in his account of the battle, that "at this period the event of the action was doubtful, and victory alternately presided over each army."[32]

No sooner would the British defeat one group of defenders than "they found it necessary to return and attack another body of them that had appeared in their rear," Charles Stedman explained.[33] Stevens was wounded in the thigh and had to be carried from the battlefield. Cornwallis had his horse shot out from under him as he personally led his troops against the Virginians. Charles O'Hara was critically injured and had to relinquish command of his forces to Lieutenant Colonel James Stuart. Ultimately, the British bayonet carried the day. The second line of militia began to emulate the North Carolinians in abandoning their positions and fleeing to the rear. But Edward Stevens, whose leg was being dressed and bandaged at a field hospital near the courthouse, could take extreme pride in the performance of his Virginians. "The brigade behaved with the greatest bravery, and stood till I ordered their retreat," he later declared.[34]

Greene and the Continentals waited expectantly throughout the ferocious fighting that was occurring at the edge of the corn field and in the woods between it and the courthouse. The popping sound of musket fire came closer and closer. Finally, Virginia militiamen began to emerge from the forest and run across the open ravine to get away from the redcoats. William Washington's cavalry came upon the scene and rode to the top of a hill at the south end of the clearing.

The first contingents of the British army to break out of the woods and enter the ravine just west of the courthouse were Webster's men. Without waiting for other elements of Cornwallis's army to arrive, Lieutenant Colonel Webster foolishly threw his troops against the American right. The Continentals bided their time until the British were within twenty yards, and then let loose a crushing volley. His knee shattered, Webster came to realize that he was greatly outnumbered. Limping and crawling all the way, the chastened lieutenant colonel led his men back into the forest. He would never recover from his crippling wounds.

Gradually, more and more elements of the British army appeared at the edge of the woods opposite the courthouse. The Second Battalion of Guards under Stuart arrived and attacked the Second Maryland Regiment on the American left, which surprisingly offered little resistance and began to give way. This initial advantage, however, almost turned into a catastrophe for the British. Gunby's First Marylanders, who were on Stuart's immediate left, launched a vigorous assault against the left flank of the advancing redcoats. The two combatants "appeared so near that the blazzes from the muzzles of their guns seemed to meet," commented one observer.[35]

At about the same time, Washington's dragoons fell upon Stuart's right flank, thereby achieving a double envelope much like that which had turned the tide at Cowpens two months before. Riding fast as they swung their sabers, the patriot cavalry hacked the unsuspecting redcoats to pieces. Vicious hand-to-hand fighting was occurring throughout the ravine—an orgy of shooting, clubbing and stabbing performed in a natural amphitheater. Lieutenant Colonel Stuart was among the many who were killed in this merciless melee. It was a slaughter pen.

Cornwallis recognized that he must take bold action to rescue the situation, but even his loyal officers were amazed by what the earl decided to do. He ordered his artillerymen to load their cannon with grape shot and fire directly at the boiling mass of humanity that lay before them. Obviously knowing that many of his own troops would be killed and gruesomely hurt, Cornwallis nonetheless watched dispassionately as soldiers on both sides reeled under a massive shower of shrapnel. Stunned, the First Maryland and Washington's dragoons staggered about as the survivors from Stuart's

Guards returned to the British lines. Meanwhile, additional elements of Cornwallis's army were coming to the edge of the woods after finally overwhelming Stevens's Virginians. Seeing that the tide of battle was swinging in the earl's favor and not wanting to risk a fight to the finish, Nathanael Greene instructed his army to disengage and begin an orderly retreat toward the Dan. It was about 3:30 P.M.

Technically, the Battle of Guilford Court House was a British victory. Cornwallis captured Greene's artillery pieces and took control of the battlefield. "On the whole . . . the laurels for military achievement must be awarded to the British," Christopher Ward insists.[36] But the American army was still intact, and the earl had suffered enormous casualties. Of the 1,924 British and hessian soldiers of all ranks who had fought at Guilford Court House, 93 were killed, 413 were wounded, and 26 were missing—a staggering 27% of the British army.

Almost completely out of food, still forced to sleep unprotected from the elements, and possessing only meager medical supplies, the redcoats spent a gloomy night in the clearing around the courthouse on March 15. Charles Stedman described what it was like:

> The night was remarkable for its darkness, accompanied with rain which fell in torrents. Near fifty of the wounded, it is said, sinking under their aggravated miseries, expired before the morning. The crys of the wounded and dying, who remained on the field of action during the night exceeded all description. Such a complicated scene of horror and distress, it is hoped, for the sake of humanity, rarely occurs, even in a military life.[37]

"Greene had damaged Cornwallis so severely that the British command was no longer capable of acting offensively," asserts John Pancake.[38] "If ever a general won a Phyrric victory," writes Don Higginbotham, "it was Lord Cornwallis, whose army virtually ceased to exist as a fighting force."[39] Nathanael Greene, whose performance at Guilford Court House has been criticized, especially his spacing of the militia lines too far apart and his undue cautiousness at the end, understood that he had greatly weakened his adversary. Writing on March 18, the Fighting Quaker stated:

> I have never felt an easy moment since the enemy crossed the Catawba until since the defeat of the 15th, but now I am perfectly easy, being persuaded it is out of the enemy's power to do us any great injury. Indeed, I think they will retire as soon as they can get off their wounded.[40]

Greene's assessment of the situation was accurate.

Chapter Fifteen

Greene Returns To South Carolina

On March 18, leaving some of his most critically wounded behind, Charles Cornwallis led his weakened and exhausted army out of Guilford Court House and headed for Cross Creek on the Cape Fear River. There he hoped to find supplies that Colonel Nisbet Balfour, the commander of the British garrison in Wilmington, North Carolina, had supposedly shipped inland. "This whole Country is so totally destitute of subsistence, that forage is not nearer than nine miles, and the Soldiers have been two days without bread," the redcoat general complained.[1]

As Cornwallis marched toward the coast, he could not help but notice the absence of any meaningful support from the Loyalists. George Germain's strategy of sending British soldiers into the Southern hinterland to induce hordes of Tories to gather under the Royal standard was in shambles, as was Cornwallis's military reputation. With the exception of Tarleton's blunder at Cowpens, the redcoats had won every major battle since marching out of Charleston the summer before. "British victories in the field had meant nothing in the face of the American's clever maneuvering and the stubborn resistance of the partisans," says John Pancake.[2]

Nathanael Greene pursued the redcoat general and his tattered troops as far as Ramsey's Mill on the Deep River. There the Fighting Quaker ordered Light Horse Harry Lee to maintain contact with the earl, while Greene turned the main patriot army of some 1,500 men southward. "I am determined to carry the war immediately into South Carolina," the Fighting Quaker told General Washington in a dispatch dated March 29.[3] Although the British had some 8,000 soldiers in South Carolina, they were vulnerable because they were mostly Tories, principally from the North, who were widely scattered in isolated outposts stretching from Georgetown on the coast to Augusta, Georgia on the Savannah River.

Fundamental to Greene's plan for the conquest of South Carolina was for the partisans, especially Pickens, Sumter, and Marion, to interdict the routes by which supplies and reinforcements traveled to the enemy garrisons.

Like any army of occupation, the British had to haul provisions overland through unfriendly territory, but this already difficult task was becoming even more arduous since local support for the king had diminished to a modicum in the Carolinas by 1781. One scholar writes, "There were so few committed Loyalists and so many committed rebels; there were also so many rivers to obstruct the passage of an army; above all, it was virtually impossible to find adequate provisions and forage in that inhospitable land."[4]

After Cornwallis had arrived in Wilmington on April 7, Greene summoned Lee to rejoin him. Greene ordered the famous calvary officer to find the Swamp Fox so that together Light Horse Harry and Marion could make trouble for Colonel Francis Lord Rawdon, the 26-year-old officer who had assumed command of British forces in South Carolina. "These military friends," Lee wrote, "very cordially rejoiced at being again united in the great attempt of wrestling South Carolina from the enemy."[5]

On April 23, Lee and Marion attacked and overran Fort Watson, a small stockade located 60 miles northwest of Charleston on the Santee River. "The commandant, finding every resource cut off, hung out the white flag," Lee proclaimed.[6]

The first major battle in Greene's campaign to retake South Carolina occurred on April 25 at Hobkirk's Hill, a small, sandy promontory about a mile and a half north of Camden. Rawdon, who had a garrison of some 900 men in the town, clashed with Greene's army of about 1,200.

The Fighting Quaker thought that Thomas Sumter was about to join him, but the Carolina Gamecock, much to Greene's chagrin, persisted in pursuing his own objectives. "Sumter refuses to obey my orders, and carries off with him all the active force of this unhappy State on rambling, predatory excursions, unconnected with the operations of the army," the exasperated patriot general complained.[7] It was experiences such as this that caused the Fighting Quaker to be so harsh in his judgment of militia.

The Battle of Hobkirk's Hill demonstrated again that Nathanael Greene did not excel as a tactician. Indeed, the patriot general was caught completely off guard by a humiliating, surprise bayonet attack. Believing that he must either inflict a crippling defeat upon the Fighting Quaker or abandon his post and fall back toward Charleston, Rawdon made the bold decision to strike at the larger American army encamped on Hobkirk's Hill. Unfortunately for the patriots, they were busily consuming "a comfortable supply of provisions" when the redcoats and Tories fell upon them in the late morning.[8] "General Huger told me that . . . a number of officers with himself were washing their feet, and a number of soldiers were washing their kettles in a small rivulet that run by their camp, when their picket was engaged with the enemy," William Moultrie reported.[9]

Seeking to turn both of Rawdon's flanks, Greene was surprised to learn that John Gunby's First Maryland Regiment, which had performed so magnificently at Guilford Court House, became disorganized during the counterattack and gave way to the enemy, thereby placing Greene's center in jeopardy. "Previously being ordered not to fire and now ordered to halt," said William R. Davie, "while the British were coming up with charged bayonets, before the colonel could be understood and repeat the charge, the enemy was among them and made them give way."[10]

Greene had no choice but to order his army to withdraw. He retreated two or three miles to the north, almost to the exact spot where Cornwallis and Gates had fought the previous August. Rawdon occupied Hobkirk's Hill and was technically correct in claiming victory, but the British had paid a heavy price. "The victory was indisputably Rawdon's, but like Cornwallis's at Guilford, it was a victory too expensively bought," says Christopher Hibbert in *Redcoats and Rebels.*[11] Rawdon had suffered 258 casualties, including 38 killed.

Just two days later, on April 27, the young redcoat colonel was forced to begin to evacuate Camden and retreat to Monck's Corner, only thirty miles from Charleston, because he lacked sufficient strength to protect his lines of communication with the coast. Rawdon "burned the gaol, mills and many private houses . . . and retired with his army to the south side of the Santee River . . . by which movement he gave up . . . a large extent of country," stated William Moultrie, who was still a prisoner of the British in Charleston.[12]

It was a sad day for the king's fortunes in the Carolina backcountry. Marching dejectedly with the British were the Tories who had fought alongside the redcoats at Hobkirk's Hill "together with the Wives, Children, Negroes and Baggage of almost all of them."[13]

It meant nothing for the British to win battles like Hobkirk's Hill if they could not control the countryside through which their reinforcements and supplies had to come. "The genius of Nathanael Greene lay in the fact that his strategic objectives relied less on good fortune than on planning that could be adapted to any contingency," John Pancake asserts.[14] Said Nathanael Greene, "There are few generals that has run oftener, or more lustily than I have done. But I have taken care not to run too far, and commonly have run as fast forward as backward, to convince our Enemy that we are like a Crab, that could run either way."[15]

Over the next several weeks, as the heat and humidity of summer began to return to the Carolinas, the patriots picked off redcoat outposts like so many peaches hanging on a tree. The Tory garrison at Orangeburg, South Carolina surrendered to Thomas Sumter on May 11. Lee and Marion captured Fort Motte, a supply depot near the confluence of the Wateree and the Congaree, on May 12. The resourceful pair of patriot commanders used flaming arrows to burn down the house in which the defenders were ensconced. "The . . . house was a large, pleasant edifice intended for the summer residence of the respectable owner. . . . Nevertheless the obligations of duty were imperative," Lee explained.[16] On May 15, Fort Granby at present-day Columbia fell, and the Swamp Fox took control of Georgetown on May 23.

After several days of heavy fighting, Thomas Brown, whose Florida Rangers had been terrorizing the backcountry for years and who now commanded the Loyalists at Augusta, capitulated to Lee and Pickens on June 4. According to Light Horse Harry Lee, a woman asked to speak to the notorious Tory and said to him,

> Colonel Brown, in the late day of your prosperity I visited your camp and on my knees supplicated for the life of my son, but you were deaf to my intreaties. You hanged him, though a beardless youth, before my face. These eyes have seen him scalped by the savages under your immediate command, and for no better reason than that his name was M'Koy. As you are now a prisoner . . . for the present I lay aside all thoughts of revenge; but when you resume your sword I will go five hundred miles to demand satisfaction at the point of it for the murder of my son.[17]

Such were the emotions engendered in the South during the American Revolution. Brown, who had never forgiven the Whigs for his "toe roasting" episode, was taken to Savannah and paroled to the British.

Even Light Horse Harry Lee, the perpetrator of "Pyle's Hacking Match," was appalled by the level of violence that continued in the Carolina backcountry. An especially despicable event took place just after the patriots captured Augusta. A Whig horseman rode up to the door of a house where Colonel Benjamin Grierson was held prisoner, stood up in his stirrups, pulled his pistol, and shot the Colonel dead. It was cold-blooded murder, plain and simple. The killer rode away and was never caught. "In no part of the South was the war conducted with such asperity as in this quarter. It often sank into barbarity," Lee proclaimed.[18]

The only remaining British garrison in the Carolina hinterland by early June was Ninety Six, so named because it was ninety-six miles from the major Cherokee town of Keowee. Long a hotbed of Loyalism, it was here that Patrick Ferguson had trained the Tory militiamen who had fought at Kings Mountain the previous October. It was toward this same place that Banastre Tarleton had initially headed after he had left Winnsborough in January 1781.

Emotions were intense when Nathanael Greene and his army of about 1,000 men arrived at Ninety Six on May 22. The patriots had long dreamt of the day when they could capture the outpost which had been the most enduring symbol of British power in the backcountry. Accompanied by Colonel Thaddeus Kosciuszko, the Polish engineer who had been with him ever since Charlotte, the Fighting Quaker rode out to inspect the enemy's entrenchments that very afternoon.

Colonel John Harris Cruger, the New York Tory who had come South in 1779 and who had commanded a regiment during d'Estaing's siege of Savannah, had erected formidable defensive works at Ninety Six, including a star-shaped redoubt, called "the star," from which the Tories could direct crossfire to prevent attackers from camping at the foot of the walls.

Rawdon had sent orders to Cruger to evacuate Ninety Six, but they had never arrived. Consider how the Tories must have felt when they looked out and saw Greene's Continentals and militia. With no help within 150 miles, they labored in the sweltering heat, placing sandbags atop the parapet to protect themselves from sharpshooters. At night, black slaves were sent out to fetch water from a nearby stream for the defenders, who were under the immediate command of Major Green.

During the same languid summer nights, accompanied by the same cacophonous chorus of crickets and frogs, slaves were digging zigzags and parallels for Greene under Kosciuszko's watchful eye. The plan was to burrow a tunnel beneath the walls of the star and to blow an opening through which the patriots could enter and overwhelm Major Green and the defenders before they could recover from the blast. Progress was painfully slow, partly because the red clay of the piedmont was almost like stone and partly because Green wisely sent small bands of troops out from the star to attack and kill the workers. In one embarrassing incident the defenders grabbed some of the digging tools and took them back into the redoubt.

Nathanael Greene's hopes for a methodical approach to capturing Ninety Six by siege were disrupted in mid-June, when Thomas Sumter sent word that Rawdon had left Charleston on June 7 and was on his way with a relief expedition. Reckoning that he was not strong enough to fight Rawdon and Cruger combined, Greene wasted no time in ordering that a direct assault be launched against the star redoubt at noon on June 18.

The commander of this heroic onslaught was Lieutenant Colonel Richard Campbell. The scheme was for an advanced party to chop its way through the abatis that surrounded the redoubt, enter the trench at the base of the walls, and provide covering fire for a second wave that would carry long poles with hooks on the ends to pull the sandbags off the parapet. The main body of troops would then storm the star and use the fallen sandbags as a sort of stairway to move over the walls and subdue the defenders.

The battle began with an hour-long artillery duel between the two armies. Cannon balls and grape shot screamed through the stultifying air. Then the order to attack was given. Campbell's troops, mostly Virginia militia, dashed toward the abatis and cut their way through to the trench on the far side.

Difficulties arose, however, when the second wave tried to pull the sandbags off the parapet. The walls of the star were too high, the sandbags were too securely fastened, and the enemy fire was too intense. For almost an hour the patriots struggled mightily to surmount the redoubt, only to be repulsed again and again with severe losses. The fighting was vigorous on both sides, with soldiers not infrequently using their muskets as clubs.

The carnage was ghastly. The stench of death was made sickeningly pungent by the torrid heat that engulfed both armies. "Finding the enemy defended their works with great obstinacy, and seeing but little prospect of succeeding without heavy loss, I ordered the attack to be pushed no further," Greene explained.[19]

A British officer took special delight in describing the aftermath of this horrific engagement, in which the outnumbered defenders, most of whom were Tories from New York and New Jersey, had doggedly refused to give way: "The Americans covered their shame in the trenches, nor was it till the next day that they recollected themselves so far as to ask permission to bury their dead. The groans also of their wounded assailed their ears and called aloud for that relief which ought to have been much earlier administered."[20]

Nathanael Greene suffered 150 casualties in this ill-fated attempt to capture Ninety Six and its star. On June 19 he marched his army toward Charlotte to get out of Rawdon's way.

Indicative of the predicament in which the British found themselves, Rawdon arrived and ordered Cruger to abandon Ninety Six and return to Charleston, where the British commander hoped to obtain enough reinforcements to renew the offensive later that summer. After briefly pursuing Greene, Rawdon recognized that his army was incapable of continuing the chase. "Clad in their heavy wooden uniforms, unused to the hundred-degree heat and the enervating humidity of the Carolina country, they simply had reached the limit of their endurance," says Pancake about the redcoats and their Loyalist allies.[21]

Greene spent July and most of August 1781 in the High Hills of the Santee, a twenty-mile string of sand and clay hills that rise up to 200 feet above the left bank of the Wateree River. Here the Rhode Islander could rest his army and wait for militia to join him. By August 22, having a force of some 2,400 men, about three-fourths of whom were either Continentals or seasoned veterans, Greene felt strong enough to take the offensive against the redcoats.

This was a far cry from the hectic weeks following Morgan's victory at the Cowpens, when Greene had raced toward the Dan, rejecting any thought of marching toward the British. By August 1781 the tables had turned. Greene knew that Rawdon's successor as British commander in South Carolina, Colonel Alexander Stewart, had brought an army of some 2,000 men inland from Charleston and had established a camp on the right bank of the Santee. The Fighting Quaker left the High Hills, headed north to Camden where he crossed the Wateree, and took a circuitous route toward the confluence of the Congaree and the Wateree, where he expected to find the redcoats.

Stewart, who had under his command such battle-tested veterans as the Third, Sixty-third, and Sixty-fourth Regiments, plus the New York and New Jersey Loyalists who had fought so valiantly at Ninety Six, had moved his camp eastward a short distance to Eutaw Springs. It was a serene spot just to the south of the Santee River opposite Nelson's Ferry and astride a road that roughly paralleled the river. It took its name from the springs, really an underground river, that fed a small creek that meandered along the northern edge of an open field about eight acres in size where the redcoats and the Tories had pitched their tents in neat rows.

Not far from the creek was a two-story brick house which would play a pivotal role in the upcoming engagement. From the upper windows one could obtain a panoramic view of the surrounding countryside. Except for a thicket of bramble and blackjack oak on the steep banks of the creek, the woods west of the field were fairly open. Moss dripped from the limbs of massive coastal oaks, adding to the rural charm of the place.

The Battle of Eutaw Springs was to be the last of Greene's major clashes with the British in the Carolinas, and it was also to be the bloodiest.

Greene lost almost 25% of his men, and Stewart suffered casualties of about 42%. William Washington was seriously wounded and taken prisoner. Richard Campbell, who had led the charge against the star redoubt at Ninety Six, took a musket ball in the chest and fell dead to the ground.

For almost four hours the two armies tore at one another in savage hand-to-hand combat. Otho Williams described the terrible deeds that were done on September 8, 1781, on the banks of the Santee River: "If the two lines on this occasion did not actually come to the mutual thrust of the bayonet, it must be acknowledged that no troops ever came nearer. They are said to have been so near that their bayonets clashed and the officers sprang at each other with their swords, before the enemy actually broke away."[22]

Troops on both sides fought tenaciously at Eutaw Springs because many were deserters who knew that they would be hanged if captured. "At the close of the war, we fought the enemy with British soldiers, and they fought us with those of America," Greene half jokingly remarked.[23] Survival, not patriotism or dedication to some abstract political principle, was the primary motivation for many of the combatants who struggled and died at Eutaw Springs.

The Battle of Eutaw Springs served no real purpose other than to confirm that the British had no chance of reviving Germain's defunct Tory recruiting strategy. Local support for the king had become so anemic that Stewart and his men had no idea that Nathanael Greene and his army were only a few miles away and closing fast. "Notwithstanding every exertion being made to gain intelligence of the enemy's situation," he later told Cornwallis, "they rendered it impossible, by waylaying the bye-paths and passes through the different swamps."[24]

Early on the morning of September 8, British foragers, who were busily digging sweet potatoes, bumped into the leading elements of the patriot force. After a brief cavalry skirmish with the enemy, the foragers ran back toward the redcoat camp to warn Stewart. Scrambling to meet the impending attack and realizing that he could not match the strength of Greene's cavalry, the redcoat commander ordered one of his officers to place sharpshooters in the upper windows of the brick house to retard the advance of the patriot dragoons if the British were compelled to retreat. Stewart also sent about 300 men under Major John Majoribanks to the thicket on the south bank of the creek to provide covering fire for the redcoats and the Tories in case they had to withdraw.

The main body of Stewart's command, which unlike Ferguson's at Kings Mountain or Cruger's at Ninety Six contained substantial numbers of British regulars, formed a single defensive line across the road in the open woods west of the field where they had pitched their tents. On the left were the Sixty-third and Sixty-fourth Regiments, Cruger's Loyalists were in the middle, and the Third Regiment and Major Majoribanks were on the right. Major John Coffin's cavalry and a small contingent of infantry were stationed south of the road and constituted the only British reserve. The artillery pieces, except for one that was sent down the road to skirmish with Greene's gunners, were distributed along the line of defenders.

Faintly at first, then gradually more pronounced, came the sounds of the drums of the patriot army. Not since Savannah had large numbers of British regulars waited in the South for rebels to attack. Clearly, the initiative had passed to the patriots. It was just before 9:00 A.M.

Greene brought his men to the battlefield with the militia in the lead. Just as at Guilford Court House, the Continentals were situated behind the irregulars and were expected to deliver the decisive blow. Francis Marion commanded the South Carolina militia on the right of the first line, while Andrew Pickens headed those on the left. In between were North Carolinians under a French officer, the Marquis de Malmady. The Continentals consisted of Marylanders on the left under Otho Williams, Virginians in the center under Richard Campbell, and North Carolinians on the right under Jethro Sumner. Light Horse Harry Lee and his dragoons covered Greene's right flank, and Colonel John Henderson's cavalry protected his left. Making up Greene's reserve were Robert Kirkwood's Delaware Continentals and William Washington's cavalry.

The battle commenced with the exchange of artillery fire. "As soon as the skirmishing parties were cleared away from between the two armies, a steady and desperate conflict ensued," said Otho Williams. "That between the artillery of the first line and that of the enemy was bloody and obstinate in the extreme."[25] Much like what had transpired at Cowpens, some of the redcoats eventually broke formation and rushed forward helter-skelter when they saw elements of the patriot militia beginning to fall back after delivering several volleys. At this critical moment, Greene ordered Sumner's North Carolina Continentals and Lee's cavalry to attack the British left, while Henderson and Washington fell upon the British right. Meanwhile, Stewart committed Coffin and the reserve to try to shore up the crumbling British defenses, but a bayonet attack by the remaining Continentals, including Kirkwood's Delaware regiment, sent the redcoats and Cruger's Tories reeling back through the open woods and through the clearing where they had been encamped.

Stewart, knowing that it would be the job of the patriot dragoons to pursue the British and to keep them from reforming, sent additional sharp-shooters into the brick house to pick off the enemy as they advanced into the open field. But the most obstinate resistance was offered by Major Majoribanks in the thicket of bramble and blackjack oak along the banks of the creek on the British right. Fearing that Majoribanks could threaten the flank of the Maryland Continentals, Greene ordered William Washington to dislodge the redcoats. It was during this effort that Washington was wounded and captured. Finding the thicket virtually impenetrable, Washington decided to attempt to ride around Majoribank's right. Otho Williams described what happened:

> With this view, he ordered his troops to wheel by sections to the left, and thus brought nearly all his officers next to the enemy, while he attempted to pass their front. A deadly and well-directed fire, delivered at that instant, wounded or brought to the ground many of his men and horses, and every officer except two.[26]

The battlefield at Eutaw Springs was fast becoming a scene of almost total confusion. Riderless horses, terrified by the screaming, yelling, and shooting coming from all around them, galloped through the British camp, knocking over tents and scattering provisions over the blood-stained ground. The sharpshooters continued to blast away from the upper windows of the brick house. By this time most of the redcoats and Tories were racing through the open field with no other thought than trying to get away from their pursuers.

If the patriots had maintained their pace and if the Fighting Quaker had been willing to throw all of his available strength into the fray at this most opportune moment, the victory over Stewart might have been total. But Greene's troops, many of whom were "thirsty, naked, and fatigued," could not resist the temptation of stopping in the British camp and rummaging through the enemy's discarded belongings, including the liquor, with the result that the American officers were "nearly abandoned by their soldiers, and the sole marks for the party who now poured their fire from the windows of the house."[27]

When Greene learned that Majoribanks had succeeded in capturing several artillery pieces that had been brought up to fire into the brick house, the patriot general predictably broke off the engagement and retreated into the woods to the west of the open field. Stewart was too weak to follow, and Greene marched unmolested to his camp in the High Hills of the Santee. The British returned to Charleston and never ventured into the countryside again.

After Eutaw Springs, the only British garrisons in the Carolinas and Georgia were Savannah, Charleston, and Wilmington. "The conquered states were regained, and our exiled countrymen were restored to their deserted homes—sweet rewards of our toil and peril," proclaimed Light Horse Harry Lee.[28] Unable to control the hinterland, the redcoats had no choice but to stay close to the sea, where the seemingly invincible Royal Navy could protect them and assure the uninterrupted flow of supplies. But the British were about to lose control of the seas for the second time in the South, and this time the loss would be fatal.

Chapter Sixteen

Yorktown

It was in Virginia, not South Carolina, that the culminating campaign of the revolutionary war in the South was to occur. The largest of the colonies, Virginia had also contributed the greatest number of leaders to the patriot cause, including George Washington, Horatio Gates, Daniel Morgan, and Light-Horse Harry Lee. Virginia escaped significant military incursions by the British until May 1779, when Royal troops landed and briefly occupied Portsmouth, near the mouth of the Chesapeake Bay, and pillaged and burned several nearby towns and tobacco plantations.

In December 1780, Henry Clinton, who wanted to establish a firm foothold on the Chesapeake to support future large scale naval operations, sent a force of some 1,600 men under Benedict Arnold to Virginia. Arriving at Hampton Roads, the inlet between the Atlantic Ocean and the Chesapeake Bay, and proceeding up the James River, these troops landed about twenty-five miles below Richmond in early January 1781. Arnold occupied the Virginia capital without a fight on January 5 and destroyed much of the city.

General Washington, who continued to command the main patriot army in and around Peekskill, New York, in the Highlands of the Hudson, knew that capturing the treasonous Arnold would go a long way toward boosting the sagging morale of the American rebels. Recognizing that Arnold would be virtually powerless to oppose a combined land and naval attack, Washington ordered some 1,200 New England and New Jersey Continentals to move south under the command of the Marquis de Lafayette. These men were to cooperate with an equal number of French troops, who were sailing from Newport, Rhode Island with Admiral Sochet Destouches, to seal off the mouth of the Chesapeake Bay and then put ashore.

Unhappily for Washington, Admiral Arbuthnot and a small British fleet bested Destouches in a naval engagement on March 16, which meant that Lafayette would have to depend almost solely upon his own resources to fight the redcoats. Furthermore, the British troops in Virginia received a new commander, Major General William Phillips, and 2,600 reinforcements on March 26. To counter this move, Washington ordered General "Mad Anthony" Wayne and about 1,000 Pennsylvania Continentals to Virginia; sadly, the Pennsylvanians did not arrive until early June, by which time events had taken an ominous turn for the patriots.

On April 10, 1781, Charles Cornwallis sent a dispatch from his base in Wilmington, North Carolina to Major General Phillips. In this dispatch, the earl set forth the fundamental tenets of his evolving strategy. In this document, one can detect the germ of the idea that contributed to the calamitous encirclement of the British army at Yorktown the following October. Stating that he was "quite tired of marching about the country in quest of adventures," the redcoat general advanced the reasons why he did not intend to return to South Carolina to assist Lord Rawdon.[1]

In the earl's opinion, Wilmington was too far from Camden to allow his army to get to the garrison on the Wateree before Greene arrived. Cornwallis went on to argue that Rawdon, if he could withstand the Rhode Islander's initial onslaught, would be strong enough to protect the string of outposts in South Carolina on his own. The earl contended that attempting to help Rawdon would serve no good purpose and would draw his own army away from Virginia, where he believed the crucial battles must be won if the South was to be subdued. Cornwallis proposed that he march his force of some 1,400 exhausted and battered men northward from Wilmington to join Phillips's larger army in Virginia, where "we then have a stake to fight for, and a successful battle may give us America."[2]

In a communique he sent to Clinton on April 10, Cornwallis declared that Virginia was far more suitable for offensive operations than was North Carolina, where "numberless rivers and creeks" made "interior navigation" virtually impossible. "Until Virginia is in a manner subdued," he proceeded to tell the British commander in chief, "our hold upon the Carolinas might be difficult, if not precarious."[3] Cornwallis believed that on the broad expanse of Chesapeake Bay and along the mighty rivers that penetrated its western shore—the James, the York, the Rappahannock, and the Potomac—the British could assemble and transport into the interior a force of sufficient strength to conduct a war of conquest. "By a war of conquest," he told Phillips, "I mean, to possess the country sufficiently to overturn the Rebel government, and to establish a militia and some kind of mixed authority of our own."[4] No longer would Royal forces depend so heavily upon support from the Loyalists, "the contrary of which I have sufficient experienced," he declared to Clinton.[5]

Such notions of venturesome boldness were totally incongruous with

Clinton's concept of what the British army should do in Virginia. "And all my former correspondence with His Lordship . . . had clearly evinced that, so far from proposing to commence solid operation in the Chesapeake before I should be reinforced, I did not even think any operation there safe unless we were certain of a permanent naval superiority," he later maintained.[6] Cornwallis's concept of defeating the rebels by means of a "war of conquest" was completely out of step with official British policy, which still held that the Loyalists would eventually have to shoulder the responsibility for winning the war. One wonders whether the earl ever comprehended that he was involved in a political struggle.

Perhaps because it offered the only prospect for rescuing his tarnished military reputation, or perhaps because George Germain, with whom the earl continued to communicate directly, also championed the importance of operations on the Chesapeake, Cornwallis was determined to go to Virginia and stay on the offensive. "If our plan is defensive mixed with desultory raids," he proclaimed derisively, "let us quit the Carolinas and stick to our salt pork at New York, sending now and then a detachment to steal tobacco, etc."[7]

Cornwallis marched his army out of Wilmington in mid-April. He reached Petersburg, Virginia on May 20, where he assumed command of an army of more than 7,000 troops. Unfortunately, Major General Phillips had died from illness a few days earlier. Lafayette's army, which was encamped in nearby Richmond, was outnumbered by roughly three to one.

The circumstances which prompted Cornwallis to leave the Carolinas and the degree of complicity that Henry Clinton had in this fateful decision have been the subject of considerable controversy over the years. Not surprisingly, especially when one considers the disastrous outcome of British operations along the Chesapeake in 1781, Clinton insisted that Cornwallis directly and knowingly violated his instructions to remain in the Carolinas until the pacification of that region was certain. The British commander in chief discussed this matter at length in his history of the campaign:

> Wherefore, having by my written instructions to Lord Cornwallis *clearly and positively directed His Lordship to regard the security of Charleston as a primary object, and not to make any offensive move that should be likely to endanger it,* and it being an incontestable fact that his move into Virginia exposed that post to the most imminent danger, I am extremely sorry I am obliged in this place to assert that His Lordship *disobeyed my orders and acted contrary to his duty in doing so.*[8]

The situation was not as sharply defined as Henry Clinton claimed. In the realm of British military practice, where politics reigned supreme and where commanders made sure that subordinates could be held accountable if anything went wrong, there was no formal chain of command in the modern sense of the term. Instructions, including those that Clinton sent to Cornwallis, were little more than suggestions that could be modified by field commanders if local circumstances so dictated.

The problem for the British was not that Clinton issued imprecise instructions or that Cornwallis disobeyed his orders. It was not even that Cornwallis and Clinton profoundly distrusted one another, which they undeniably did. The overarching difficulty for the British had its roots in the Carolinas, especially in the seemingly endless list of small engagements like Kettle Creek, Williamson's Plantation, and Pyle's Hacking Match which had demonstrated that the Royal military was not strong enough to control the countryside and provide ongoing protection for the Loyalists. Lacking this capacity, the British had no chance of succeeding, no matter how many battles they won. In truth, the surrender of the earl's army at Yorktown was merely the final episode in the unfolding drama of a flawed policy that had manifested itself as early as Moore's Creek Bridge. In a real sense, the culminating campaign on the Chesapeake was anticlimactic.

To his credit, Henry Clinton came closer than most British officers to recognizing that winning the allegiance of the rank-and-file population of the colonies was the single most important objective of British policy. He certainly understood this far better than Cornwallis did. On July 18, 1781, Clinton told Germain:

> I can say little more to Your Lordship's sanguine hopes of the speedy reduction of the southern provinces than to lament that the present state of the war there does not altogether promise so flattering an event. Many untoward incidents, of which Your Lordship was not apprised, have thrown us too far back to be able to recover very soon even what we have lately lost there. For, if as I have often before suggested the good will of the inhabitants is absolutely requisite to retain a country after we have conquered it, I fear it will be some time before we can recover the confidence of those in Carolina, as their past sufferings will of course make them cautious of forwarding the King's interests before there is the strongest certainty of his army being in a condition to support them.[9]

Although Cornwallis advocated the launching of a major offensive in

Virginia, where Tory support was weak, Clinton favored pursuing the more realistic objective of landing troops on the upper Chesapeake and the taking of Baltimore, "where, I am told, we have many friends."[10] It was toward this end that the British commander in chief wanted Cornwallis to assume a defensive stance and choose a harbor on the coast to fortify, so that major squadrons of the Royal Navy could safely enter the Chesapeake.

Charles Cornwallis was a fighter. On May 26 the earl sent a communique to Clinton in which he explained the course of military operations he intended to pursue:

> I shall now proceed to dislodge LaFayette from Richmond, and with my light troops to destroy any magazines or stores in the neighborhood which may have been collected either for his use or General Greene's army. From thence I propose to move to the Neck at Williamsburg . . . and keep myself unengaged from operations which might interfere with your plans for the campaign until I have the satisfaction of hearing from you.[11]

Although he had promised not to "run about the country in quest of adventures," the earl could not resist the seductive prospect of chasing La-Fayette's army out of Richmond and maybe even destroying it.[12]

Cornwallis marched his army out of Petersburg on May 24, crossed the James River about twenty-five miles below Richmond, and moved northward to New Castle on the Pamunkey River, which he reached on May 29. Meanwhile, LaFayette, recognizing that Cornwallis was trying to prevent him from uniting with Wayne, evacuated the Virginia capital on May 27. The Frenchman dashed toward the South Anna River, which he crossed beginning on May 29, and proceeded northward to Ely's Ford on the Rappahannock. Disappointed at not having blocked LaFayette's line of retreat, Cornwallis reverted to his original plan of concentrating his energies upon destroying patriot supply and ammunition depots.

After marching to Cook's Ford on the North Anna River, the earl diverted the main army southward and sent Banastre Tarleton and his dragoons westward toward Charlottesville, where the rebel legislature was in session. Riding into town on June 4 with sabers slashing, Tarleton's troops seized some of the members of the legislature and barely missed capturing Governor Thomas Jefferson. Not strong enough to hold the town, the British raiders rode southeastward and reunited with Cornwallis at Elk Hill on the James River about fifty miles west of Richmond, where the main army made camp on June 7. The earl ordered Major John Simcoe to attack nearby Point of Forks and seize supplies placed there by von Steuben.

Meanwhile, far off in northern Virginia, LaFayette and Mad Anthony Wayne united their forces on June 10 near Racoon Ford on the Rapidan River. Still too weak to confront Cornwallis, LaFayette's army of about 4,500 men nonetheless began to move southward toward the main body of British troops so it could keep track of the earl's activities. Cornwallis broke camp at Elk Hill on June 15 and occupied Richmond the next day.

After five days, the British initiated a leisurely march down the peninsula between the James and York Rivers and established themselves at Williamsburg on June 25, where Cornwallis awaited instructions from Clinton. A dispatch from the British commander in chief, dated June 11, 1781, arrived in Williamsburg on June 26. In it Clinton recommended that Cornwallis send as many troops as he could spare to the northern Chesapeake to participate in a major attack upon Philadelphia. Clinton reiterated, however, that the earl should retain a sufficient number of soldiers "to take a defensive station in any healthy situation you choose, be it at Williamsburg or Yorktown."[13]

Cornwallis responded to Clinton on June 30, saying that he had "lost no time in taking measures for complying with the requisitions contained in your dispatch." The earl, however, proceeded to question the likelihood that his weakened command could meet all eventualities that might arise from assuming a defensive stance. "I submit it to Your Excellency's consideration," he proclaimed, "whether it is worth while to hold a sickly, defensive post in this bay, which will always be exposed to a sudden French attack and which experience has now shown makes no diversion in favor of the southern army."[14]

Clinton and Cornwallis were engaged in a game of cat and mouse, as each maneuvered to pin the blame upon the other for whatever unfortunate developments might ensue. To obviate the circumstance that Cornwallis could claim that he did not have enough men to do the job, Clinton sent a letter to the earl on July 8 which authorized him to keep as many soldiers as he deemed necessary to "hold a station in Chesapeake for ships of the line as well as frigates." The British commander in chief continued:

> I therefore beg leave to request *that you will without loss of time examine Old Point Comfort and fortify it,* determining such troops as you may think necessary for that purpose and garrisoning it afterward. But, if it should be Your Lordship's opinion that Old Point Comfort cannot be held without having possession of York . . . and that the whole cannot be done with less than 7000 men,

you are at full liberty to detain all the troops now in Chesapeake, which I believe amount to somewhat more than that number.[15]

Cornwallis kept all his soldiers with him in Virginia. After inspecting Old Point Comfort and finding it unacceptable, the earl transported his 7,000 man force from Portsmouth, to which he had marched in July in preparation for sending troops to Clinton, to Yorktown on August 1. There he began erecting fortifications. According to Cornwallis, Yorktown was "the only harbor in which we can hope to be able to give effectual protection to line-of-battle ships."[16]

The Marquis de Lafayette and his army of about 5,000 men were encamped in Williamsburg. Even before Cornwallis arrived in Virginia, the young Frenchman and other patriot leaders were urging General Washington to send large numbers of reinforcements southward from the Highlands of the Hudson. The problem for Washington was that he had only 3,500 Continentals with which to oppose Clinton's 10,500 troops in New York City. Even if the Comte de Rochambeau, who commanded about 4,000 French troops at Newport, Rhode Island, joined Washington, the patriots would be outnumbered. Moreover, as long as the British retained control of the seas, Clinton could easily dispatch additional men and supplies to match whatever strength the patriots could assemble on the Chesapeake.

Washington decided that the most effective way to assist LaFayette was to bring Rochambeau to the Hudson, so that the two armies could keep Clinton pinned down in New York City. Toward this end, Washington and his subordinates met with Rochambeau in Wethersfield, Connecticut on May 22. The two generals agreed that the French army would march to the Hudson as soon as possible and that the Franco-American army would "make a serious demonstration against the weakened base at New York."[17]

Provisions were made in this so-called Wethersfield plan to reconsider the proper mode of operations should the French navy wrest control of the seas from the British. Washington and Rochambeau knew that a powerful French fleet under Admiral de Grasse had recently sailed from France for the West Indies, but they were not certain that it would be ordered to North America and, if so, when and where it would make its appearance. "Should the West India fleet arrive upon the coast, the force thus combined may either proceed in the operation against New York, or may be directed against the enemy in some other quarter, as circumstances shall dictate," Washington told Rochambeau.[18]

The Wethersfield Plan meant that LaFayette could do little more than keep Cornwallis under surveillance. Indeed, the Marquis's only battle with the British army occurred on July 9, when Cornwallis was ferrying his troops across the James River near Jamestown Island on his way from Williamsburg to Portsmouth. Tricked into believing that only a small contingent of redcoats remained north of the river, Mad Anthony Wayne launched an attack near Greenspring Plantation in the late afternoon and was severely repulsed. Understandably, in early August LaFayette was content to stay in his camp at Williamsburg and await developments. They were not long in coming.

On June 9, 1781, Rochambeau received a dispatch from de Grasse in which the French admiral announced that he would sail to North America and arrive sometime after July 15. He further declared that operations must commence shortly thereafter, because the French fleet would remain along the coast for only a brief period. As to where he would land, de Grasse left that decision to the commanders in North America. Interestingly, it was Rochambeau, not Washington, who made the fateful decision to bring the French fleet to the Chesapeake. Several days before he told his American counterpart about de Grasse's communique, the French general penned a reply in which he suggested that the admiral "enter the Chesapeake on his way, as there might be an opportunity of striking an important stroke there."[19]

The all-important message from de Grasse reached Washington and Rochambeau on August 14. The admiral announced that he was sailing on August 13 for the Chesapeake and that arrangements for a joint land and sea operation should be undertaken immediately, because he planned to begin the return voyage to the West Indies by mid-October at the latest.

The American commander in chief and Rochambeau, whose armies had come together on the Hudson in July, understood the full implications of this news. No longer could any thought be given to a major move against Clinton in New York City. It was imperative that the Franco-American army start preparing for the 400-mile march to Virginia, where they hoped to cooperate with LaFayette and de Grasse in forcing Cornwallis to surrender. Washington explained, "Matters having now come to a crisis, and a decided plan to be determined on, I was obliged . . . to remove the French troops and a detachment from the American army to the head of Elk, to be transported to Virginia."[20]

Washington and Rochambeau began moving the Franco-American army toward Virginia on August 19. After making a feint toward Staten Island in hopes of convincing Clinton that they were preparing to attack New York City, the two commanders ordered their 6,000 men to head toward Princeton, Trenton, Philadelphia, and on to the Head of Elk at the headwaters of the Chesapeake Bay, where Admiral de Grasse was to bring transports to take their troops to the James River. There the French and American soldiers were to land and join LaFayette's 5,000-man army at Williamsburg and 3,000 additional French soldiers that de Grasse was to bring with his fleet and put ashore. "We then expected we were to attack New York in that quarter," wrote Joseph Plumb Martin, a private in Washington's army, "but after staying here a day or two, we again moved off and arrived at Trenton by rapid marches."[21]

The subterfuge worked. As late as August 27, despite receiving numerous intelligence reports that Washington and Rochambeau were headed for Virginia, the British commander in chief reported that he could not "well ascertain Mr. Washington's real intentions by this move of his army."[22] Finally, by September 2, a week after the French fleet had arrived off the Virginia capes and three days after Cornwallis had sighted "between thirty and forty sail" in Hampton Roads, Clinton came to appreciate what was afoot.[23] But even then he remained calm, because he was certain that the British fleet would be able to push de Grasse aside and open the way to Cornwallis. In addition to the New York squadron commanded by Admiral Sir Thomas Graves, Clinton could call upon the substantial sea power the British had in the West Indies. Clinton told the earl,

> By intelligence which I have this day received, it would seem that Mr. Washington is moving an army to the southward with an appearance of haste, and gives out that he expects the cooperation of a considerable French armament. . . .
>
> . . . However, as Rear Admiral Graves . . . sailed from hence on the 31 *ultimo* with a fleet of nineteen sail besides some fifty-gun ships, I flatter myself Your Lordship will have little to apprehend from that of the French.[24]

His Majesty's government had known for months that de Grasse had sailed from France with a powerful fleet and that he might be headed for the North American coast. Realizing that de Grasse would drop anchor first in the West Indies, the British assumed that Admiral Sir George Rodney and his subordinate, Samuel Hood, both in the West Indies, would be able to maintain control of the western Atlantic. On July 7, Germain stated in a dispatch to Clinton, "I have reason to believe the French fleet will push for North America and Sir George Rodney will certainly follow them, to prevent them from giving you any interruption in your operations."[25]

One week later Germain informed Clinton that the "purpose of the enemy was long known here, and Sir George Rodney has been apprised of it and will certainly not lose sight of Monsieur de Grasse."[26] But that's exactly what Rodney did. He allowed the French admiral to slip away, and then he sent Hood with only fourteen ships of the line to overtake de Grasse who, unknown to Rodney, had twenty-eight. "It was unthinkable that Britain could lose control of the seas, or so the conceit and arrogance in England permitted its leaders to believe," says John Pancake.[27]

The ultimate fate of Cornwallis's garrison at Yorktown was decided on water, not land. Nonetheless, the earl's actions contributed to his demise. Pancake goes so far as to suggest that Cornwallis was too exhausted to think clearly, or maybe that he did not know how to superintend a large army. Why, for example, did the earl, who had consistently shown himself to be a daring and resourceful commander, not march out of Yorktown and attack LaFayette and de Grasse's newly-arrived French soldiers in early September, before Rochambeau and Washington could get to Virginia? Admittedly, he would have been slightly outnumbered, but the redcoats had shown at Camden and Guilford Court House that they could carry the day against heavy odds.

The earl defended his inaction by citing instructions he had received from Clinton. In a dispatch sent to Clinton on September 17 he wrote, "If I had no hopes of relief, I would rather risk an action than defend my half-finished works. But, as you . . . promise every exertion to assist me, I do not think myself justifiable in putting the fate of the war on so desperate an attempt."[28] "From first to last," writes Pancake, "Cornwallis' behavior since coming to Virginia seems incomprehensible."[29]

All chances for assistance for the Yorktown garrison had to come by ship, but as long as de Grasse controlled the entrance to the Chesapeake Bay, no help could get through. Unlike Savannah, luck would work against the British this time. Because he took a more direct route from the West Indies, Admiral Hood had arrived off Hampton Roads on August 25, one day before the French fleet. "I am now steering for Cape Henry in order to examine the Chesapeake. From thence I shall proceed to the Capes of Delaware and, not seeing or hearing anything of de Grasse . . . shall then make the best of my way off Sandy Hook," Hood had told Clinton.[30] Observing no enemy ships, Hood had continued northward. Soon after arriving in New York, the British admiral learned that the French had entered the Chesapeake just after him. Even then, however, Hood was not concerned, because he was sure that he could "defeat any designs of the enemy."[31]

On September 5, the British fleet, now commanded by Admiral

Graves, appeared at dawn off the mouth of the Chesapeake. De Grasse, leaving four ships of the line behind to guard his transports, waited for the tide to turn and then sailed out in the late morning to meet his traditional enemy. The French had twenty-four ships of the line, and the British had nineteen.

Hood would later contend that Graves was indecisive in not ordering an attack when the French fleet was vulnerable as it sailed past Cape Henry. Knowing that a French squadron was on its way from Newport, Rhode Island with siege artillery, de Grasse sailed southeastward to draw the British fleet away from Hampton Roads. The lead elements of both fleets engaged briefly in combat late in the afternoon of September 5. "The two vans having come so close as to be almost within pistol shot, the fire was long well sustained," commented a French sailor.[32] For five days the two fleets drifted within sight of one another, but no additional fighting occurred.

On September 9, Admiral Graves, no doubt astounded by his lack of success, sent the following communique to Clinton, who had troops aboard ship at New York waiting for the signal that it was safe to sail for the Chesapeake:

> I am sorry to inform you the enemy have so great a naval force in the Chesapeake that they are absolute masters of its navigation. . . . In this ticklish state of things Your Excellency will see the little probability of anything getting into York River but by night, and of the infinite risk to any supplies sent by water. All that I can say is that every resistance the fleet can make shall not be wanting; for we must either stand or fall together.[33]

The British could not open the way. Cornwallis was trapped.

The vise around the British garrison at Yorktown was closing fast. After passing through Philadelphia in grand parade fashion on September 2, the men of Washington's and Rochambeau's Franco-American army arrived at Head of Elk on September 6 and began boarding small boats to take them southward down the Chesapeake Bay. "We passed down the bay, making a grand appearance with our mosquito fleet, to Annapolis," commented Joseph Plumb Martin.[34]

After briefly visiting his home on the Potomac for the first time during the war, General Washington rode into Williamsburg on September 15. Colonel St. George Tucker described the event: "About four o'clock in the afternoon his approach was announced. . . . The French line had just time to form. The Continentals had more leisure. He approached without any pomp or parade, attended only by a few horsemen and his own servants."[35] By September 26, all of Washington's and Rochambeau's troops were concentrated around Williamsburg where, in combination with LaFayette's and de Grasse's soldiers, they prepared for the final move against Yorktown.

Unlike d'Estaing at Savannah or Greene at Ninety Six, Washington and Rochambeau were determined to let nothing interrupt their defeating Cornwallis by methodical, classical siege operations, replete with zigzags and parallels. In a real sense, Yorktown was Charleston in reverse—in this instance the advantage belonged to the French and the Americans. The situation for Cornwallis was hopeless. Outnumbered more than two to one, he had no James Moncrief or John Maitland to save him. "A most wonderful and very observable conincidence of actions, the army commences its march from Williamsburg and approaches within two miles of York Town," wrote Colonel Johnathan Trumbull on September 28.[36]

Cornwallis had erected earthen works and redoubts roughly in a semicircle a few hundred yards inland from Yorktown. Banastre Tarleton and 700 troops were stationed in Gloucester, a small village about a mile across the York River. Inexorably, trenches brought the Allied siege artillery closer to the earl's defenses. "One-third part of all the troops were put in requistion to be employed in opening the trenches," declared Private Martin.[37]

Night after night the work went on. Soldiers were sent to the James River to help haul the massive French siege guns into place. Finally, on October 9, the French and American batteries opened up. "A simultaneous discharge of all the guns in the line followed, the French troops accompanying it with 'Huzza for the Americans,'" said a Connecticut Sergeant.[38] The fall of two key redoubts on the British left removed the last impediments to the advance of the Allied trenches. "With Such works on disadvantageous ground, against so powerful an attack, we cannot hope to make a long resistance," Cornwallis wrote to Clinton on October 11.[39]

The worst nightmare for the British had come to pass. After failing in an attempt to transport his command across the York River to Gloucester, where he had hoped to break out of the encirclement and race for Pennsylvania, Charles Cornwallis sent a message to Washington on October 17 requesting that negotiations be opened for the terms of surrender. Terms were agreed to the next day, and the official surrender ceremonies took place in a field outside Yorktown on October 19. One patriot officer wrote, "This is to us a most glorious day, but to the English, one of bitter chagrin and disappointment. Preparations are now making to receive as captives that vindictive, haughty commander and that victorious army, who, by their robberies and murders, have so long been a scourge to our brethren of the Southern states."[40]

Consider how disheartened Cornwallis must have felt. Only seventeen months before he had marched inland from Charleston, the proud commander of a seemingly invincible army. Pleading illness, he now sent Brigadier General Charles O'Hara, the spirited Irishman who had ridden across the Catawba with him at M'Cowan's Ford, to surrender his sword to the victorious American rebels and their French allies. Ironically, protocol dictated that it be given to Benjamin Lincoln, the patriot general who had surrendered and had relinquished his sword to Clinton at Charleston. According to tradition, the British, including Bloody Tarleton, walked to the parade ground as the redcoat musicians played "The World Turned Upside Down":

> If ponies rode men, and if grass
> ate cows,
> And cats should be chased in holes
> by the mouse . . .
> Summer were spring, and the
> other way 'round,
> Then all the world would be
> upside down

"I have the mortification to inform Your Excellency that I have been forced to give up the post of York and Gloucester and to surrender the troops under my command by capitulation," Cornwallis told Clinton by a dispatch dated October 20, 1781.[41]

The American Revolution technically lasted until 1783. There was still much to be done in the South, especially rounding up and attempting to reach an accommodation with the Loyalists who stayed behind, but the policies of Lord North and George Germain had been irrevocably discredited by Cornwallis's surrender at Yorktown. Britain's will to continue the war was over.

On November 18, 1781, Major James Craig evacuated Wilmington, North Carolina. On March 20, 1782, Lord North resigned as Prime Minister, taking George Germain with him. On July 11, 1782, the British left Savannah. On December 14, 1782, 3,800 Loyalists and 5,000 slaves joined the redcoats in sailing out of Charleston Harbor. On February 4, 1783, Great Britain announced the cessation of hostilities with the United States. It was finished. The killing would finally cease.

The American Revolution now belongs to the historians. Did Great Britain ever have a reasonable chance of prevailing? Probably not. The issue was essentially settled when the British failed to win the support of the majority of the people, especially in the South. John Pancake says,

> From Moore's Creek Bridge in 1776 to the slaughter of Pyle's regiment in 1781 Loyalists learned the bitter lesson. Assurances of support by the redcoats, even if they materialized, were always temporary. The regulars eventually moved on, leaving the King's friends to the mercy of their Whig neighbors. Small wonder that Tarleton, commenting on visitors to the British camp in 1781, observed, "The generality of these visitants seemed desirous of peace, but averse to every exertion that might procure it; . . . the dread of violence and persecution prevented their taking a decided part in a cause that yet appeared dangerous."[42]

According to Rachel N. Klein:

> But while whig and loyalist forces failed to divide along clear-cut class lines, the British did attract groups that had fundamental grievances against the elites. . . . Cherokees, bandits, and slaves all gravitated to the British in opposition to an emerging social order more clearly represented by the whigs. Had the British been fully able to accept their "disaffected" allies, those groups might have done them considerable military service. As it was, leading loyalists were involved in a series of contradictions. By their various associations, they alienated potential supporters and sealed the fate of the British war effort in the South.[43]

Nathanael Greene made the most significant military contributions to the patriot victory, but his most important accomplishment was not that he won. It was that he didn't lose.

Enough said.

NOTES

Chapter 1

1. Hugh F. Rankin, *The Moores Creek Bridge Campaign, 1776* (The Moores Creek Battleground Association, 1986), 1.
2. Ibid., 2.
3. Henry Steele Commager and Richard B. Morris, eds., *The Spirit of 'Seventy Six. The Story Of The American Revolution As Told By Participants* (Harper & Row, 1967), 338, 339.
4. Ibid., 337–338.
5. George F. Scheer and Hugh F. Rankin, eds., *Rebels And Redcoats. The American Revolution Through the Eyes of Those Who Fought and Lived It* (Da Capo Press, Inc., n.d.), 132.
6. Ibid., 132.

Chapter 2

1. Commager and Morris, *Spirit of 'Seventy Six,* 61.
2. John S. Pancake, *1777. The Year of The Hangman* (University of Alabama Press, 1977), 79.
3. Commager and Morris, *Spirit of 'Seventy Six,* 61.
4. Christopher Duffy, *The Military Experience in the Age of Reason* (Athaneum, 1988), 247.
5. Henry Lumpkin, *From Savannah To Yorktown* (Paragon House Publishers, n.d.), 136.
6. Commager and Morris, *Spirit of 'Seventy Six,* 619.
7. Duffy, *The Military Experience,* 99.
8. Commager and Morris, *Spirit of 'Seventy Six,* 1064.
9. Daniel J. Boorstin, *The Americans. The Colonial Experience* (Vintage Books, 1958), 369.
10. Pancake, *1777,* 82.
11. Commager and Morris, *Spirit of 'Seventy Six,* 1064.
12. Terry W. Lipscomb, *The Carolina Lowcountry April 1775–June 1776* (South Carolina Department of Archives and History, 1991), 26.
13. Ibid., 42.
14. Ibid., 28–29.

15. Ibid., 43.
16. Ibid., 29.
17. Ibid., 43.
18. Commager and Morris, *Spirit of 'Seventy Six,* 1070.
19. Lipscomb, *Carolina Lowcountry,* 33.
20. Ibid., 33.

Chapter 3

1. Douglas L. Rights, *The American Indian in North Carolina* (Wachovia Historical Society, 1957), 170.
2. Ibid., 173.
3. Ibid., 171.
4. Ibid., 179.
5. James H. O'Donnell III, *The Cherokees of North Carolina in the American Revolution* (Department of Cultural Resources, Division of Archives and History, 1976), 18.
6. Commager and Morris, *Spirit of 'Seventy Six,* 106.
7. Jeffrey J. Crow, *The Black Experience in Revolutionary North Carolina* (Division of Archives and History, North Carolina Department of Cultural Resources, 1989), 55.
8. Ibid., 23.
9. Ibid., 57.
10. Ibid., 56.
11. Benjamin Quarles, *The Negro in the American Revolution* (W. W. Norton & Company, 1973), 19.
12. Ibid., 20.
13. Robert Middlekauff, *The Glorious Cause. The American Revolution, 1763–1789* (Oxford University Press, 1982), 316.
14. Crow, *The Black Experience,* 59.
15. Lewis Pickney Jones, *The South Carolina Civil War Of 1775* (The Sandlapper Store, Inc., 1975), 9.
16. Crow, *The Black Experience,* 55.

Chapter 4

1. Carole Watterson Troxler, *The Loyalist Experience in North Carolina* (Theo Davis Sons, Inc., 1976), viii.
2. Rachel N. Klein, *Unification of a Slave State. The Rise of the Planter Class*

in the South Carolina Backcountry, 1760–1808 (University of North Carolina Press, 1990), 81.

3. Ibid., 84.
4. Ibid., 85.
5. Troxler, *The Loyalist Experience,* viii.
6. Don Higginbotham, *The War of American Independence* (Northeastern University Press, 1983), 134.
7. Troxler, *The Loyalist Experience,* 9.
8. Edward J. Cashin, *The King's Ranger. Thomas Brown and the American Revolution on the Southern Frontier* (The University of Georgia Press, 1989), 29.
9. George Raynor, *Patriots and Tories in Piedmont Carolina* (Salisbury Printing Co., Inc., 1990), 30.
10. Ibid., 31.
11. Ibid., 32.
12. Troxler, *The Loyalist Experience,* 11.
13. Ibid., 11.
14. Barbara W. Tuchman, *The First Salute. A View of the American Revolution* (Ballentine Books, 1989), 151.
15. John S. Pancake, *This Destructive War. The British Campaign in the Carolinas 1780–1782* (University of Alabama Press, 1985), 27.
16. Ibid., 27.
17. Ibid., 26.
18. Ibid., 29.
19. Ibid., 29–30.
20. Commager and Morris, *Spirit of 'Seventy Six,* 1075.
21. Ibid., 1075.

Chapter 5

1. Higginbotham, *The War of American Independence,* 352.
2. Phillips Russell, *North Carolina in the Revolutionary War* (Heritage Printers, 1965), 55.
3. Ibid., 59–60.
4. Ibid., 63.
5. Ibid., 63.
6. Charles E. Bennett and Donald R. Lennon, *A Quest for Glory. Major General Robert Howe and the American Revolution* (The University of North Carolina Press, 1991), 89.
7. Ibid., 93.

8. Commager and Morris, *Spirit of 'Seventy Six,* 1077.

9. Ibid., 1078.

10. Ronald G. Killion and Charles T. Waller, *Georgia and the Revolution* (Cherokee Publishing Company, 1975), 187.

11. Commager and Morris, *Spirit of Seventy Six,* 1079.

12. Christopher Ward, *The War of the Revolution* (The Macmillan Company, 1952), 2:681.

13. Ward, *War of the Revolution,* 2:681.

14. John C. Dann, ed., *The Revolution Remembered. Eyewitness Accounts of the War for Independence* (University of Chicago Press, 1980), 177.

15. Commager and Morris, *Spirit of 'Seventy Six,* 1080.

16. Cashin, *The King's Ranger,* 85.

17. Alice Noble Waring, *The Fighting Elder. Andrew Pickens (1739–1817)* (University of South Carolina Press, 1962), 2.

18. Klein, *Unification of a Slave State,* 95.

19. Cashin, *The King's Ranger,* 91.

20. Scheer and Rankin, *Rebels and Redcoats,* 390.

21. Dann, *The Revolution Remembered,* 178.

22. Ibid., 181.

23. Pancake, *This Destructive War,* 33.

Chapter 6

1. Blackwell P. Robinson, *The Revolutionary War Sketches of William R. Davie* (North Carolina State University Graphics, 1976), 3.

2. Killion and Waller, *Georgia and the Revolution,* 193.

3. William B. Willcox, ed., *The American Rebellion. Sir Henry Clinton's Narrative of His Campaigns, 1775–1782, with an Appendix of Original Documents* (Oxford University Press, 1954), 149.

4. Alexander A. Lawrence, *Storm Over Savannah* (Tara Press, 1979), 13.

5. Ibid., 13.

6. Killion and Waller, *Georgia and the Revolution,* 201.

7. Lawrence, *Storm Over Savannah,* 14.

8. Ibid., 15.

9. Ibid., 15.

10. Ibid., 25.

11. Killion and Waller, *Georgia and the Revolution,* 194.

12. Ibid., 210.

13. Ibid., 195.

14. Ibid., 197.

15. Lawrence, *Storm Over Savannah*, 32.
16. Ibid., 33.
17. Killion and Waller, *Georgia and the Revolution*, 197.
18. Lawrence, *Storm Over Savannah*, 52.
19. Killion and Waller, *Georgia and the Revolution*, p. 206.
20. Ibid., 200.
21. Lawrence, *Storm Over Savannah*, 51.
22. Killion and Waller, *Georgia and the Revolution*, 206.
23. Lawrence, *Storm Over Savannah*, 54.
24. Ibid., 54.
25. Ibid., 63.
26. Ibid., 61.
27. Ibid.
28. Willcox, *The American Rebellion*, 433.
29. Ibid., 432–433.
30. Lawrence, *Storm Over Savannah*, 71.
31. Killion and Waller, *Georgia and the Revolution*, 204.
32. Ibid., 207.
33. Ibid., 202.
34. Willcox, *The American Rebellion*, 433–434.
35. Ibid., 149.
36. Lawrence, *Storm Over Savannah*, 79.
37. Ibid., 79.
38. Pancake, *This Destructive War*, 33.

Chapter 7

1. Richard Wheeler, *Voices of 1776. The Story of the American Revolution in the Words of Those Who Were There* (Penguin Books, 1991), 322.
2. Willcox, *The American Rebellion*, 423.
3. Ibid., 155.
4. Ibid., 417.
5. Ibid., 431.
6. Ibid., 434.
7. William B. Willcox, *Portrait of a General. Sir Henry Clinton in the War of Independence* (Alfred A. Knopf, 1964), 310.
8. Willcox, *Portrait of a General*, 39.
9. Wheeler, *Voices of 1776*, 322.
10. Willcox, *Portrait of a General*, 3.
11. Ibid., 15.

12. Pancake, *This Destructive War*, 59.
13. Lumpkin, *From Savannah to Yorktown*, 41.
14. Scheer and Rankin, *Rebels and Redcoats*, 396
15. Wheeler, *Voices of 1776*, 325.
16. Scheer and Rankin, *Rebels and Redcoats*, 396.
17. Ibid., 397.
18. Ibid., 398.
19. Ibid.
20. Wheeler, *Voices of 1776*, 328.
21. Commager and Morris, *Spirit of 'Seventy Six*, 1108–1109.
22. Ibid., 1109.
23. Ward, *War of the Revolution*, 2:703
24. Scheer and Rankin, *Rebels and Redcoats*, 399.
25. Ibid.
26. Willcox, *The American Rebellion*, 171.

Chapter 8

1. Robert W. Coakley and Stetson Conn, *The War of the American Revolution* (Center of Military History United States Army, 1975), 42–43.
2. Willcox, *The American Rebellion*, 188.
3. Stephen Conway, "The great mischief Complain'd of: Reflections on the Misconduct of British Soldiers in the Revolutionary War," *William and Mary Quarterly* (July, 1990): 370.
4. Pancake, *This Destructive War*, 81.
5. Wheeler, *Voices of 1776*, 324.
6. Commager and Morris, *Spirit of 'Seventy Six*, 1122.
7. Conway, *William and Mary Quarterly* (1986): 383.
8. Ibid., 378–379.
9. Wheeler, *Voices of 1776*, 326.
10. Ibid.
11. Commager and Morris, *Spirit of 'Seventy Six*, 1114.
12. Charles Bracelen Flood, *Rise, and Fight Again. Perilous Times Along the Road to Independence* (Dodd, Mead & Company, 1976), 260.
13. J. Tracy Power, "The Virtue Of Humanity Was Totally Forgot: Buford's Massacre, May 29, 1780," *South Carolina Historical Magazine* (January 1992): 8.
14. Scheer and Rankin, *Rebels and Redcoats*, p. 402.
15. Commager and Morris, *Spirit of 'Seventy Six*, 1115.
16. Ibid., 1112.

17. Ibid., 1111.
18. Power, *South Carolina Historical Magazine* (January 1992): 5.
19. Higginbotham, *The War of American Independence*, 361.
20. Pancake, *This Destructive War*, 71.
21. Power, *South Carolina Historical Magazine* (January 1992): 14.
22. Willcox, *The American Rebellion*, 181.
23. Willcox, *Portrait of a General*, 321.
24. Higginbotham, *The War of American Independence*, 360.
25. Klein, *Unification of a Slave State*, 79.
26. Lyman C. Draper, *King's Mountain and Its Heroes: History of the Battle of King's Mountain, October 7, 1780, and the Events Which Led to It* (Dauber & Pine Bookshops, Inc., 1929), 136.
27. Robinson, *Revolutionary War Sketches*, 12.
28. Commager and Morris, *Spirit of 'Seventy Six*, 1120.
29. Flood, *Rise and Fight Again*, 271.

Chapter 9

1. Flood, *Rise and Fight Again*, p. 266.
2. Ibid., 267.
3. Ward, *War of the Revolution*, 2:715.
4. Flood, *Rise and Fight Again*, 283.
5. Scheer and Rankin, *Rebels and Redcoats*, 404.
6. Ward, *War of the Revolution*, 2:718.
7. Flood, *Rise and Fight Again*, 285.
8. Ibid., 288.
9. Ibid., 291.
10. Commager and Morris, *The Spirit of 'Seventy Six*, 1127.
11. Dann, *The Revolution Remembered*, 194.
12. Willcox, *Portrait of a General*, 222.
13. Ibid., 442.
14. Ibid., 223.
15. Franklin Wickwire and Mary Wickwire, *Cornwallis The American Adventure* (Houghton Mifflin Co., 1970), 145.
16. Scheer and Rankin, *Rebels and Redcoats*, 406–407.
17. Ibid., 407.
18. Ibid.
19. Ibid.
20. Robinson, *Revolutionary War Sketches*, 18.
21. Higginbotham, *The War of American Independence*, 360.

22. Dann, *The Revolution Remembered,* 195.

23. Commager and Morris, *Spirit of 'Seventy Six,* 1131.

24. Ibid., 1133.

25. Flood, *Rise and Fight Again,* 332.

26. Ibid., 333.

27. Scheer and Rankin, *Rebels and Redcoats,* 410.

28. Willcox, *Portrait of a General,* 454.

29. Pancake, *This Destructive War,* 107.

30. Lumpkin, *From Savannah to Yorktown,* 67.

31. Flood, *Rise and Fight Again,* 341.

32. Ibid., 337.

33. Christopher Hibbert, *Redcoats and Rebels. The American Revolution Through British Eyes* (Avon Books, 1990), 273.

34. Higginbotham, *The War of American Independence,* 362.

35. Dann, *The Revolution Remembered,* 202.

36. Draper, *Kings Mountain,* 506.

37. Ibid., 498.

38. Ibid., 506.

39. Ibid., 499.

40. Troxler, *The Loyalist Experience,* 24.

41. Ibid., 28.

42. Ibid., 27.

43. Pancake, *This Destructive War,* 109.

44. Robinson, *Revolutionary War Sketches,* 23.

45. Ibid.

46. Wheeler, *Voices of 1776,* 353.

47. Ibid.

Chapter 10

1. Draper, *Kings Mountain,* 510.

2. Ward, *War of the Revolution,* 2:740.

3. Draper, *Kings Mountain,* 508.

4. Ibid., 507.

5. Ibid., 508.

6. Ibid., 509.

7. Ward, *War of the Revolution,* 2:740.

8. Hank Messick, *King's Mountain. The Epic of the Blue Ridge "Mountain Men" in the American Revolution* (Little, Brown and Company, 1976), 92.

9. Draper, *Kings Mountain,* 541.

10. Flood, *Rise and Fight Again,* 352.

11. Ibid., 355.

12. Messick, *King's Mountain,* 99–100

13. Ibid., 128.

14. Ibid., 127.

15. Lumpkin, *From Savannah to Yorktown,* 95.

16. Draper, *Kings Mountain,* 510.

17. Messick, *King's Mountain,* 129.

18. Scheer and Rankin, *Rebels and Redcoats,* 417.

19. Ibid.

20. Draper, *Kings Mountain,* 549.

21. Ibid., 538.

22. Ibid., 552.

23. Ibid., 543.

24. Wheeler, *Voices of 1776,* 356.

25. Ibid.

26. Messick, *King's Mountain,* 140.

27. Draper, *Kings Mountain,* 543.

28. Wheeler, *Voices of 1776,* 356.

29. Messick, *King's Mountain,* 154.

30. Scheer and Rankin, *Rebels and Redcoats,* 418.

31. Ibid.

32. Draper, *Kings Mountain,* 539.

33. Scheer and Rankin, *Rebels and Redcoats,* 418.

34. Messick, *King's Mountain,* 154.

35. Hibbert, *Redcoats and Rebels,* 283.

36. Messick, *King's Mountain,* 155.

37. Draper, *Kings Mountain,* 510.

38. Wheeler, *Voices of 1776,* 357.

39. Ibid.

40. Willcox, *Portrait of a General,* 226.

41. Wickwire and Wickwire, *Cornwallis,* 216.

42. Ward, *War of the Revolution,* 2:745.

43. Coakley and Coan, *American Revolution,* 73.

44. Willcox, *Portrait of a General,* 228.

45. Commager and Morris, *Spirit of 'Seventy Six,* 1148–49.

46. W. J. Wood, *Battles of the Revolutionary War. 1775–1781* (Algonquin Books of Chapel Hill, Chapel Hill, NC), 207.

Chapter 11

1. M. F. Treacy, *Prelude to Yorktown: The Southern Campaign of Nathanael Greene 1780–1781* (The University of North Carolina Press, 1963), 59.
2. Theodore Thayer, *Nathanael Greene. Strategist of the American Revolution* (Twayne Publishers, 1960), 296.
3. Elswyth Thane, *The Fighting Quaker: Nathanael Greene* (Aeonian Press, Inc., 1977), 62.
4. Ibid., 26.
5. Ibid., 125.
6. Thayer, *Nathanael Greene*, 227.
7. Ibid., 243.
8. Wheeler, *Voices of 1776*, 358.
9. Treacy, *Prelude to Yorktown*, 58.
10. Charles Royster, *Light-Horse Harry Lee and the Legacy of the American Revolution* (Cambridge University Press, 1986), 23.
11. Hugh F. Rankin, *Greene and Cornwallis: The Campaign in the Carolinas* (Department of Cultural Resources, Division of Archives and History, Raleigh, NC, 1976), 4–5.
12. Treacy, *Prelude to Yorktown*, 59.
13. Ibid., 56.
14. Rankin, *Greene and Cornwallis*, 6.
15. Commager and Morris, *Spirit of 'Seventy Six*, 1152.
16. Flood, *Rise and Fight Again*, 361.
17. Commager and Morris, *Spirit of 'Seventy Six*, 1152.
18. Thayer, *Nathanael Greene*, 289.
19. Thane, *The Fighting Quaker*, 191.
20. Pancake, *This Destructive War*, 129.
21. Ibid., 128.
22. Don Higginbotham, *Daniel Morgan. Revolutionary Rifleman* (The University of North Carolina Press, 1961), 9.
23. Thane, *The Fighting Quaker*, 188.
24. Pancake, *This Destructive War*, 139.
25. Rankin, *Greene and Cornwallis*, 18.
26. Robert D. Bass, *Gamecock. The Life and Campaigns of Thomas Sumter* (Holt, Rinehart and Winston, 1961), 116.

Chapter 12

1. Pancake, *This Destructive War*, 131.
2. Commager and Morris, *Spirit of 'Seventy Six*, 1155.

3. Rankin, *Greene and Cornwallis,* 32.

4. Wheeler, *Voices of 1776,* 360.

5. Scheer and Rankin, *Rebels and Redcoats,* 427.

6. Higginbotham, *Daniel Morgan,* 131.

7. Ibid., 132.

8. Ibid.

9. Scheer and Rankin, *Rebels and Redcoats,* 428.

10. Ibid.

11. Commager and Morris, *Spirit of 'Seventy Six,* 1153.

12. Scheer and Rankin, *Rebels and Redcoats,* 428.

13. Ibid., 429.

14. Higginbotham, *Daniel Morgan,* 136.

15. Ibid.

16. Pancake, *This Destructive War,* 138.

17. Commager and Morris, *Spirit of 'Seventy Six,* 1158.

18. Scheer and Rankin, *Rebels and Redcoats,* 430.

19. Higginbotham, *Daniel Morgan,* 137.

20. Ibid.

21. Scheer and Rankin, *Rebels and Redcoats,* 430.

22. Ibid.

23. Wheeler, *Voices of 1776,* 362.

24. Higginbotham, *Daniel Morgan,* 139.

25. Scheer and Rankin, *Rebels and Redcoats,* 431.

26. Higginbotham, *Daniel Morgan,* 140.

27. Wheeler, *Voices of 1776,* 363.

28. Scheer and Rankin, *Rebels and Redcoats,* 432.

29. Higginbotham, *Daniel Morgan,* 141.

30. Commager and Morris, *Spirit of 'Seventy Six,* 1159.

31. Higginbotham, *Daniel Morgan,* 142.

32. Commager and Morris, *Spirit of 'Seventy Six,* 1157.

33. Wheeler, *Voices of 1776,* 363.

34. Flood, *Rise and Fight Again,* 381.

35. Commager and Morris, *Spirit of 'Seventy Six,* 1159.

Chapter 13

1. Ward, *War of the Revolution,* 2:770.

2. Commager and Morris, *Spirit of 'Seventy Six,* 1160.

3. Thayer, *Nathanael Greene,* 310.

4. Pancake, *This Destructive War,* 157.

5. Ibid., 159.

6. Thomas E. Baker, *Another Such Victory* (Eastern Acorn Press, 1981), 24.

7. Flood, *Rise and Fight Again*, 382.

8. Willcox, *Portrait of a General*, 261.

9. Higginbotham, *The War of American Independence*, 368.

10. Scheer and Rankin, *Rebels and Redcoats*, 435.

11. Pancake, *This Destructive War*, 161.

12. Flood, *Rise and Fight Again*, 382.

13. Ward, *War of the Revolution*, 2:766.

14. Flood, *Rise and Fight Again*, 383.

15. Scheer and Rankin, *Rebels and Redcoats*, 436.

16. Flood, *Rise and Fight Again*, 385.

17. Ibid., 386.

18. Ibid., 387.

19. Pancake, *This Destructive War*, 164.

20. Higginbotham, *Daniel Morgan*, 155.

21. Scheer and Rankin, *Rebels and Redcoats*, 440.

Chapter 14

1. Commager and Morris, *Spirit of 'Seventy Six*, 1162.

2. Pancake, *This Destructive War*, 174.

3. Commager and Morris, *Spirit of 'Seventy Six*, 1162.

4. Ibid., 1162–1163.

5. Ibid., 1163.

6. Pancake, *This Destructive War*, 172.

7. Ibid., 167.

8. Royster, *Light-Horse Harry*, 35–36.

9. Russell, *North Carolina*, 209.

10. Commager and Morris, *Spirit of 'Seventy Six*, 1163.

11. Royster, *Light-Horse Harry*, 38.

12. Ward, *War of the Revolution*, 2:918.

13. Wheeler, *Voices of 1776*, 369.

14. Baker, 31.

15. Scheer and Rankin, *Rebels and Redcoats*, 444.

16. Commager and Morris, *Spirit of 'Seventy Six*, 1163.

17. Ibid., 1163–1164

18. Baker, 35.

19. Ibid., 36.

20. Scheer and Rankin, *Rebels and Redcoats*, 445.

21. Baker, 45.

22. Scheer and Rankin, *Rebels and Redcoats,* 446.

23. Ibid.

24. Baker, 50.

25. Wheeler, *Voices of 1776,* 370.

26. Ibid.

27. Ibid., 372.

28. Baker, 53.

29. Ibid.

30. Ibid., 54.

31. Wheeler, *Voices of 1776,* 372.

32. Rankin, *Greene and Cornwallis,* 74.

33. Baker, 59.

34. Ibid., 61.

35. Ibid., 65.

36. Ward, *War of the Revolution,* 2:793

37. Baker, 76.

38. Pancake, *This Destructive War,* 186.

39. Higginbotham, *The War of American Independence,* 370.

40. Commager and Morris, *Spirit of 'Seventy Six,* 1164.

Chapter 15

1. Pancake, *This Destructive War,* 188.

2. Ibid., 186.

3. Commager and Morris, *Spirit of 'Seventy Six,* 1167.

4. Hibbert, *Redcoats and Rebels,* 308.

5. Wheeler, *Voices of 1776,* 378.

6. Ibid., 379.

7. Pancake, *This Destructive War,* 193.

8. Ward, *War of the Revolution,* 2:802.

9. Wheeler, *Voices of 1776,* 379.

10. Commager and Morris, *Spirit of 'Seventy Six,* 1177.

11. Hibbert, *Redcoats and Rebels,* 309–310.

12. Wheeler, *Voices of 1776,* 380.

13. Pancake, *This Destructive War,* 200.

14. Ibid., 187.

15. Ibid., 204.

16. Wheeler, *Voices of 1776,* 382.

17. Ibid., 384.

18. Robert D. Bass, *Ninety Six. The Struggle for the South Carolina Back Country* (The Sandlapper Store, Inc.), 394.

19. Wheeler, *Voices of 1776,* 384.

20. Commager and Morris, *Spirit of 'Seventy Six,* 1185.

21. Pancake, *This Destructive War,* 214.

22. Commager and Morris, *Spirit of 'Seventy Six,* 1189.

23. Pancake, *This Destructive War,* 217.

24. Ward, *War of the Revolution,* 2:827.

25. Commager and Morris, *Spirit of 'Seventy Six,* 1187.

26. Ibid., 1190.

27. Ibid., 1191.

28. Wheeler, *Voices of 1776,* 386.

Chapter 16

1. Commager and Morris, *Spirit of 'Seventy Six,* 1201.

2. Ibid.

3. Ibid.

4. Ibid.

5. Ibid.

6. Willcox, *Portrait of a General,* 287.

7. Commager and Morris, *Spirit of 'Seventy Six,* 1201.

8. Willcox, *Portrait of a General,* 288–289.

9. Ibid., 309.

10. Ibid., 549.

11. Ibid., 522.

12. Commager and Morris, *Spirit of 'Seventy Six,* 1201.

13. Willcox, *Portrait of a General,* 530.

14. Ibid., 536.

15. Ibid., 543.

16. Ibid., 553.

17. Henry P. Johnston, *The Yorktown Campaign and the Surrender of Cornwallis 1781* (Eastern Acorn Press, 1981), 75.

18. Ibid., 76.

19. Ibid., 80.

20. Ibid., 83–84.

21. Joseph Plumb Martin, *Private Yankee Doodle. Being a Narrative of Some of the Adventures, Dangers and Sufferings of a Revolutionary Soldier* (Eastern Acorn Press, 1988), 222.

22. Willcox, *Portrait of a General,* 562.

23. Ibid., 563.

24. Ibid.

25. Ibid., 540.

26. Ibid., 546.

27. Pancake, *This Destructive War,* 225.

28. Willcox, *Portrait of a General,* 571.

29. Pancake, *This Destructive War,* 228.

30. Willcox, *Portrait of a General,* 561–562.

31. Willcox, *Portrait of a General,* 562.

32. Commager and Morris, *Spirit of 'Seventy Six,* 1220.

33. Willcox, *Portrait of a General,* 567.

34. Martin, *Private Yankee Doodle,* 224.

35. Commager and Morris, *Spirit of 'Seventy Six,* 1224.

36. Ibid., 1227.

37. Martin, *Private Yankee Doodle,* 230.

38. Commager and Morris, *Spirit of 'Seventy Six,* 1232.

39. Willcox, *Portrait of a General,* 581.

40. Commager and Morris, *Spirit of 'Seventy Six,* 1241.

41. Willcox, *Portrait of a General,* p. 583.

42. Pancake, *This Destructive War,* 243.

43. Klein, *Unification of a Slave State,* 108.

CHRONOLOGY

Of Major Events In The
American Revolutionary War in the South

1775

23 March: Virginia Convention passed resolution that colony should immediately take measures to defend itself. Patrick Henry delivered his "liberty or death" speech.

19 April: Mail seized from British ship in Charleston, South Carolina disclosed that the British Government intended to coerce colonies into submission. This news provided warning to patriots in the Carolinas and Georgia.

20–21 April: Virginia Governor Lord Dunmore (John Murray) seized provincial powder supply in Williamsburg. Outbreak of fighting with patriot militia was barely averted.

21 April: Patriots in Charleston, South Carolina removed powder from public magazines.

10 May: Second Continental Congress convened in Philadelphia, Pennsylvania, with delegates from all colonies except Georgia in attendance.

11 May: Patriots in Savannah, Georgia removed powder from royal magazine.

31 May: Patriots in Mecklenburg County, North Carolina passed the Mecklenburg Resolves, which proclaimed British law to be null and void.

31 May: Josiah Martin, Governor of North Carolina, fled from his place in New Bern and occupied Fort Johnston on the Cape Fear River.

2 June: South Carolina Provincial Congress proclaimed that residents were "ready to sacrifice their lives and their fortunes" for the patriot cause.

8 June: Lord Dunmore vacated his palace in Williamsburg, Virginia and went aboard the British warship *Fowey* at Yorktown.

10 July: Georgia sent out first patriot vessel commissioned for naval warfare.

18 July: Josiah Martin forced by patriot threat to go aboard British sloop *Cruzier* in Cape Fear River.

23 August: King George III of Great Britain declared 13 American colonies to be in rebellion and ordered the suppression of American defiance of British authority.

15 September: William Campbell, Governor of South Carolina, compelled by loss of control of affairs to go aboard British sloop *Tamar*.

10 October: General William Howe replaced General Thomas Gage as Commander-in-Chief of British Army forces in the American colonies.

24–25 October: British landing party repulsed with heavy losses when it attempted to occupy Hampton, Virginia.

7 November: Lord Dunmore ordered Virginia placed under martial law.

22 November: Patriots won almost bloodless encounter with small Loyalist force at Reedy Creek, South Carolina (south of modern Greenville) and captured Tory leaders.

9 December: British force sent by Lord Dunmore to stop patriots who were advancing on Norfolk, Virginia was badly defeated with 62 casualties at Great Bridge, Virginia.

13 December: Patriots occupied Norfolk, Virginia.

1776

1 January: Lord Dunmore ordered British Navy to bombard and set fire to Norfolk, Virginia when patriots refused to allow British landing party to come ashore.

20 January: General Henry Clinton sailed from Boston with 1200 troops to oversee British expedition against the Carolinas.

11 February: Sir James Wright, Royal Governor of Georgia, fled from Savannah and took refuge on a British warship.

27 February: Continental Congress resolved to establish Southern Department of the Continental Army, consisting of Virginia, the Carolinas, and Georgia.

27 February: Loyalist force consisting mainly of Scotch Highlanders clashed with patriot force at Moore's Creek Bridge about 17 miles from Wilmington, North Carolina. Patriots achieved a decisive victory.

7 March: Governor Wright failed in his attempt to recapture Savannah, Georgia by armed force, thereby assuring that the Georgia capital would remain in patriot hands.

9–13 March: Maryland ship *Defense* attacked and repulsed British sloop *Otter* in Chesapeake Bay, and two Maryland militia companies occupied Northampton County, Virginia.

12 April: North Carolina led American colonies in instructing its delegates in the Continental Congress to vote for independence.

15 May: Virginia Convention ordered Richard Henry Lee and the other Virginia delegates to the Continental Congress to propose independence.

4 June: General Clinton and Admiral Sir Peter Parker arrived with expeditionary force off Charleston, South Carolina.

4 June: General Charles Lee, named by the Continental Congress as the first commander of the Southern Department, arrived in Charleston, South Carolina.

28 June: Admiral Parker and British Navy launch a major but unsuccessful attack against Fort Sullivan on Sullivan's Island, South Carolina.

2 July: Continental Congress approved resolution of independence which had been introduced by Richard Henry Lee of Virginia on June 7th.

4 July: Continental Congress approved formal Declaration of Independence.

8–10 July: Patriot forces attacked and captured Gwynn Island in Chesapeake Bay, where Governor Dunmore had taken refuge. Dunmore was compelled to flee, first up the Potomac River, where he carried out raids against several plantations, and eventually to New York.

July: Cherokees under Chief Dragging Canoe launched a major offensive against patriot settlements on the frontier of Virginia and the Carolinas. Patriot militia eventually crushed the rebellion with devastating consequences for the ability of the Native Americans to provide meaningful support for the British.

August: General Robert Howe, commander of the Southern Department of the Continental Army, mounted unsuccessful invasion of British East Florida.

1777

7–9 February: Patriots defenders of Fort McIntosh in present Camden County, Georgia were overwhelmed by British and Tory troops moving north from St. Augustine, Florida.

1778

21 March: General Clinton, who was to relieve Howe as British commander in North America, was ordered to dispatch 3000 troops to East Florida.

4 May: Congress ratified treaties of alliance and of amity and commerce between the United States and France.

6 June: Members of the Carlisle Peace Commission arrived in Philadelphia.

25 September: Congress appointed General Benjamin Lincoln to replace Robert Howe as Commander of the Southern Department of the Continental Army. Virginia and North Carolina are urged to come to the aid of South Carolina and Georgia.

27 November: Archibald Campbell and 3500 troops set sail from New York for attack against Georgia.

29 December: General Robert Howe and patriot troops were defeated at Savannah, Georgia, and Archibald Campbell and his British and Tory force took control of the town.

1779

9 January: Patriot defenders of Fort Morris at Sunbury, Georgia were compelled to capitulate after 3-day siege by British force, which included Native Americans.

29 January: British force under Archibald Campbell occupied Augusta, Georgia and summoned Tories to gather under the Royal standard.

3 February: Patriots under General William Moultrie successfully defended Beaufort, South Carolina from British attack.

14 February: Colonel Andrew Pickens defeated band of 700 North Carolina Tories at Kettle Creek, Georgia and prevented their joining the British at Augusta.

3 March: Patriot force of mostly North Carolina militiamen was severely defeated at Briar Creek, Georgia by British force that was retreating from Augusta to Savannah.

11–12 May: General Benjamin Lincoln marched main Southern Continental Army from South Carolina into Georgia, where he occupied Augusta. Augustine Prevost countered by dispatching redcoats across the lower Savannah River. When General Moultrie and his patriot troops gave way, the British decided to advance all the way to Charleston, South Carolina.

20 June: Patriot army attacked British rear guard at Stono Ferry, South

Carolina. In this brief but bloody engagement the British held their ground but soon retreated southward.

21 June: Spain declared war on Great Britain.

11–12 September: Admiral D'Estaing's French fleet arrived off Georgia coast and began landing troops at Beaulieu Plantation, 14 miles below Savannah, Georgia.

16 September–10 October: Combined force of Americans under General Benjamin Lincoln and French under Admiral D'Estaing laid siege to Savannah, Georgia.

9 October: Franco-American army attacked Augustine Prevost's defenses at Savannah, Georgia and after suffering heavy losses failed to take the town.

26 December: General Henry Clinton and sizeable British army set sail from New York on mission to capture Charleston, South Carolina and invade the Carolinas.

1780

10–11 February: General Clinton's troops landed on Simmons Island and began their methodical campaign to overwhelm General Benjamin Lincoln's army in Charleston, South Carolina.

14 March: British garrison at Fort Charlotte at present site of Mobile, Ala. was defeated by Spanish army led by Spanish Governor Bernardo de Galvez of Lousiana.

1 April: Having brought ships into Charleston Harbor and having sealed off virtually all avenues of escape, the British began classical siege operations against General Lincoln's army in Charleston, South Carolina.

14 April: Colonel Banastre Tarleton carried out surprise attack against patriot force at Monck's Corner, South Carolina, thereby eliminating any possibility for Lincoln's army to evacuate Charleston.

24 April: patriot sortie at Charleston, South Carolina inflicted tactical defeat

on elements of the British attackers but Lincoln's army lacked strength to press the attack.

12 May: General Lincoln's American army after six-week siege surrendered to General Clinton. Now in possession of Charleston, South Carolina, the British now made preparations for a major invasion of the Carolina backcountry.

29 May: Colonel Tarleton and his dragoons inflicted a devastating defeat in the Waxhaws on Continental troops under Abraham Buford. This infamous episode earned Tarleton the nickname, "Bloody Tarleton."

20 June: Large body of Loyalists defeated by patriot militia at Ramsour's Mill (in modern Lincolnton, North Carolina).

12 July: Colonel Thomas Sumter led patriot militia in victory over Tories, including some of Tarleton's dragoons, at Williamson's Plantation (near present Rock Hill, South Carolina).

13 July: Congress selected Major General Horatio Gates to take command of the Southern Department of the Continental Army.

30 July: Patriot force persuaded Loyalist garrison at Fort Anderson (10 miles southeast of Cowpens) to surrender without firing a shot.

1 August: Bloody but inconclusive skirmish between patriots and elements of Major Patrick Ferguson's command occurred at Green Spring, South Carolina.

1 August: Thomas Sumter led attack against fortified Tory stronghold at Rocky Mount, South Carolina. Lacking artillery, the patriot force could not dislodge the defenders.

6 August: Sumter's partisans attacked and defeated the Tory garrison at Hanging Rock, South Carolina, about 20 miles east of Rocky Mount.

15 August: Sumter captured British force guarding Wateree Ferry, South Carolina, together with a large stock of supplies and wagons enroute to the British garrison at Camden, South Carolina.

16 August: Major engagement occurred about seven miles north of Camden, South Carolina between the British army of General Charles Cornwallis and the American army of Major General Horatio Gates. The British achieved a decisive victory and therefore made preparations for moving into North Carolina.

18 August: Near Musgrove's Mill, South Carolina on the north bank of the Enoree River, patriots achieved a victory over a large band of Tories.

18 August: Colonel Tarleton surprised Sumter's command at Fishing Creek, South Carolina and killed 150 patriots.

20 August: Brigadier General Francis Marion surprised the British guards who were escorting 150 American prisoners to Charleston at Nelson's Ferry (Great Savannah), South Carolina on the Santee River and released the patriots.

4 September: Francis Marion and about 50 followers routed a much larger Tory force at Blue Savannah, South Carolina.

14–18 September: Patriots took outposts guarding Augusta, Georgia, but were unable to capture the city because of the arrival of British reinforcements.

21 September: Colonel William R. Davie led patriot troops in surprise attack against Tory band at Wahab's Plantation, about 20 miles southwest of Charlotte, North Carolina.

26 September: Cornwallis and his army occupied Charlotte, North Carolina after brief but sharp skirmish with patriot militia led by William R. Davie.

29 September: Francis Marion defeated small Tory force at Black Mingo Creek, South Carolina.

7 October: Patriot force of 900 frontiersmen decisively defeated Tory force of approximately the same size headed by Major Patrick Ferguson at Kings Mountain on the North Carolina-South Carolina border. This battle was a major turning point in the war in the South.

26 October: Marion dispersed a Tory force which had gathered near Tear-court Swamp, South Carolina.

30 October: Congress approved the appointment of Nathanael Greene as commander of the Southern Army.

9 November: Sumter's patriot militia inflicted heavy casualties on force of 140 troops that attacked him at Fishdam Ford, South Carolina, 25 miles northwest of British headquarters at Winnsborough, South Carolina.

20 November: Sumter and about 1000 militia decisively defeated Tarleton and approximately 270 dragoons at Blackstocks, South Carolina. Sumter was severely wounded in this engagement.

3 December: General Greene took command of the Southern Army from Horatio Gates in Charlotte, North Carolina.

4 December: Colonel William Washington's cavalry secured the surrender of approximately 100 Tories who had occupied a fortified barn at Rudgeley's Mill, South Carolina.

12–13 December: Marion skirmished with British force at Halfway Swamp, South Carolina.

28 December: Patriot force of 280 Continental cavalry and mounted infantry defeated 250 Loyalists at Hammond's Store, South Carolina (near modern Newberry).

30 December: Benedict Arnold, now a British Brigadier, arrived at Hampton Roads, Virginia to initiate raids up the James River.

1781

5–7 January: Arnold occupied Richmond, Virginia and burned tobacco warehouses and some private and public buildings before vacating the city.

8 January: 40 mounted rangers from Arnold's force overwhelmed 150 patriot militia at Charles City Court House, Virginia.

17 January: Daniel Morgan won a resounding victory over Banastre Tarleton at Cowpens, South Carolina in a classic double envelopment of the Redcoats and Tories just after dawn. The Battle at Cowpens constituted a major turning point in the American Revolutionary War in the South.

24 January: Henry Lee and Francis Marion raided Georgetown, South Carolina and captured the British commander. Lacking necessary siege equipment, Lee and Marion soon withdrew.

1 February: Cornwallis's army, after occupying Ramsour's Mill, North Carolina, moved to the Catawba River and crossed at M'Cowan's Ford where General William Lee Davidson, commander of the patriot militia, was killed in a brief but sharp skirmish. Afterward, Tarleton dispersed patriot militia at Tarrant's Tavern (near modern Mooresville, North Carolina).

1 February: British under Major James Craig occupied Wilmington, North Carolina.

14 February: Nathanael Greene crossed Dan River into Virginia, leaving Cornwallis in control of the two Carolinas.

25 February: Henry Lee's Continentals surprised and destroyed contingent of local Tory militia at Haw River, North Carolina, in infamous engagement known as "Pyle's Hacking Match."

2 March: Henry Lee skirmished with advanced guard of British army under Tarleton at Clapp's Mill, North Carolina.

6 March: Tarleton's cavalry and 1,000 British infantry attacked contingent of Greene's army at Wetzell's Mill, North Carolina. Weaker patriot force refused to participate in a major engagement and therefore withdrew.

15 March: Major battle between Greene and Cornwallis occurred at Guilford Court House, North Carolina (in modern Greensboro). Technically, the battle was a British victory, but because of heavy losses Cornwallis was compelled to retreat toward the coast.

16 March: French and British fleets clashed in the first "Battle of the Capes" at the entrance to Chesapeake Bay. British were able to maintain control and thereby assure supply routes to Arnold's troops in Virginia.

23 April: Fort Watson, South Carolina (now under the waters of Lake Marion) fell to patriots.

25 April: Greene, after returning to South Carolina, was attacked by Lord Rowdon's troops at Hobkirk's Hill, just outside Camden, South Carolina. Although victorious, Rawdon soon had to retreat to Charleston, South Carolina, because he was unable to protect his route of supply.

25 April: Major General William Phillips, who succeeded Arnold as commander of British troops in Virginia, defeated patriot militia defending Petersburg, Virginia.

27 April: Benedict Arnold dispersed patriot militia at Osborne's Virginia, which was on the James River 15 miles below Richmond.

29 April: General Lafayette and 1200 Continentals sent south by General Washington arrived in Richmond, Virginia.

10 May: Lord Rawdon abandoned Camden, South Carolina and retreated to Charleston.

10 May: Spanish captured Pensacola, Florida after two-month siege, thereby causing the loss of British control of West Florida.

11 May: British outpost at Orangeburg, South Carolina surrendered to Thomas Sumter.

12 May: Henry Lee and Francis Marion overwhelmed the defenders of Fort Motte, South Carolina.

15 May: Henry Lee captured Fort Granby, South Carolina (in modern Columbia, South Carolina).

20 May: Charles Cornwallis and 1500 soldiers reached Petersburg, Virginia, where the Earl took command of all 7200 British troops in Virginia.

22 May-19 June: General Greene and about 1000 Continentals lay siege to the British post at Ninety-Six, South Carolina. Frontal assault on final day failed to dislodge the Tory defenders of the Star Redoubt.

4 June: Banastre Tarleton raided Charlottesville, Virginia, where he barely missed capturing Governor Thomas Jefferson and the other members of Virginia legislature.

5 June: British troops attack major patriot supply depot at Point of Fork (Fort Union), Virginia and destroyed supplies.

10 June: General Wayne and 1000 Continentals joined Lafayette in Virginia to harass Cornwallis.

26 June: British and patriot armies clashed at Spencer's Tavern, Virginia, near Williamsburg, with light casualties on both sides.

6 July: General Wayne attacked what he thought was the rear guard of Cornwallis's army at Greenspring (near Jamestown), Virginia. After brief but sharp engagement, the patriots were forced to withdraw after suffering 140 casualties.

9–24 July: Tarleton carried out a series of raids on south side of the James River as far west as Bedford County.

17 July: Patriots attacked and forced the withdrawal of the British garrison at Monck's Corner, South Carolina. Marion engaged the retreating British at Quimby's Creek Bridge, South Carolina, on the left bank of the Cooper River some 15 miles from Charleston.

1 August: Cornwallis occupied Yorktown, Virginia, as well as Gloucester Point across the York River.

21 August: Washington, learning that the French fleet was headed for the mouth of Chesapeake Bay, began marching his army southward toward Virginia.

25 August: Rochambeau's French army joined Washington's in New Jersey and started marching toward the Chesapeake.

26 August: French fleet of 34 warships under Admiral Francois Comte de Grasse arrived off the Virginia capes.

2 September: French troops from de Grasse's fleet commenced landing below Yorktown, Virginia.

5 September: Second "Battle of the Capes" occurred between British and French fleets outside entrance to Chesapeake Bay. Action, which continued for several days, was indecisive, but British were unable to break through to British garrison at Yorktown, Virginia.

8 September: Nathanael Greene fought bloody engagement with British troops at Eutaw Springs, South Carolina. Both sides suffered heavy casualties, but victory technically belonged to the British, even though they soon withdrew to Charleston, South Carolina.

12 September: Force of 1000 Loyalists made surprise attack upon Hillsborough, North Carolina, and took more than 200 prisoners, including Governor Thomas Burke. After withdrawing, Loyalists were attacked at Cane Creek (Lindley's Mill).

14 September: Washington and Rochambeau arrived on the peninsula between the James and York rivers in Virginia and make final preparations for marching toward Yorktown, Virginia.

28 September-19 October: Combined American and French forces laid siege to Yorktown, Virginia.

3 October: At Gloucester Point, directly across the York River from Yorktown, Virginia, French troops and patriot militia attacked a foraging party sent out by Banastre Tarleton and began formal siege operations against Gloucester Point, thereby depriving Cornwallis of his only avenue of escape.

14 October: American and British troops capture Redoubts 9 and 10 in British defense line at Yorktown, Virginia.

16–17 October: Because of storm Cornwallis was unable to ferry his troops across the James River to Gloucester Point.

19 October: Cornwallis's army of approximately 10,000 troops surrendered to 11,000 Americans and 9,000 French soldiers at Yorktown, Virginia.

This event would prove to be decisive in ending Parliamentary support for continuing the effort to defeat the American rebellion.

18 November: British evacuated Wilmington, North Carolina.

27 November: British outpost at Fair Lawn, South Carolina fell to patriot militia.

1 December: Nathanael Greene attacked British garrison at Dorchester, South Carolina, prompting the defenders to withdraw toward Charleston, South Carolina.

28–29 December: Henry Lee launched unsuccessful attack against Johns Island, South Carolina.

1782

27 February: British House of Commons officially advised King George III to terminate war with America.

11 July: British evacuated Savannah, Georgia.

11–13 September: 250 Indians and 40 Loyalists failed in their effort to capture Fort Henry, Virginia.

27 September: Formal peace negotiations between American and British commissioners opened in Paris, France.

30 November: The United States and Great Britain signed preliminary treaty of peace recognizing American independence.

14 December: Charleston, South Carolina, the last British outpost in the South, was evacuated by the British, who took 3800 Loyalists and 5000 slaves with them.

1783

4 February: Great Britain announced end of hostilities with the United States.

11 April: Congress of the United States announced end of hostilities.

15 April: Congress of the United States ratified preliminary treaty of peace with Great Britain.

3 September: Definitive treaties of peace were signed by Great Britain, France, Spain, and The Netherlands.

BIBLIOGRAPHY

Baker, Thomas E., *Another Such Victory. The story of the American defeat at Guilford Courthouse that helped win the War for Independence* (Eastern Acorn Press, 1981).

Bass, Robert D., *Gamecock. The Life and Compaigns of Thomas Sumter* (Holt, Rinehart and Winston, 1961).

Bass, Robert D., *Ninety Six. The Struggle for the South Carolina Back Country* (The Sandlapper Store, Inc.).

Bennett, Charles E. & Lennon, Donald R., *A Quest for Glory. Major General Robert Howe and the American Revolution* (The University of North Carolina Press, 1991).

Boorstein, Daniel J., *The Americans. The Colonial Experience* (Vintage Books, 1958).

Cashin, Edward J., *The King's Ranger. Thomas Brown and The American Revolution On The Southern Frontier* (The University of Georgia Press, 1989).

Coakley, Robert W. & Conn, Stetson, *The War of the American Revolution* (Center Of Military History United States Army, 1975), pp. 42–43.

Commager, Henry Steele & Morris, Richard B., eds., *The Spirit of 'Seventy Six. The Story Of The American Revolution As Told By Participants* (Harper & Row, 1967).

Crow, Jeffrey J., *The Black Experience in Revolutionary North Carolina* (Division of Archives and History, North Carolina Department of Cultural Resources, 1989).

Dann, John C., ed., *The Revolution Remembered, Eyewitness Accounts of the War for Independence* (University of Chicago Press, 1980).

Draper, Lyman C., *King's Mountain And Its Heroes: History Of The Battle Of*

King's Mountain, October 7, 1780, And The Events Which Led To It (Dauber & Pine Bookshops, Inc., 1929).

Duffy, Christopher, *The Military Experience in the Age of Reason* (Athaneum, 1988).

Flood, Charles Bracelen, *Rise, And Fight Again. Perilous Times Along the Road to Independence* (Dodd, Mead & Company, 1976).

Hibbert, Christopher, *Redcoats And Rebels. The American Revolution Through British Eyes* (Avon Books, 1990).

Higginbotham, Don, *Daniel Morgan. Revolutionary Rifleman* (The University of North Carolina Press, 1961).

Higginbotham, Don, *The War Of American Independence* (Northeastern University Press, 1983).

Johnston, Henry P., *The Yorktown Campaign And The Surrender Of Cornwallis 1781* (Eastern Acorn Press, 1981).

Jones, Lewis Pickney, *The South Carolina Civil War Of 1775* (The Sandlapper Store, Inc., 1975).

Killion, Ronald G. & Waller, Charles T., *Georgia and the Revolution* (Cherokee Publishing Company, 1975).

Klein, Rachel N., *Unification of a Slave State. The Rise Of The Planter Class In The South Carolina Backcountry, 1760–1808* (University of North Carolina Press, 1990).

Lawrence, Alexander A., *Storm Over Savannah* (Tara Press, 1979).

Lipscomb, Terry W., *The Carolina lowcountry April 1775–June 1776* (South Carolina Department of Archives and History, 1991).

Lumpkin, Henry, *From Savannah To Yorktown* (Paragon House Publishers, n.d.).

Martin, Joseph Plumb, *Private Yankee Doodle. Being A Narrative Of Some Of*

The Adventures, Dangers And Sufferings Of A Revolutionary Soldier (Eastern Acorn Press, 1988).

Messick, Hank, *King's Mountain. The Epic of the Blue Ridge "Mountain Men" in the American Revolution* (Little, Brown and Company, 1976).

MiddleKauff, Robert, *The Glorious Cause. The American Revolution, 1763–1789* (Oxford University Press, 1982).

O'Donnell, James H. III, *The Cherokees of North Carolina in the American Revolution* (Department of Cultural Resources, Division of Archives and History, 1976).

Pancake, John S., *1777. The Year of The Hangman* (University of Alabama Press, 1977).

Pancake, John S., *This Destructive War. The British Campaign in the Carolinas 1780–1782* (University of Alabama Press, 1985).

Quarles, Benjamin, *The Negro In The American Revolution* (W. W. Norton & Company, 1973).

Rankin, Hugh F., *Greene and Cornwallis: The Campaign in the Carolinas* (Department of Cultural Resources, Division of Archives and History, Raleigh, N.C., 1976).

Rankin, Hugh F., *The Moores Creek Bridge Campaign, 1776* (The Moore Creek Battleground Association, 1986).

Raynor, George, *Patriots and Tories in Piedmont Carolina* (Salisbury Printing Co., Inc., 1990).

Rights, Douglas L., *The American Indian in North Carolina* (Wachovia Historical Society, 1957).

Robinson, Blackwell P., *The Revolutionary War Sketches of William R. Davie* (North Carolina State University Graphics, 1976).

Royster, Charles, *Light-Horse Harry Lee & the Legacy of the American Revolution* (Cambridge University Press, 1986).

Russell, Phillips, *North Carolina In The Revolutionary War* (Heritage Printers, 1965).

Scheer, George F. & Rankin, Hugh F., eds., *Rebels And Redcoats. The American Revolution Through the Eyes of Those Who Fought and Lived It* (Da Capo Press, Inc., n.d.).

Thane, Elswyth, *The Fighting Quaker: Nathanael Greene* (Aeonian Press, Inc., 1977).

Thayer, Theodore, *Nathanael Greene. Strategist of the American Revolution* (Twayne Publishers, 1960).

Trecy, M. F., *Prelude To Yorktown: The Southern Campaign Of Nathanael Greene 1780–1781* (The University of North Carolina Press, 1963).

Troxler, Carole Watterson, *The Loyalist Experience In North Carolina* (Theo Davis Sons, Inc., 1976).

Tuchman, Barbara W., *The First Salute. A View of the American Revolution* (Ballentine Books, 1989).

Ward, Christopher, *The War Of The Revolution* (The Macmillan Company, 1952), Vol 2.

Waring, Alice Noble, *The Fighting Elder. Andrew Pickens (1739–1817)* (University of South Carolina Press, 1962).

Wheeler, Richard, *Voices of 1776. The Story of the American Revolution in the Words of Those Who Were There* (Penguin Books, 1991).

Wickwire, Franklin and Mary, *Cornwallis The American Adventure* (Houghton Mifflin Co., 1970).

Willcox, William B., ed., *The American Rebellion. Sir Henry Clinton's Narrative Of His Campaigns, 1775–1782, With An Appendix Of Original Documents* (Oxford University Press, 1954).

Willcox, William B., *Portrait Of A General. Sir Henry Clinton In The War of Independence* (Alfred A. Knopf, 1964).

Wood, W. J., *Battles Of The Revolutionary War. 1775–1781* (Algonquin Books of Chapel Hill, Chapel Hill, N.C.).

Articles

Conway, Stephen, "The great mischief Complain'd of: Reflections on the Misconduct of British Soldiers in the Revoluytionary War." *(William And Mary Quarterly,* July 1990.

Mason, Keith, "Localism, Evangelicalism, and Loyalism: the Sources of Discontent in the revolutionary Chesapeake." *Journal of Southern History,* February, 1990.

Olwell, Robert A., "Slavery and Political Independence in South Carolina, May 1775–March 1776." *Journal of Southern History,* February, 1989.

Power, J. Tracy, " 'The Virtue Of Humanity Was Totally Forgot': Buford's Massacre, May 29, 1780." *(South Carolina Historical Magazine,* January, 1992).

INDEX